UPPER INTERMEDIATE BUSINESS ENGLISH COURSE BOOK

NEW EDITION

MARKET LEADER

David Cotton   David Falvey   Simon Kent

PEARSON
Longman

FINANCIAL
TIMES

Map of the book

	Discussion	Texts	Language work	Skills	Case study
Unit 1 Communication page 6	What makes a good communicator?	Reading: Internal communication – *Financial Times* Listening: An interview with a marketing manager for mobile media	Words to describe good and bad communicators Idioms	Dealing with communication breakdown	HCPS: Improve communication in a global company Writing: e-mail
Unit 2 International marketing page 14	Discussion of international brands	Reading: Coffee culture – *Financial Times* Listening: An interview with a marketing specialist	Marketing collocations Noun compounds and noun phrases	Brainstorming	Zumo – creating a global brand: Reposition a sports drink for the global market Writing: e-mail
Unit 3 Building relationships page 22	Discuss business relationships and do a quiz	Reading: AIG knows everyone – *Financial Times* Listening: An interview with a Chinese business executive	Words to describe relations Multi-word verbs	Networking	Getting to know you: Discuss ways to promote customer loyalty Writing: sales letter
Unit 4 Success page 30	Defining success Comparing similarities and differences between two companies	Reading: Steve Jobs – *Guardian* Listening: An interview with the founder of a successful business	Present and past tenses Prefixes	Negotiating	Camden FC: Negotiate a sponsorship deal for a football team Writing: press release or letter
Unit 5 Job satisfaction page 38	Discuss motivation and do a quiz on stress Discuss what makes a job satisfying	Perks that work - *Virginia Business Online* Listening: An interview with the Human Resources Director of a large company	Words for describing motivating factors Passives	Handling difficult situations	Office attraction: Devise a policy on close relationships at work Writing: guidelines
Unit 6 Risk page 46	Discuss everyday risk and risk in business	Reading: Planning for the future – *Financial Times* Listening: An interview with the Chief Executive of a risk management company	Words for describing risk Adverbs of degree	Reaching agreement	Suprema cars: Consider options to improve a car manufacturing company's profits Writing: report
Unit 7 e-commerce page 54	Discuss the use of the Internet	Reading: Internet shopping – *Financial Times* Listening: An interview with a marketing director of a computer company selling online	Internet terms Conditionals	Presentations	KGV Europe: Decide whether a music retailer should trade on the Internet Writing: e-mail
Revision unit A page 62					

Grammar reference: page 130   **Writing file:** page 138   **Activity file:** page 146

Introduction

What is Market Leader and who is it for?

Market Leader is a multi-level business English course for businesspeople and students of business English. It has been developed in association with the *Financial Times*, one of the leading sources of business information in the world. It consists of 14 units based on topics of great interest to everyone involved in international business.

This new edition of the Upper Intermediate level features new authentic texts and listenings throughout, reflecting the latest trends in the business world. If you are in business, the course will greatly improve your ability to communicate in English in a wide range of business situations. If you are a student of business, the course will develop the communication skills you need to succeed in business and will enlarge your knowledge of the business world. Everybody studying this course will become more fluent and confident in using the language of business and should increase their career prospects.

The authors

David Falvey *(left)* has over 20 years' teaching and managerial experience in the UK, Japan and Hong Kong. He has also worked as a teacher trainer at the British Council n Tokyo, and is now Head of the English Language Centre and Principal Lecturer at London Metropolitan University.

Simon Kent *(centre)* has over 15 years' teaching experience including three years as an in-company trainer in Berlin at the time of German reunification. He is currently a Senior lecturer in business and general English, as well as having special responsibility for designing new courses at London Metropolitan University.

David Cotton *(right)* has over 35 years' experience teaching and training in EFL, ESP and English for Business, and is the author of numerous business English titles, including *Agenda, World of Business, International Business Topics,* and *Keys to Management*. He is also one of the authors of the best-selling *Business Class*. He is a Senior Lecturer at London Metropolitan University.

What is in the units?

Starting up

You are offered a variety of interesting activities in which you discuss the topic of the unit and exchange ideas about it.

Vocabulary

You will learn important new words and phrases which you can use when you carry out the tasks in the unit. A good business dictionary, such as the *Longman Business English Dictionary*, will also help you to increase your business vocabulary.

Discussion

You will build up your confidence in using English and will improve your fluency through interesting discussion activities.

Reading

You will read authentic articles on a variety of topics from the *Financial Times* and other newspapers and online business websites. You will develop your reading skills and learn essential business vocabulary. You will also be able to discuss the ideas and issues in the articles.

Listening

You will hear authentic interviews with businesspeople. You will develop listening skills such as listening for information and note-taking.

Language review

This section focusses on common problem areas at upper intermediate level. You will become more accurate in your use of language. Each unit contains a Language review box which provides a review of key grammar items.

Skills

You will develop essential business communication skills such as making presentations, taking part in meetings, negotiating, telephoning, and using English in social situations. Each Skills section contains a Useful language box which provides you with the language you need to carry out the realistic business tasks in the book.

Case study

The Case studies are linked to the business topics of each unit. They are based on realistic business problems or situations and allow you to use the language and communication skills you have developed while working through the unit. They give you the opportunities to practise your speaking skills in realistic business situations. Each Case study ends with a writing task. A full writing syllabus is provided in the Market Leader Practice File.

Revision units

Market Leader Upper Intermediate also contains two revision units, based on material covered in the preceding seven Course Book units. Each revision unit is designed so that it can be done in one go or on a unit-by-unit basis.

UNIT 1 Communication

Everything that can be said can be said clearly.

Ludwig Wittgenstein (1889–1951),
Austrian philosopher

Starting up

A What makes a good communicator? Choose the three most important factors.

- fluency in the language
- an extensive vocabulary
- being a good listener
- physical appearance
- a sense of humour
- grammatical accuracy
- not being afraid of making mistakes
- an awareness of body language

B What other factors are important for communication?

C Discuss these questions.

1 What forms of written and spoken communication can you think of? For example: *e-mails*, *interviews*

2 Which of the above do you like using? Why?

3 What problems can people have with them?

4 How can these problems be solved?

Vocabulary
Good communicators

A Which words below apply to good communicators? Which apply to bad communicators?

> articulate   coherent   eloquent   fluent   focussed
> hesitant   inhibited   extrovert   persuasive   rambling
> responsive   sensitive   succinct   reserved

 Vocabulary file page 171

6

B **Which of the words in Exercise A have the following meanings?**

1 concise

2 reluctant to speak

3 talking in a confused way

4 able to express ideas well

5 clear and easy to understand

6 good at influencing people

7 outgoing

8 reacting in a positive way

C **Complete this talk by a communication expert with the verbs from the box.**

~~listen~~ digress interrupt explain engage clarify confuse ramble

'Good communicators really ...*listen*... to people and take in what is said. They maintain eye contact and have a relaxed body language, but they seldom ....¹ and stop people talking. If they don't understand and want to ....² something they wait for a suitable opportunity.

When speaking, effective communicators are good at giving information. They do not ....³ their listener. They make their points clearly. They will avoid technical terms, abbreviations or jargon.

If they do need to use unfamiliar terminology they ....⁴ by giving an easy to understand example. Furthermore, although they may ....⁵ and leave the main point to give additional information and details where appropriate, they will not ....⁶ and lose sight of their main message. Really effective communicators who have the ability to ....⁷ with colleagues, employees, customers and suppliers are a valuable asset for any business.'

D 🎧 1.1 **Listen to the talk and check your answers.**

E **Think of a good communicator you know. Explain why they are good at communicating.**

➡ *Vocabulary file* page 171

Listening

Improving communications

▲ Anuj Khanna

A 🎧 1.2 **Listen to the first part of an interview with Anuj Khanna, Marketing Manager of Netsize, a marketing agency for mobile media, and answer the questions.**

1 According to Anuj Khanna:

a) why have communications improved in recent years?

b) how can they improve in the future?

2 What example does he give of banks improving communications with customers?

B 🎧 1.3 **Listen to the second part of the interview.**

1 What are the consequences of the following communication breakdowns?

a) problems in air traffic control systems

b) delays in fixing communication systems

c) faults in cash machines

2 Which of the following developments in communication does Anuj Khanna expect to see in the future?

a) more privacy for customers

b) more freedom for companies to communicate with customers

c) more control by customers over the messages they receive

d) more communication between machines

C **How do you think business communication will change in the future?**

Reading
Internal communication

Ⓐ What are the advantages and disadvantages for companies of using e-mail?

Ⓑ Select three of the items below which, in your opinion, best contribute to improving communication.

trust	flexi-time
open plan offices	small teams
voice mail	strong corporate identity
e-mail	frequent meetings
mobile phones	staff parties

Communication – it's much easier said than done

By Clare Gascoigne

Trust is key in an open organisation

Getting staff to talk to each other ought to be the least of your problems, but internal communication can be one of the
5 hardest nuts to crack in business.
'Communication comes up in every department. The repercussions of not communicating are vast,' says
10 Theo Theobald, co-author of *Shut up and Listen! The Truth About How to Communicate at Work.*
Poor communication can be a purely practical problem.
15 Gearbulk, a global shipping business with branches around the world, faced language and geographical difficulties, as well as a huge amount of paperwork. With
20 up to 60 documents per cargo, it was a logistical nightmare to track and monitor jobs, while tighter security regulations after 9/11 meant customs documents had to
25 be ready before a ship was allowed to sail.
Installing an automated system means data is now entered only once but can be accessed by anyone
30 in the company, wherever they are.
'Reporting is faster by a matter of months,' says Ramon Ferrer, Vice President of Global IT at Gearbulk. 'An operational team
35 carrying a voyage all the way across the world doesn't always have to be talking to each other – and we don't waste time duplicating the same information.'
40 Given today's variety of communication tools, it seems strange that we still have a problem communicating. But the

I PREFERRED IT WHEN HE HID BEHIND HIS COMPUTER SENDING SILLY E-MAILS

brave new world of high-tech can
45 create barriers – senior managers hide behind their computers, staff use voice mail to screen calls, and employees sitting next to each other will send e-mails rather than
50 speak.
'Managers should get up, walk round the office and talk to people,' says Matt Rogan, Head of Marketing at Lane4, a leadership
55 and communications consultancy. 'Face-to-face communication can't be beaten.'
Theobold recommends checking e-mail only three times a day,
60 allocating a set period of time to deal with it. 'If you leave the sound on, the temptation is as great as a ringing phone. People will interrupt meetings to check their e-mails.'
65 Another problem is simply hitting the 'reply all' button, bombarding people with information. 'We had unstructured data coming at staff from left,
70 right and centre, leaving it up to individuals to sort out,' says Gearbulk's Ferrer. 'Our new system has reduced e-mails and changed

the way people work. It will remind
75 you about work flow.'
Information overload also means people stop listening. But there may be a deeper reason why a message fails to get through, according to
80 Alex Haslam, Professor of Psychology at Exeter University.
'Everyone thinks a failure to communicate is just an individual's error of judgment, but it's not
85 about the person: it's about the group and the group dynamics,' he says. 'Just training people to be good communicators isn't the issue.'
90 The problem is that employees develop common loyalties that are far stronger than the need to share information. This can even extend to questions of safety.
95 In the mid-1990s there were a lot of light air crashes in Australia because the two government departments responsible for air safety weren't communicating,'
100 says Haslam. 'The government was trying to save money and both groups felt threatened. The individuals were highly identified with their own organisation and
105 unwilling to communicate with the other department.'
A company is particularly at risk when cost-cutting is in the air. Individuals withdraw into
110 departmental loyalties out of fear. Sending such people on yet another 'how to communicate' course will be pointless. Instead, Haslam believes that identifying the sub-
115 groups within an organisation and making sure each group feels valued and respected can do far more to encourage the sharing of information. The key to
120 communication, he says, is trust.

From the *Financial Times*

FINANCIAL TIMES

C Read the article and complete the chart below.

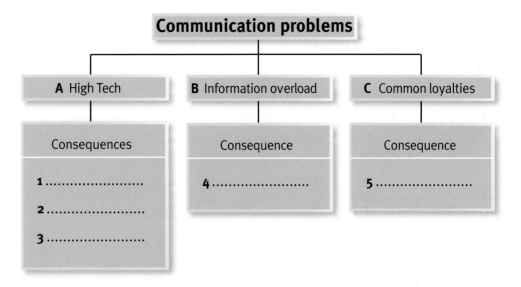

Communication problems

A High Tech	B Information overload	C Common loyalties
Consequences	**Consequence**	**Consequence**
1 .... 2 .... 3	4	5 ....

D Read the article again and answer these questions.

1 What communication problems did Gearbulk have?
2 How did Gearbulk overcome the problems?
3 What solutions does Theobald recommend for the above problems?
4 According to the author, why do staff often receive too many e-mails?
5 Why weren't the two government departments (responsible for air safety) communicating?
6 What does the author think about sending people on communication courses?

E Which word in each group does not form a word partnership with the word in bold?

1 **waste**	time	resources	information
2 **face**	trouble	problems	difficulties
3 **duplicate**	information	time	work
4 **install**	systems	factories	equipment
5 **save**	money	time	experience
6 **develop**	truth	loyalty	motivation
7 **share**	support	information	ideas
8 **allocate**	time	ideas	resources
9 **interrupt**	e-mails	conversations	meetings

F Discuss these questions.

1 'Face-to-face communication can't be beaten.' Do you agree?
2 How could communication be improved in your organisation?
3 How will communication change in the office of the future?

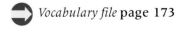 *Vocabulary file* page 173

Language review
Idioms

page 130

A Complete these idioms with the missing words from the box.

point	bush	grapevine	stick	wavelength	wires
	nutshell	picture	tail	purposes	

a) to put it in a ....

b) to get straight to the ....

c) to hear it on the ....

d) to put you in the ....

e) to get the wrong end of the ....

f) to be on the same ....

g) can't make head or .... of it

h) to talk at cross ....

i) to beat about the ....

j) to get our .... crossed

B Which of the idioms in Exercise A mean the following?

1 to fail to understand anything

2 to share similar opinions and ideas

3 to summarise briefly

4 to misunderstand

5 to delay talking about something

6 to give the latest information

7 to talk about the most important thing

8 to hear about something passed from one person to another

C Complete the sentences with the idioms from Exercise A.

1 OK, I'll .... I'm afraid we're going to have to let you go.

2 'You and your boss seem to agree on most things.' 'Yes, we are ....'

3 Some important decisions were taken at yesterday's meeting. Let me ....

4 I think we are .... I mean next month, not this month.

5 He never gives you a straight answer. He's always ....

6 I .... that he's been fired. Is it true?

7 It's a very complicated system, but to .... it works exactly like a big kettle.

8 If you think our biggest problem is market share then you have ....

9 This report makes no sense at all. I ....

10 Everyone arrived for the meeting at different times. We must have ....

D Ask your partner the following questions.

1 What have you heard on the grapevine recently?

2 When was the last time you got the wrong end of the stick?

3 When is it necessary to put someone in the picture?

4 In what situations is it good to beat about the bush?

5 In what situations is it good to get straight to the point?

6 Can you give an example of when you were talking at cross purposes?

7 Is there anything you can't make head or tail of?

Skills

Dealing with communication breakdown

A What expressions can you use on the phone in the following situations?

1 you don't hear what someone says
2 the person speaks too fast or too quietly
3 you don't understand a word or expression they use
4 you want to check the spelling of something
5 you want more information about a subject
6 the connection is not good and you can't continue the conversation
7 you want to check the key points

B 🎧 1.4 Listen to the telephone conversation between Bernard and Koichi. Which of the problems mentioned in Exercise A do the speakers have when communicating?

C 🎧 1.5 Listen to the two speakers in a similar conversation. Explain why the second conversation is better. Give as many reasons as you can.

D 🎧 1.5 Listen to the conversation again and complete these extracts with words or expressions from the conversation.

1 That's good. .... while I get a pen.

2 Sorry Bernard, I .... Could you .... a little, please? I need to take notes.

3 Let me .... that, 200 posters, pens and pencils and 50 bags. .... it.

4 Seel ... sorry, could you .... me, please, Bernard, I don't think I know the company?

5 'They've placed an order for 18 of the new lasers...' 'Sorry, ... 80 lasers?'

6 Sorry, I don't follow you. What .... 'roll-out' .... ?

7 But I need details about the company. Sorry, it's .... Could you ....? I can't hear you very well.

8 Sorry, I still can't hear you. I'll .... ; maybe the line will be better.

E Now match each extract 1–8 to the points you discussed in Exercise A.

F Work in pairs. Role play. Marketing Manager: turn to page 151; Overseas agent: turn to page 150. While doing the role play, practise some of the expressions you can use for dealing with breakdowns in communication.

Useful language

Asking for repetition
Sorry, could you repeat that?
I didn't (quite) catch that.
Could you speak up, please?
Could you say that again, please?

Asking for clarification
Would/Could you spell that, please?
Can I read that back to you?
What do you mean by ...?

What does ... mean?
Sorry, I'm not with you.
Sorry, I don't follow you.
Could you give me some more details, please?
Could you let me have more information?
Could you explain that in more detail?
Could you clarify that?
Could you be more specific, please?

Solving a problem
Sorry, it's a bad line. Can I call you back?

Summarising the call
Let me go over what we've agreed.
Let me just summarise ...

HCPS

Background

HCPS is a private health care organisation based in Geneva, Switzerland. It offers advice and treatment to wealthy people and company employees all over the world. Its advertising emphasises that it provides a personal health service tailored to the individual's needs.

The HCPS group was formed a year ago, following a takeover of HCP by Sanicorp, another health care organisation. Since the takeover, the company has become more centralised, with more decisions being made by the top management at head office. The working language of the group is English.

Communication problems

Following the takeover, a number of serious communication problems have arisen.

Read the e-mails sent by Gloria Richter, Office Manager, and by Ursula Krieger, Sales Director.

In your opinion, what is the most important problem mentioned in the e-mails?

To...	Gunther Schmidt	
From...	Gloria Richter	
Subject:	E-mails; staff lounge	Date: March 3

There are some communication problems I wish to bring to your attention.

1 Each day we receive a huge number of e-mails from colleagues inside the company and from overseas customers. Some are important, many are not. My staff seem to spend all day checking and sorting e-mails, which is time-consuming and results in them neglecting other duties.

2 My staff don't understand why you got rid of the staff lounge after the takeover. They say that it used to be a good place to meet people from other departments and to exchange ideas. Most of them still have not met anyone from Sanicorp yet.

To...	Chris Wright
From...	Ursula Krieger
Subject:	Communications problems
Date:	March 18

Since the takeover, problems have arisen and they need resolving soon.

1 A lot of middle managers are really confused about who they should report to. We know management are planning a reorganisation, but isn't it time they told us what's happening?

2 Several department heads are unhappy because they can't get a quick answer when they want to spend money, even small sums. When they ask their present line manager for authority to buy something, for example, a piece of equipment, the usual reply is 'it's not up to me anymore'.

Desiree Roland Consultants SA

The President of HCPS, Susan Westbrook, recently contacted a firm of management consultants, Desiree Roland Consultants SA, based in France. She asked them to analyse the communication problems in HCPS and to send in a report. The consultants interviewed staff at all levels in the company.

🎧 1.6 Listen to some typical comments and complete the table with information from the listening extracts.

Task

You are members of Desiree Roland Consultants. Work in small groups. Make a list of all the communication problems in the company.

Then rank the problems in order of importance.

What actions do you suggest to solve the communication problems?

Discuss your ideas in groups, then meet as one group and work out an action plan.

Which actions should be taken:
a) immediately?
b) in the near future?
c) later, when convenient?

Which actions will require:
a) a lot of investment?
b) some investment?
c) very little investment?

Type of problem	Description of problem
Organisation	....
Documents	....
Location of premises	....
Customer relations	....
Other problems	....

🎧 1.7 Now listen to the President of the company, Susan Westbrook, talking to Chris Wright, Managing Director. Who do you agree with, the President or the Managing Director? Why?

Writing

Write a follow-up e-mail from the consultants detailing their recommendations.

 Writing file page 139

> *The last stage of fitting the product to the market is fitting the market to the product.*
>
> Clive James,
> Australian writer and broadcaster

Starting up

A Think of one brand in each of these categories which is marketed internationally.

| food | drink | electrical equipment | clothing | construction |

B Discuss these questions.

1 What are the advantages for a company of expanding beyond its domestic market?

2 What kinds of problems do companies face when they go international?

3 What methods can companies use to enter overseas markets?

 *Vocabulary file* page 171

Vocabulary
Collocations

A Complete these statements with suitable expressions from the box.

buying habits	economic situation
government bureaucracy	income distribution
monetary regulations	political stability

1 Because of tight .... company profits could not be taken out of the country.

2 Red tape and other examples of .... hinder a company's entry into a market.

3 The country is attractive to exporters because it has enjoyed .... for the last 50 years.

4 The purchasing behaviour of consumers can be described as their ....

5 The .... is improving leading to a rise in employment.

6 .... is a term used by economists to describe how wealth is shared in a country.

B Discuss these questions.

1 What are some of the main benefits of political stability?

2 How would you describe the present economic situation of your country compared to 10 years ago?

3 Is it possible to achieve equal income distribution in a country? Explain why or why not.

C Look at the words and phrases below. Underline the odd one out.

1 a) growing market   c) expanding market
  b) developing market   d) declining market

2 a) questionnaire   c) promotion
  b) focus group   d) survey

3 a) market sector   c) market segment
  b) market research   d) market niche

4 a) international market   c) domestic market
  b) overseas market   d) worldwide market

5 a) launch a product   c) bring out a product
  b) withdraw a product   d) introduce a product

6 a) slogan   c) discount
  b) free sample   d) special offer

7 a) retailer   c) wholesaler
  b) distributor   d) manufacturer

D Complete this exercise and then compare answers with a partner.

1 Give an example of an expanding market in your country.

2 Give some examples of products or services which are targeted at niche markets.

3 Another name for a home market is a .... market.

4 If a product has a design fault a company may decide to .... it, correct the fault and relaunch it at a later date.

5 'Just do it' is an example of a ....

6 What's the difference between a retailer and a wholesaler?

Reading
Coffee culture

A **Answer these questions.**

1 Which hot drinks are popular in your country?
2 What is your favourite hot drink?
3 Which five words do you associate with coffee?

Coffee culture comes to coffee-growers

By John Authers and Mark Mulligan

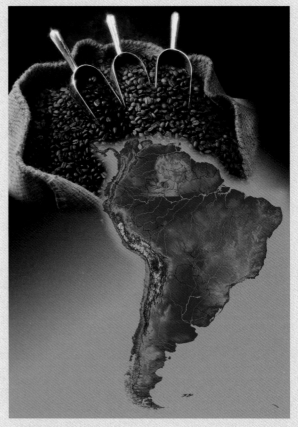

In Chile, they prefer tea to coffee and instant rather than freshly brewed.

In Argentina, by contrast, breakfast is with a frothy cappuccino, a heart-starting espresso, or a caffè latte. In Brazil, after-dinner coffee is served free at any self-respecting restaurant.

That Latin America is not one great homogeneous culture often surprises travellers. However, even the most subtle differences in the consumer profile of a Colombian and a Venezuelan will not have been lost on Starbucks, one of the fastest-growing global brands.

After searches for local partners, and a successful trial run in Mexico City, Starbucks arrived in South America.

With no conventional advertising, the Seattle-based company opened stores in Lima and Santiago within 24 hours of each other.

Neither Peru nor Chile has a mass-market café culture, although European and US-style coffee houses have begun springing up in the upmarket districts of both their capitals.

Despite this cultural peculiarity, a Starbucks survey found that Chileans on average drink only 150 cups of coffee a year, compared with 345 in the US and more than twice that number in many European countries. Of the 800g of coffee per capita bought in supermarkets and from speciality shops each year, 90 per cent of it is instant.

In Argentina, per capita consumption is about 4kg a year, mostly in whole or ground coffee beans. Despite being a coffee-grower, Peru has a similar pattern of coffee consumption.

The irony is not lost on Julio Gutiérrez, head of Latin America at Starbucks Coffee International. 'We've been doing business in Latin America for decades,' he says. 'We haven't had any stores but we've been buying Latin American coffee since the beginning.'

'Expansion will depend entirely on how long it takes to find the right partner in each of those countries,' he says. 'If we don't find anyone, we may think about going in ourselves.'

Anyone who knows the Starbucks story can already visualise potential outlets in the most fashionable neighbourhoods of the region's capital cities. From a single store in Seattle's Pike Place Market in 1971, Starbucks today owns 3,907 stores in North America and licences a further 1,378. They also own 437 and franchise 1,180 outlets in the rest of the world.

It first expanded from its home market to Japan in 1996 and is now present in more than 30 countries. Last year alone, the Starbucks' living-room-in-a-coffee-house format was introduced to Mexico, Germany, Spain, Austria, Puerto Rico, Greece, Oman, Indonesia and southern China. Starbucks 'corners', or mini-outlets, are found in airline offices, sports stadiums, airports, hotels and bookshops. Copy-cat coffee-bar chains have emerged, only to be swallowed by Starbucks or forced to merge with competitors.

Fortune and fame, however, have not come without their critics. Some analysts say the company was forced to globalise because it had saturated its home market. Others say the Japanese experience has not been a happy one. Security concerns forced the company to retreat from Israel, and the anti-globalisation movement now has Starbucks stores on its hit list.

In aspiring societies such as Chile and Mexico, American companies are generally well regarded and any novelty from abroad is guaranteed to arouse curiosity.

Both the Lima and Santiago Starbucks have been packed since opening their doors, and the company has rolled out 15 stores in Mexico City since launching its first – cleverly located beside the US embassy – a year ago.

Roman Perez-Miranda, head of Latin America for Interbrand, agrees. 'Mexico is the closest Latin America gets to the US, both geographically and culturally,' he says. 'It was an obvious starting-point for Starbucks in the region.'

From the Financial Times

FINANCIAL TIMES

B Read the article quickly and identify the country or countries where the statement is true.

| Argentina | Peru | Chile | Brazil | Colombia | Venezuela | Mexico | US |

1 People in this country would rather drink tea than coffee.
2 People in this country would rather drink instant coffee.
3 In this country coffee is usually free after dinner in restaurants.
4 In this country people drink 345 cups of coffee a year.
5 In this country people drink 4kg of whole or ground coffee beans per year.

C Answer these questions.

1 Where and when did Starbucks begin?
2 How many stores does it own in **a)** North America? **b)** the rest of the world?
3 How many stores does it allow others to operate in **a)** North America? **b)** the rest of the world?
4 Which overseas market did Starbucks enter first?
5 In what sort of places can you find Starbucks' sales-points?
6 According to the article what four problems has Starbucks had?

D Which of the following verbs can form a word partnership with a) a product, b) a market?

1 retreat from
2 launch
3 pull out of
4 break into
5 penetrate
6 introduce
7 saturate
8 withdraw
9 get a foothold in
10 roll out
11 license
12 phase out

E Which of the verbs in Exercise D are connected to a) entering a market, b) leaving a market? Use a good dictionary to help you.

Listening
Adapting to markets

A 2.1 Listen to the first part of the interview with Paul Smith, a marketing specialist. What questions should you consider before entering an overseas market?

B 2.2 Listen to the second part of the interview. What problems or challenges does Paul Smith mention?

C What problems might a foreign producer of the following products have in trying to market their goods in your country: a) luxury cars, b) shampoos, c) breakfast cereals?

▲ Paul Smith

Language review
Noun compounds and noun phrases

1 A compound noun is two nouns together. Noun compounds are common in business because they are shorter and more convenient than noun phrases. For example:
an export licence rather than *a licence to export*
a consumer protection law rather than *a law for the protection of consumers*

2 Longer noun phrases are also common. They may consist of adverbs, adjectives and compound noun. The following pattern is typical:

Adverb	Adjective / *-ing* participle	Noun / Gerund	Head noun
increasingly	difficult long-term expanding	market marketing overseas	conditions strategy sales

 page 130

A Find noun phrases in the article on page 16 which have similar meanings to the phrases below.

1 the key facts about someone who buys goods or services (paragraph 3)

2 the activity of visiting outlets that sell hot beverages to a lot of people (paragraph 6)

3 places that sell unusual products that are different in some way (paragraph 7)

4 the amount of goods or materials used by each person in a particular period of time (paragraph 8)

5 a group of people trying to stop international companies controlling the world economy (paragraph 13)

B One word in each group does not make a compound noun with the word in bold. Cross it out.

1 **marketing**   campaign / budget / leader / strategy
2 **market**   research / survey / check / sector
3 **product**   market / range / features / manager
4 **advertising**   campaign / exchange / agency / slogan
5 **brand**   awareness / loyalty / image / contract
6 **sales**   figures / conditions / forecast / targets
7 **price**   promotion / rise / product / range

C The words in each of the noun phrases below are in the wrong order. Write the phrases in their correct form.

1 impressive figures sales really

2 department new public relations

3 highly research market ambitious programme

4 overseas expanding operations

5 rapidly sheet balance improving

6 extremely rate exchange volatile

7 highly marketing report confidential

Skills
Brainstorming

A Brainstorming is a useful way of generating creative ideas in meetings. Decide which tips below are good advice and which ones you disagree with. Then compare your answers with a partner.

1 Explain the purpose of the meeting clearly.
2 Ask each person to speak in turn, starting with the most senior.
3 Announce the time limit for the meeting.
4 Avoid criticising or judging ideas during the session.
5 Encourage ideas, however unusual they may be.
6 Don't interrupt when people are offering suggestions.
7 Make sure everyone keeps to the point.
8 Don't spend time on details.

B 2.3 Listen to the first part of an authentic brainstorming meeting between three members of the Marketing Department at Business Solutions Limited. Then answer these questions.

1 What is the purpose of the meeting?
2 What types of promotion are mentioned by participants?

C 2.4 Now listen to the rest of the meeting and answer these questions.

1 What other ideas for promoting the website are mentioned by participants?
2 When is the next meeting? What information will the participants get then?

D Match the comments made by the participants to the headings in the Useful language box below. You can use the Audio scripts on pages 158 and 159 to check the context of the comments. (Some comments can be put under more than one heading.)

1 Fire away.
2 Excellent!
3 I think we'd reach a wide audience …
4 We should definitely do some of that.
5 Absolutely!
6 What about press advertising?
7 That might be one way …
8 Would it be worth it sponsoring some kind of event?
9 It would be great to do a presentation …
10 What about that?

Useful language

Stating objectives
The purpose of the meeting this morning is to …
What we need to achieve today is …
Our objective here is to …

Making suggestions
I think we could …
I suggest we …
One thing we could do is …

Expressing enthusiasm
That's great!
That's the best idea I've heard for a long time.
That's an excellent suggestion.

Encouraging contributions
Don't hold back.
Say whatever comes to mind.
Any other ideas?
At this stage we want all your

ideas, however crazy you think they are.

Agreeing
Yes, that's a good idea because …
Absolutely because …
Exactly because …
You're (absolutely) right because …

E Choose one of the situations below and hold a brainstorming meeting.

1 Your company has developed a new sports or music magazine. Brainstorm ideas for an advertising campaign.
2 Your company will shortly be receiving a visit from some important Chinese businesspeople who wish to set up a joint venture with your firm. Brainstorm ideas for suitable gifts for the three Chinese visitors.

Zumo - creating a global brand

Background

The best-selling sports drink, Zumo, is produced by Zumospa, a food and drinks company based in Valencia, Spain. In the last financial year, Zumo contributed €30 million to Zumospa's annual sales revenue, accounting for 20% of the company's total turnover. It is, in fact, Zumospa's cash cow, generating more revenue than any other of its products.

At present, Zumo is sold only in Europe. However, the sports drink market is the most rapidly growing segment of the world beverage market. Zumospa is now looking outside Spain for markets and would like to make Zumo a global brand.

Key features of Zumo

- Contains caffeine, vitamins and glucose.
- Has a secret ingredient, 'herbora', made from roots of rare African plants.
- Scientific studies show that the body absorbs Zumo faster than water or other soft drinks.
- The unique formula contributes to Zumo's taste and thirst-quenching properties.

2.5 Listen to this excerpt from a radio programme, Business Today. Ricardo Gonzales, Zumospa's President, discusses Zumospa's plans to globalise.

Make notes on the company results, future plans and competitive advantage.

Marketing

- Launched in the mid-1980s. Positioned as an energy product for fitness-conscious people, especially sportsmen and women, between the ages of 20 and 45.
- Distributed mainly through grocery stores, convenience stores and supermarkets. Also through sports clubs. Additionally, sales are generated through contracts with professional leagues, such as football, golf and tennis associations.
- Press, TV and radio advertising is backed up by endorsement contracts with famous European footballers and tennis stars.
- Zumo is offered in four flavours and its price is in the medium range.

Developing a global brand

Zumospa needs to reposition it for the global market. Initial research suggests that Zumo is perceived as a Spanish drink, and its close identification with Spain may not be suitable when developing a global brand.

Zumospa would like to launch a global campaign focussing first on South America, Mexico, the Southern states of the US and Japan, where they have regional offices. A decision has been taken to use a standardised advertising theme in these markets, although the copy of the advertisements and language of the TV and radio commercials will be adapted to local needs.

Before setting up focus groups in these areas and commissioning market surveys, the Marketing Department of Zumospa have organised an informal departmental meeting to brainstorm ideas for their global marketing strategy.

Brainstorming Session

1 Does Zumo need a new name? If so, what?
2 Introduce new Zumo varieties for different market segments e.g. Diet Zumo? Other versions?
3 Redesign Zumo bottle/can? If so, how?
4 Create a new slogan? Suggestions?
5 Ideas for TV or radio advertisement? Also, newspapers and magazines?
6 Price – medium range?
7 How to compete against similar products from Coke, Pepsi, Heinz, etc?
8 New market opportunities for Zumo?
9 Create a special division to market Zumo worldwide?
10 Apply to be official sponsor at next Olympic Games?

Writing

As Marketing Manager for Zumospa, write an e-mail to the directors of the company informing them of the key ideas which came out of the brainstorming session you attended. You should indicate which ideas you favour and why.

➡ *Writing file* page 139

Task

You are members of the Marketing Department of Zumospa. Work in groups and brainstorm the points listed in the rough notes. One person in the group should take notes. Then meet as one group and select some of the best suggestions for further study.

UNIT 3 Building relationships

‘ *A relationship is like a shark, you
know. It has to constantly move
forward or it dies.* ’
Woody Allen, American film-maker and actor

Starting up

A **Discuss these questions.**

1 What are the most important relationships for you **a)** at your place of work
or study? **b)** outside your place of work or study?

2 What benefits do you get from each relationship?

B **Ward Lincoln, Business Relations Manager with an international training
organisation, is talking about areas for companies to consider in order to
build strong business relationships. What factors do you think he will
mention?**

C 🎧 3.1 **Listen to the interview and check the predictions you made in
Exercise B.**

D **Answer the questions in the quiz. Then turn to page 153 to find out how good
you are at building relationships.**

---

1 You are in a room with a group of people
who don't know each other. Do you

a) wait for someone to say something?

b) introduce a topic of conversation?

c) introduce yourself?

2 When you are introduced to people, do you
remember

a) their name?

b) their face?

c) their clothes?

3 On festive occasions, e.g. New Year, do you

a) send greeting cards to everyone you
know?

b) send e-mails?

c) reply only to cards received?

4 Do you think small talk is

a) enjoyable?

b) a waste of time?

c) difficult to do well?

5 Do you prefer
  a) not to socialise with colleagues?
  b) to socialise often with colleagues?
  c) to socialise with colleagues only if you have to?

 6 Do you like to have conversations
  a) with people who share your interests?
  b) with almost anyone?
  c) with people who are your social equals?

Vocabulary
Describing relations

A The verbs below are often used with the word *relations*. Use them to complete the table.

break-off	build-up	cement	foster	cut off	develop	disrupt
encourage	establish	endanger	improve	jeopardise	maintain
strengthen	promote	restore	resume	damage	sour	undermine

Positive meaning	Negative meaning
build up relations	break off relations

B Choose the correct verb in each sentence.

1 Sales staff who are impolite to customers *disrupt / damage* the reputation of a company.

2 We are planning to *promote / establish* branch offices in Singapore.

3 By merging with a US company, we greatly *strengthened / maintained* our sales force.

4 Our image has been *fostered / undermined* by poor after-sales service.

5 Thanks to a new communications system, we are *souring / improving* relations with suppliers.

6 A strike at our factory *resumed / disrupted* production for several weeks.

7 We could not agree on several points so we *broke off / cut off* talks regarding a joint venture.

8 The success of our new product launch was *resumed / jeopardised* by an unimaginative advertising campaign.

9 In order to gain market share in China, we are *building up / cutting off* a sales network there.

10 Relations between the two countries have been *endangered / fostered* by official visits and trade delegations.

C Match the following sentence halves. Then make five more sentences with the verbs in Exercise A and B.

1 Widespread rumours of a hostile take-over bid are certain

2 The Accounts Department's very slow payment of invoices

3 The long-term contracts, which will run for the next five years,

4 The excellent relations the company enjoys with the local community

5 As a result of the government's imposition of currency controls,

a) are a credit to its highly effective PR Department.

b) have cemented relations between the two companies.

c) its close relations with several major foreign investors have been jeopardised.

d) is causing stormy relations with some of the company's suppliers.

e) to strain relations between the two leading French software companies.

Listening
Relationships in a global market

▲ Agnes Chen

A 🎧 3.2 **Listen to the first part of the interview with Agnes Chen, a Chinese business executive, who travels frequently on overseas trips. Make notes on the following points.**

1 Doing business in South America
2 Doing business in China
3 The best way to build a business relationship

B 🎧 3.3 **Listen to the second part of the interview and give an oral summary of it using the following words and phrases.**

clear objectives	beginning	achieve and deliver	trust
time to time	promise	deliver	face-to-face contact
review	open and sharing relationship		

Reading
AIG knows everyone

A **What area of business do you think the company American International Group (AIG) is involved in? Is it a) tobacco? b) insurance? c) oil? d) packaging? Skim the article quickly to find the answer.**

B **What do the following numbers in the article refer to?**

166   1992   1919   80,000   130

C **Who are the following people mentioned in the article: *Maurice Greenberg, Cornelius Vander Starr, Edmund Tse*?**

D **According to the article what are the main factors responsible for AIG's success in Asia?**

E **Read the article and answer these questions.**

1 What objective does AIG have in China?
2 What does Mr Greenberg see as his role in the company?
3 Why is Asia important to AIG?

F **Find three verbs in the article which combine with the noun *relationships* to mean *develop*.**

G **Find phrases (adjective and noun) in the article which mean the following.**

1 unused possibilities (paragraph 3)
2 continuing in the same place for a great length of time (paragraph 5)
3 unlimited entry (paragraph 8)
4 representatives connected to a company (paragraph 10)
5 developing sales areas (paragraph 12)
6 important talks (paragraph 13)
7 most important countries (paragraph 13)

H **Discuss these questions.**

1 What can spoil relations between companies?
2 A foreign company is opening a branch in your country. What factors should it consider?
3 In your experience are certain nationalities better at building relationships than others? If so, which ones?
4 How can you build good business relationships?

Vocabulary file page 173

AIG knows everyone in Asia

By Shawn Donnan et al

AIG, American International Group, has grown from a small Shanghai-based underwriting agency into the world's largest insurer by market value. It has a capitalisation of $166bn, and is firmly embedded in Asia's corporate culture. Indeed, with roots dating back more than half a century, and the constant focus on the region by Maurice Greenberg, its Chairman, AIG has an unrivalled scale of operations and a wealth of political and business connections.

For other US and European insurers, the company is both a benchmark and a powerful competitor. 'They know anyone who is anyone in Asia.'

However, in order to continue to prosper, AIG will have to succeed in China – probably the insurance market with the biggest untapped potential in the world.

After 17 years of lobbying by Mr Greenberg, AIG was the first foreign insurer to be allowed into China, in 1992. It now operates in eight cities but admits making only 'a small profit' in the country. Today, turning its pioneering presence into a commercial success is AIG's biggest challenge.

In China as with the rest of Asia, AIG's main advantage over its competitors is its long-standing presence. The group was founded in Shanghai in 1919 by Cornelius Vander Starr, a 27-year-old American entrepreneur.

That historical accident, and Mr Starr's quest to expand to the rest of Asia in the ensuing 10 years, are still benefiting the company. Over the past nine decades, AIG built on those foundations through endlessly pursuing close relationships with Asia's governments, regulators and powerful businessmen.

Edmund Tse, who runs the Asian operations and life assurance worldwide, says AIG's policy is to build relationships with as many influential people as possible. 'If you want to do business, you have to be friends with senior leaders,' he says. 'You need to be friends with the head of state, the minister of finance, the minister of trade, the [central] bank governor and the insurance regulator.'

AIG believes its three decades spent courting China will be rewarded with unrestricted access to its vast insurance market. 'The Chinese always remember good friends,' says Mr Tse.

But if its 'friendship' with China is not enough to tap the country's potential, AIG may lose its main growth engine. And without a strong Asia, AIG would be a much weaker company.

AIG may be a company of 80,000 employees and 350,000 affiliated agents in 130 countries but much of its success is down to individual relationships.

Many of those relationships have been forged by Maurice Greenberg, the company's chairman and chief executive.

Mr Greenberg says that playing the long game has given AIG an edge, particularly in terms of investing in emerging markets. He courted the Chinese for 17 years before being granted a licence in 1992.

Mr Greenberg knows quite a few people. His style has always been to discuss big issues – corporate, political and economic – with anyone he meets. One analyst refers to AIG as a 'sovereign corporate nation' as Mr Greenberg insists on representing the company in high-level discussions. 'If you're dealing with the premier or president of a country, he is not thrilled to have a deputy come and see him. Even if a country is not one of the leading nations in the world, that country is important. It's important to him and it's important to us.'

From the *Financial Times*

FINANCIAL TIMES

Language review
Multi-word verbs

Multi-word verbs are particularly common in spoken English. They are made with a verb and particles such as *at, away, down* and *off*. Four types are:

1 Without an object
*I'm going to be **tied up** in meetings all day.*

2 With an object – separable
*In the excitement of **beating off** the competition, managers become carried away.*
*In the excitement of **beating** the competition **off**, managers become carried away.*

3 With an object – inseparable
*I'll **look into** the matter immediately.*

4 With two particles
*Organisations are beginning to **wake up to** these lost opportunities.*

 page 131

A 🎧 3.4 **Two managers are talking about building relationships with agents. Put the conversation in the correct order. Then listen and check your answers.**

- [ ] **a)** Well, I hope you get a result. I must be going. I've got to draw up an agency agreement myself, I've put it off far too long already.

- [ ] **b)** What exactly was the problem?

- [ ] **c)** Yes. Our results were terrible. We tried to build up market share but it just didn't happen. We just managed to hold on to what we had.

- [ ] **d)** Unfortunately, our agent let us down. We thought we could count on him to boost sales but he had no commitment, no motivation.

- [ ] **e)** He should be. He's got a very good track record. We'd set up a meeting on Friday, but he had to call it off – something came up.

- [1] **f)** How's it going in France, Gina? We didn't do too well there last year.

- [ ] **g)** Well, I suppose you terminated his contract then.

- [ ] **h)** Good. Let's hope he'll be better than the last one.

- [ ] **i)** All the best. Speak to you soon.

- [ ] **j)** Yes, there was no way we could renew it. We sounded out a few possible replacements and found someone else. We get on really well.

B **Underline all the multi-word verbs in the conversation in Exercise A. Then match each one to a verb phrase with a similar meaning below.**

1 have a friendly relationship

2 depend on / rely on

3 make bigger / stronger

4 keep / maintain

5 postpone / delay

6 find out opinions / intentions

7 disappoint

8 arrange

9 compile / write down

10 cancel

C **Rephrase these comments using the multi-word verbs from Exercise A.**

1 We can't hold the meeting tomorrow.
   *We'll have to **call** the meeting **off** tomorrow.*

2 Let's have the presentation next week – we're too busy at the moment.

3 We always know our suppliers will meet their deadlines.

4 We have now established a first class distribution network in Europe.

5 Could you please prepare a contract as soon as possible?

6 Could you fix a meeting with them for next week?

7 We've kept the same market share as we had last year.

8 The new sales manager is very popular with his team.

Skills

Networking

A 🎧 3.5 **Networking is a vital part of establishing good business relationships. Listen to four conversations at business conferences. For each one decide whether the statements are true or false.**

1 **a)** The first speaker introduces herself straightaway.
  b) The second speaker doesn't remember her until she introduces herself.

2 **a)** The second speaker knows that Henry Willis is in New York.
  b) The second speaker offers to contact the New York office.

3 **a)** Both speakers know Jon Stuart.
  b) The second speaker isn't able to offer any help.

4 **a)** Both speakers have been doing business in Asia for some time.
  b) In the end they establish an area of common interest.

B 🎧 3.6 **Listen to the telephone conversation, then answer the questions.**

1 What is the purpose of the call?

2 Does it have a successful outcome? Why? Why not?

C 🎧 3.6 **Now listen again and complete the extracts from the conversation.**

1 I .... you don't .... me .... Silvana said it would probably be OK.

2 Is it a .... time to ring or could I call you .... at a better time?

3 Silvana .... that you might be able to .... me on franchising contracts.

4 Mmm, I don't know. I could maybe give you a little help, but I know someone .... in that area.

5 You haven't got her phone number ....
.... ?

6 Can I .... when I call her?

D **Work in pairs and role play these situations.**

1 The owner of a department store visits Moscow to find a supplier of amber jewellery. He/She phones a Russian contact recommended by a colleague. The owner wants to find out if the Russian is interested in doing business with his/her company.

2 You are networking at a conference about sports goods. You are either
  a Sales Manager, turn to page 146
  or a Sports Goods Wholesaler, turn to page 155.

Useful language

Mentioning people you know
Harry Kaufman suggested I gave you a call.
I was given your name by Jon Stuart.

Giving advice
I suggest you give her a call.
You could try to track him down through our New York office.

Asking for help / contacts
Can I mention your name when I call him?
He mentioned that you might be able to help me.
You haven't got his phone number by any chance?
Is this a convenient time or shall I call back later?

Referring to previous meetings
Haven't we met somewhere before?
We both went to that presentation ...

Establishing common interests
Maybe we could help you out there.
Are you in sales or product development?

CASE STUDY

Background

Kimsoong, a Korean car manufacturer, has its European headquarters near Paris. It has retail sales franchises in most European countries which not only sell cars and motor accessories but also have servicing facilities. The larger outlets also offer fast-fitting of tyres and exhausts, and deal in used cars.

Over the last ten years Kimsoong, with its reputation for reliability at low prices, have built up market share at the lower end of the market. Their basic models include many 'extras' which other manufacturers charge for. Kimsoong also makes large donations to environmental groups and is seen as an organisation with a social conscience. Furthermore, its R&D Department is developing an 'eco-car' which uses an alternative power source.

Problems

Intense competition is forcing Kimsoong to consider new ways of generating business. Management believe that if the company looks after existing customers well, they may buy three or four Kimsoong vehicles over a ten-year period. Therefore, Kimsoong's new strategy is to hold on to existing customers and increase customer loyalty. They also hope to develop a more accurate buyer profile (At present, data is from questionnaires sent to customers following sales but only 40% are returned). However, because of pressure on profits, they need to achieve these objectives at a low cost.

Solutions

A customer loyalty programme will be developed by the Customer Services Department at head office. It will be available to all European franchises and costs will be shared 50/50 with head office. Its aims are:

- to build up long-term customer relationships, thereby increasing profits
- to increase customer loyalty
- to draw up an accurate buyer profile
- to encourage staff to be more active in building up good customer relations.

Kimsoong customer profile

Age		Sex		Occupation	
Under 30	48%	Male	52%	Student	8%
31–40	27%	Female	48%	Self-employed	15%
41–50	15%			Employed	75%
Over 51	10%			Retired	2%

Interests (in order of importance)		Percentage of repeat buyers	Income group	
1 Eating / drinking	5 Health / fitness	15%	Higher income	2%
2 Sport	6 Reading		Middle income	82%
3 Travel	7 The arts		Lower income	16%
4 Environment	8 Politics			

Reason for not repeating purchase		After-sales care (customer rating)		Customers' priorities (in order of importance)
Bought a competitor's model	52%	Excellent	4%	1 Economy
Dissatisfied with service	26%	Very good	12%	2 Price
Relocated	8%	Good	17%	3 Reliability
No longer drive	5%	Fair	61%	4 After-sales service
Don't know	9%	Poor	6%	5 Length of warranty
				6 Performance
				7 Comfort

Task

Work in small groups. You work in Customer Services at head office.

1 Think of five ideas to include in Kimsoong's customer loyalty programme.

2 🎧 3.7 Listen to two directors of the company exchanging ideas about how to foster customer loyalty. Make notes on the five suggestions they make.

3 Consider your ideas and those of the directors. Choose the best four ideas to include in the company's programme.

4 Meet as one group. Discuss your ideas and decide on the best four to include in the customer services programme.

Writing

Choose a company you are familiar with. Write a sales letter to Roger Eastwood, one of a group of priority customers. Outline a special offer which you are making to this priority customer group. Make your letter appear as personalised as possible.

 Writing file page 138

Success

The only place where success comes before work is in the dictionary.
Vidal Sassoon, hairstylist

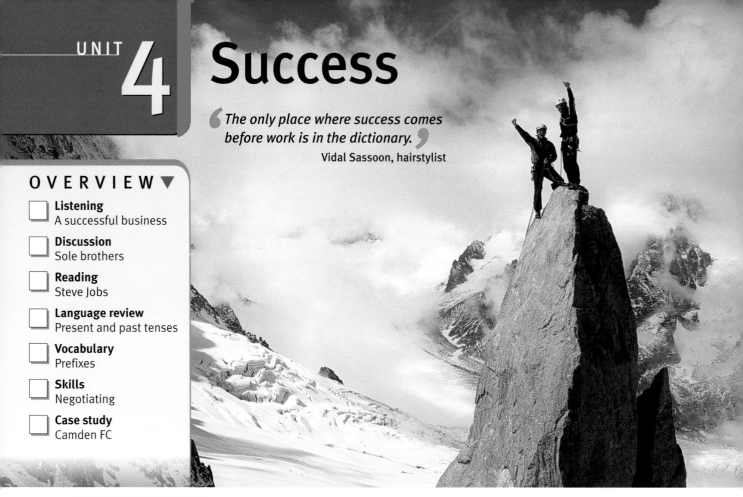

Starting up

A What makes people successful? Add more words to the list below. Then choose the five most important.

charisma	drive	looks	nepotism	discipline
dedication	imagination	luck	ruthlessness	money

B Talk about a person you know who is successful. Why are they successful?

➡ *Vocabulary file* pages 171–173

C What are the best indicators of an individual's level of success? How important are the following in your culture?

exotic holidays	cosmetic surgery	designer clothes	domestic help
chauffeur(s)	expensive jewellery	top-of-the-range car(s)	
influential friends	leisure activities	pedigree pets	luxury home(s)

D Complete these statements using words from the box.

leader	customer	brand	profit	headquarters
workforce	subsidiaries	people	innovation	shares

A successful business ...

a) is always making money and increasing its ....

b) is often the market ....

c) is moving forward and interested in ....

d) has a motivated ....

e) has a loyal .... base.

f) has a world-famous .... and an instantly recognised logo.

g) issues .... which are worth millions on the stock market.

h) has its .... in a prestigious location.

i) has branches and .... all over the world.

j) treats its employees well and is .... orientated.

Listening
A successful business

▲ Catherine Ng

A 🎧 **4.1 Catherine Ng established an electronic watch company with six employees in 1979. The company now has over 500 employees. Listen to the first part of the interview and say whether these statements are true or false.**

1 The Swiss believed the quartz watch would lead to huge growth in the market.
2 Catherine Ng's floor space increased by 1,400 sq ft by the end of the first year.
3 In the short term she developed luxury goods.
4 Products with time modules became more valuable.
5 The company cut prices for all products.
6 They started making more clocks and fewer watches.

B 🎧 **4.2 Listen to the second part of the interview and answer the following questions.**

1 What are the main factors of Catherine Ng's success?
2 What advice does she give people looking for success?

Discussion
Sole brothers

A Work in pairs. One of you reads about Puma below; the other reads about Adidas Saloman on page 155. Then use the points below to give an oral summary of your text to your partner.

- Name of founder
- Founding date
- Type of products
- Chief Executive Officer
- Date of going public
- Sponsorship
- Diversification
- Expansion

B Discuss what the companies have in common, and how they are different.

Sole Brothers
PUMA

In 1948 Rudolf Dassler left his brother's company Adidas to set up his own shoe company, Puma.
After successes with its products on the football pitch and athletics track, Puma became a limited partnership.

It had further successes at the Olympic Games and World Cups with players such as the famous Brazilian footballer Pelé wearing Puma shoes.

In the 1970s it had success with tennis shoes and by 1981 many American football stars were using Puma shoes. Later, the tennis stars Martina Navratilova and Boris Becker won the Wimbledon Tournament wearing Puma shoes.

In 1986 Puma became a corporation and went public on the Munich and Frankfurt stock exchanges.

At that time, Puma introduced many innovations in shoe design such as the 'Trinomic' and 'disc system' shoes.

Jochen Zeitz was appointed CEO in 1993 and a year later Puma made a profit for the first time since going public.

After more athletic successes, Puma established Puma North America as a wholly owned subsidiary.

In 1998 Puma linked sport and fashion when it launched a collection with the fashion designer Jil Sander. It also placed products in top Hollywood movies.

In 2000, Puma launched www.puma.com. It was successful in the first year of its operation. It also continued to link fashion and clothing, cooperating with many leading designers.

The company also launched clothing and footwear for business travellers to wear on business trips.

Puma products are very popular. New models of their shoes are snapped up by fashion-conscious people. Their products are outsourced and distributed in more than 80 countries. Puma are planning a world-wide roll-out of their concept stores to expand their market.

Reading
Steve Jobs

A **Before you read the article say what you know about the following:**

1 Bill Gates
2 Steve Jobs
3 Tim Berners-Lee

The Guardian profile: Steve Jobs

By Duncan Campbell

Jobs is a co-founder of Apple, the man behind the astonishing success of the computer animation firm Pixar - of *Toy Story* and *Finding*
5 *Nemo* fame - a billionaire regarded as a visionary in the industry.

Born to an Egyptian Arab father and an American mother in Green Bay, Wisconsin, 49 years ago,
10 Steven Paul was adopted soon after his birth by Paul and Clara Jobs, who lived in Mountain View in Santa Clara, California.

After completing high school in
15 California, Jobs went north to Reed College in Portland, Oregon, but dropped out after one term. Back in California, he became a regular at the Homebrew
20 Computer Club, along with another young man, five years his senior, with his own visions of the future: Steve Wozniak.

In 1976, when Jobs was 21, he
25 and Wozniak started their own business, the Apple Computer Company, in Jobs' family garage. With a mission to produce affordable personal computers the
30 pair went to market with the Apple I shortly afterwards. A local company ordered 25 of the prototype and the pair were on their way. The almost instant
35 success of Apple I and its sister Apple II launched them. By the age of 25 Jobs was worth $165m.

Apple was the first landmark in Jobs' career but by 1985 he was on
40 his way out after John Sculley, who had joined the company from Pepsi-Cola, decided it was time to

drop the pilot. Four years later Jobs returned with another
45 computer company, NextStep, which never achieved the success of Apple but reminded people that he was far from finished.

What was later hailed as Jobs'
50 second coming started with his involvement in Pixar, the animation company he bought from the Star Wars director, George Lucas, and renamed. The hit movie
55 *Toy Story* instantly established it as one of the key players in Hollywood, a success only added to with the release of *Finding Nemo*.

Pixar made Jobs a billionaire.
60 His triumph there also reminded people of his ability to predict the technological future. Apple asked him to return. He came back in 1997 and within a year the ailing
65 company was once more making handsome profits.

His latest venture may turn out to be the most influential. Since the emergence of high-speed Internet
70 the music industry has complained that it is being brought to its knees by the pirates of downloading. The dream of hundreds of companies has been a way to harness the
75 desire for music on the Internet and turn it into profit. Jobs believes that iTunes is the answer.

But then Jobs does not believe in underselling his companies. 'This
80 will go down in history as the turning point for the music industry,' he told Fortune magazine at the launch of iTunes in the US.

85 Journalists who have followed Jobs' career have also seen another side of his personality when he has walked out of interviews, irritated at the line of questioning and
90 refusing intrusions into his personal life. He is not known for his patience.

'We can't have a heroic figure without a fatal flaw,' was the
95 assessment of David Plotnikoff, writing a profile earlier this year in local paper. 'Jobs ... exudes arrogance of a certain blastfurnace intensity that people find hard to
100 overlook ... With Jobs, it was never enough to say "We're right on this and they're wrong". No, it was always "We're right on this and they're idiots".'

105 But Plotnikoff added: 'There is simply no way the Mac could have been born without that supreme confidence.' If there has been a theme to Jobs' success it has been
110 his genius, as it were, for finding other geniuses and promoting their brilliance.

From the Guardian

B **Answer the following questions.**

1 Why were the following dates important?
   a) 1976 **b)** 1985 **c)** 1997

2 What was Steve Jobs' first success?

3 What made him:
   a) a millionaire? **b)** a billionaire?

4 Why did he leave Apple?

5 Why did he come back?

6 How long did it take to turn Apple round?

7 Why does Jobs think his latest venture will be a turning point for the music industry?

8 Why do you think Steve Jobs is successful?

Language review
Present and past tenses

Complete the rules with the words *present simple, present continuous, present perfect* or *past simple*.

1 We use the .... to describe actions and situations which are generally true: *We sell our products into many markets.*

2 We use the .... to describe completed actions or events which took place at a particular time or over a period of time in the past: *She telephoned me yesterday; He became Chief Executive in 2005.*

3 We use the .... to describe current or temporary situations: *Petrol is getting more expensive by the week; She's working in Poland on a fixed-term contract.*

4 We use the .... to describe life experiences, present results of past actions or announce news: *The company has done well recently.*

➡ page 131

A Discuss these questions about the article on page 32.

1 In paragraphs three, four and seven which tense is mainly used and why?

2 Find examples of the present perfect in paragraphs eight and ten and say why it is used.

3 In paragraphs one, nine and eleven find one example of the present simple and say why it is used.

B Research Steve Jobs on the Internet and write a final paragraph saying what he is doing now.

C Write an article on TOYS"Я"US ™ for a business magazine. Use the notes below, putting the verbs in brackets into appropriate tenses.

THE COMPANY
One of world's largest toy retailers
(sell) merchandise through more than 1,500 stores
685 toy stores in US, 605 international toy stores, and 216 BABIES"Я"US ™ stores

HOW THE COMPANY STARTED
1948 Charles Lazarus (begin) business for children only
(set up) first baby furniture store Washington DC
1957 Lazarus (open) first toy supermarket
1978 TOYS"Я"US ™ (become) public company

RECENT EVENTS
(open) Times Square flagship store New York 2001
recently (lose) number one US position to Wal-Mart
significantly (expand) video merchandising in US stores
(evolve) into a 11 billion dollar business

WHAT IT IS DOING NOW
(try) to regain number one position from Wal-Mart
now (focus) on BABIES"Я"US ™
(work) hard to be number one baby product specialist store chain in world

Vocabulary
Prefixes

A The following words formed with a prefix are from the article on page 32: *co*-founder, *re*named, *under*selling. Match the common prefixes from the box with the correct meaning below.

*over*produce   *mis*interpret   *out*-vote   *co*-founder   *re*named
ultra-sophisticated   *ex*-president   *de*activate   *under*selling

1 too much
2 better / more than
3 badly
4 extremely
5 former
6 opposite
7 with
8 too little
9 again

B Underline the odd one out in each group.

1	**under**	perform / rate / charge / profit
2	**co**	producer / worker / boss / author
3	**re**	launch / engineer / locate / decide
4	**over**	spend / estimate / supply / lose
5	**mis**	manage / judge / calculate / look
6	**out**	perform / bid / class / win
7	**ultra**	efficient / cautious / modern / big
8	**ex**	boss / director / employee / staff
9	**de**	merge / nationalise / regulate / grow

C Complete the sentences with the correct word from Exercise B.

1 Several sales staff *underperformed* last year and didn't meet their targets.
2 Smith and Turner were the two .... of the report.
3 We will .... our product as soon as we have finished the modifications.
4 We .... the number of people who would buy our product in Asia.
5 Because the company has been .... for years we are close to bankruptcy.
6 They had to .... their rivals to take over the company.
7 Our .... factory has state-of-the-art machinery.
8 My .... was impossible to work with so I left the company.
9 Many state companies in Eastern Europe are being ....

 Vocabulary file pages 171–173

Skills
Negotiating

A **Three key skills in negotiating are:**

1 signalling (drawing attention to what you're about to say)
2 checking understanding
3 summarising.

Study the examples of each in the Useful language box.

Useful language

Signalling	Checking understanding	Summarising
I'd like to make a suggestion. I think we should leave this point and come back to it later.	Sorry, could you repeat that?	Can we just summarise the points we've agreed so far?
I want to ask a question. How are we going to pay for this?	Are you saying you don't have that quantity in stock?	OK, so we're agreed. You'll pay for delivery and get everything to us by the end of June.
	So what you're saying is you will ...	

B **Now read the negotiation between the Commercial Director of a car manufacturer and the General Manager of a business equipment firm. Underline any examples of *signalling*, *checking understanding* or *summarising*.**

Director   We're willing to give you a 12% discount on our list price if you buy over 30 vehicles – that's OK. It'll mean you'll be paying just under £14,400 for each vehicle. But that's providing you don't have any special requirements which cost us more money.

Manager   Special requirements? What do you mean exactly?

Director   Oh, I don't know, if you want the interior of the car to be changed, for example. The price we've agreed is for our standard model. Or if you wanted a modification which costs money, more storage compartments, for example.

Manager   Right. It's true, some of our top sales staff can be fussy. I don't know though, we'd still like a 12% discount, given the size of our order.

Director   Mmm, OK, let me make a suggestion. We give you 12% but if someone wants extras or a modification, we'll offer you a 10% discount on that car. That's fair enough, isn't it?

Manager   OK, so you're saying you will modify the car if we ask you to?

Director   Exactly.

Manager   Right then, let's see what we've got. The price will be £14,400, providing there are no extras or modifications to the interior. You'll make small changes if we ask you to, but reduce the discount by 2%.

Director   That's it. OK. Let's talk about delivery now.

C 🎧 4.3 **Listen to some expressions, which were used later in the same negotiation. Which ones are *not* examples of *signalling*, *checking understanding* or *summarising*?**

D **Role play the following situation.**
An Italian shoe manufacturer has produced a new range of women's leather boots. A German retailer is considering placing an order for 250 pairs of each design. The Sales Manager and Chief Buyer negotiate the contract.

Sales Manager turn to page 149. Chief Buyer turn to page 147.

CASE STUDY

CAMDEN FC

Background

Camden Football Club is one of the great success stories in English football. Today, it is third in the Premier Division (the top division) and has reached the quarter finals of the European Champions League competition. The club gets huge crowds at its ground and its Polish manager, Cristos Sroda, is idolised by fans. Camden is also a great commercial success and is very profitable.

What has brought about its success? Firstly, the manager Cristos had a clear strategy for the team from the start. He developed young players who had come through the club's youth training scheme. The team was also strengthened by one or two carefully chosen foreign players.

🎧 **4.4** Listen to an interview on *Sportsline*, a weekly television programme focussing on football. The presenter of the programme talks to a football manager about Camden Football Club. Take notes of the key points.

Current situation

Camden's current four-year sponsorship deal with an insurance company is about to finish. Sophie Legrange is considering a new and better deal with United Media plc, the powerful publishing, TV production and mobile phone group. It is not only the increased money from sponsorship which appeals to Camden, however. United Media's broad range of business activities would offer many other opportunities to increase revenue.

United Media is interested in Camden because the club's success has brought it over 4m fans in the UK and 40m in the Far East. Camden played a friendly match recently in China which was watched live by a Chinese audience of over 250m.

Representatives of Camden and United Media are meeting shortly to discuss a possible sponsorship deal.

4.5 Listen to the excerpt from the radio programme *Sporting World*. How does it affect the result of your negotiation?

AGENDA

Date: 10 May
Time: 10am
Venue: Conference room, Camden Football Ground

1 Total value of the contract
2 Timing of payments
3 Advertising
4 Control of players and club activities
5 Paolo Rossetti
6 Official supplier of Camden football boots
7 Other commercial opportunities
8 Fringe benefits for players
9 Other points

Task

You are members of the negotiating team of either:
Camden FC (turn to page 147) or
United Media plc (turn to page 154).

1 Read your role card and prepare for the negotiation. Work out your objectives, priorities, strategy and tactics. Think carefully about what concessions you are willing to make. An agenda has been prepared in advance of the meeting.
2 Do the negotiation.

Writing

1 If the negotiation was successful, write a press release from the point of view of either Camden FC or United Media outlining the main points of the agreement and the benefits to the organisation you represent. The tone and style of the message should express pleasure and optimism.

or

2 If the negotiation was unsuccessful, write a letter to your opposite number in the negotiation expressing your regret that you were unable to make a deal. However, you should indicate that you might be willing to reopen negotiations in the future as clearly there could be areas of mutual benefit.

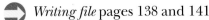 *Writing file* pages 138 and 141

Job satisfaction

'People who work sitting down get paid more than people who work standing up. '

Ogden Nash (1902–1971)

Starting up

A Which of the following would motivate you to work harder? Choose your top five and rank them in order of priority. Explain your priorities.

bonus	more responsibility	working for a successful company
bigger salary	threat of redundancy	a better working environment
commission	hard-working boss	promotion opportunities
praise	good colleagues	perks or fringe benefits

B Discuss these questions.

1 A recent US survey showed children preferred parents to go out and earn money rather than spend more time with them. What does this show, in your opinion?

2 Would you prefer a male or female boss? Why?

3 For what reasons might you change jobs? How often would you expect to do so in your lifetime? Is changing jobs often a sign of success in your culture?

 Vocabulary file pages 171–173

• *Turn to page 137 for the quiz 'Are you in danger of burning out?'*

Vocabulary

Synonyms and word building

A Match the items which are similar in meaning.

1	bureaucracy	**a)**	assessment
2	autonomy	**b)**	remuneration
3	burnout	**c)**	fringe benefits
4	pay	**d)**	severance package
5	appraisal	**e)**	independence
6	perks	**f)**	breakdown
7	golden handshake	**g)**	red tape

B Complete the sentences with words or phrases from Exercise A.

1 Most people like to have control over their work and therefore put .... near the top of their list of motivating factors.

2 Dealing with .... is a very time-consuming, demotivating problem which affects large businesses and organisations.

3 Overwork can lead to .... if not spotted early.

4 Many job satisfaction studies, perhaps surprisingly, have found that often .... is not the most motivating factor.

5 Offering .... rather than a salary increase can be a way of retaining employees in traditionally high staff turnover industries.

6 He received a very generous .... when he left the company.

7 One way for managers to monitor and develop staff and loyalty is by using .... interviews.

C Complete each sentence with the correct form of the word in bold. Sometimes you will need to use a negative form.

1 **satisfy**

a) The survey showed that staff working flexible hours were more .... with their jobs than those working fixed hours.

b) Low pay and poor working conditions create .... workers.

c) Small European companies are top of job .... league tables.

2 **motivate**

a) What are the strongest .... factors in people's lives?

b) Workers become .... if they work long hours for low pay.

c) What was your .... for becoming a salesperson?

3 **frustrate**

a) You could see the .... building up in the workforce.

b) I find talking to him .... because he never listens.

c) I felt so .... with their attitude that I decided to resign.

Discussion

Job satisfaction

1 What do you find satisfying and frustrating about your work or studies?

2 Who or what inspires you at work?

3 How true do you think the following statements are?

a) There is no such thing as company loyalty these days.

b) True fulfilment can only come with a job you love.

c) You should work to live not live to work.

Listening

Staff satisfaction survey

A Helen Tucker is Human Resources Director at Procter and Gamble. Each year, the company conducts a survey throughout their organisation to find out how satisfied their staff are in their jobs. Write down five questions that you think will appear in the survey.

B 🎧 5.1 Listen to the first part of the interview. Which of your questions does Helen Tucker mention?

▲ Helen Tucker

C 🎧 **5.1 Listen to the first part again. Note down all questions in the survey. Compare your answers with other members of your group.**

D 🎧 **5.2 Listen to the second part of the interview and answer these questions.**

1 What three ways have job priorities changed in recent years?
2 What examples does Helen Tucker give of flexible working programmes?
3 Apart from flexible working conditions, what other factors might persuade people to join Procter and Gamble?
4 Why did Procter and Gamble introduce a car share scheme?

Reading

Perks that work

A **What kind of perks would you like to have when joining a new company?**

B **In which lines are these ideas mentioned?**

1 money is a less important motivator than a caring company
2 giving employees more choice how they organise their time away from work
3 the disadvantages of offering perks
4 creating an atmosphere and culture which employees feel they belong to
5 examples of up-market perks offered by technology companies
6 the increased benefits being offered to employees

C **Look in the article to complete these word partnerships.**
For example: *personal problems*

1 personal ..*problems*..   5 common ....
2 financial ....   6 social ....
3 top ....   7 corporate ....
4 general ....   8 employee ....

D **Complete these sentences with word partnerships from Exercise C.**

1 He has resigned after having a lot of .... this year.
2 Building up .... is important with unemployment at a record low.
3 Our .... is in charge of running the company and for making joint strategic decisions with the CEO.
4 The new CEO transformed the bureaucratic .... to profit-minded entrepreneurship.
5 Companies who pollute the environment are ignoring their ethical and ....
6 The .... should get the biggest bonuses.
7 We need to use logic and .... not our emotions to make this decision.

E **Discuss these statements.**

1 Companies should be fully involved in the lives of their employees.
2 'Sick days' are a perk.
3 A pay rise is better than a job in a caring company.

Perks that work

*By **Robert Burke***

Keeping people happy is an increasingly tough trick. With unemployment at record lows, 'companies are trying just about
5 anything' to retain employees, says Jay Doherty of the New York-based human-resources consulting firm William M. Mercer Inc. Not only are
10 employees being pampered, they're getting more money, better benefits and help with personal problems such as child care and financial planning.
15 Bosses once shunned such intervention. Retention 'is no longer a human resource issue, it's a business issue,' Doherty says.
20 Because technology companies face the tightest labor markets, they have been the most aggressive in devising ways to keep workers. Herndon-based
25 Net2000 Communications, for example, puts top performers behind the wheel of luxury cars like a BMW 323i or Z3. MicroStrategy, a Vienna-based
30 data miner, goes a step further and has hosted all of its employees on Caribbean cruises.
Such perks are great for the employee, but do they make
35 sense for the company? Maybe. Doherty says all companies - including technology firms - 'have to be careful they don't create a business model that's not
40 profitable.' Don't throw money at workers who want to leave because pay raises don't always work. Perks and benefits can be effective, but they have to be
45 custom-fit to the company and the business sector. Don't add new perks just because they seem

like hot trends, he says. 'Too often there's a desperation
50 sometimes to just try anything, and it's very expensive.' MicroStrategy, which reported lower earnings earlier this year, has been rethinking its cruises,
55 for example.
Yet companies still face labor crunches that can really hurt. How do you keep workers? Start by making them feel they're part
60 of a special place with a unique culture. 'We want to hire people that are totally aligned with our values,' says Tim Huval, general manager for South Dakota-based
65 Gateway's 2,200-employee call center and manufacturing facility in Hampton. 'Honesty, efficiency, aggressiveness, respect, teamwork, caring, common sense
70 and fun. Those are values that we live by.' Richmond-based Xperts also lives by the value system. Founder and CEO William Tyler pushes pairing quality of life with
75 a sense of social responsibility.
Workers can designate which non-profit groups Xperts contributes to, for example. A strong culture makes it hard for
80 people to leave, Tyler says. 'They

don't have an urge to leave because they've found a home. They're happy.'
Notice this corporate culture
85 stuff doesn't say much about shareholders or profit. It's a decidedly employee-centric approach. 'If you ask any of them, they're all going to say,
90 "Pay me more money." But that's not the truth,' Tyler says. 'What people are looking for is, "A place that's looking out for me."'
What that means is helping
95 employees cope with problems they face outside the office. 'That is where companies can build employee loyalty,' says Barbara Bailey of William M. Mercer's
100 Richmond office. One popular tool is revamping leave policies to create 'flexible leave banks' that put all employee leave into a single category. Employees take
105 time off when they need it and don't have to call it a sick day or vacation. 'Work-life issues are huge,' Bailey says. 'You make them feel as though they're not
110 interested in looking elsewhere, because they're very happy with their life.'
From *Virginia Business Online*

Language review
Passives

- We use the passive when we are not interested in who performs an action or it is not necessary to know: *The product has been withdrawn.*
- We often use it to describe processes and procedures because we are more interested in the process itself than who carries it out: *In the final stage of manufacture, the pills are packaged and wrapped.*
- We use the passive to write in a more formal style because it is less personal than the active. It is often used in reports, minutes and business correspondence: *It was agreed that the budget would be reviewed at the next board meeting.*

➡ page 132

A Match the news extracts a)–h) to the verb forms 1–8.

1 Present simple
2 Past simple
3 Present perfect
4 Past perfect
5 Present continuous
6 Future simple
7 Modal verbs with passives
8 Passive infinitives

a) The report says supervisors *should be trained* to manage telecommuters and should define the hours and tasks expected of them.
b) Those least happy with their work/life balance were the ones who felt they *had been forced* to choose between work and home.
c) Campaigners for paternity leave say it *is* particularly *needed* in the UK where men work the longest hours in the EU.
d) Half-term *is being seen* as an increasingly attractive break by working parents in their late 30s and early 40s.
e) A survey of workers in 13 industrialised countries found the desire for a decent work/life balance *was rated* more highly than a good salary.
f) It *used to be argued* that women had not achieved pay equality because discrimination kept them in more junior jobs.
g) Efforts to encourage more women to return to work after having children *will be hampered* if employers force staff to stick to rigid hours and limit their time off.
h) Some smaller businesses *have been founded* on the principle that work/life balance makes commercial success.

B Complete the extract below with passive forms of the verbs in brackets.

Several surveys ....[1] (conduct) recently concerning the relationship between work and play. According to psychologists, activities are more likely to ....[2] (perceive) as play – and therefore attractive – rather than work – and therefore unattractive – if they ....[3] (enter) into voluntarily. In one experiment, for example, volunteers ....[4] (give) a problem-solving game to perform: some ....[5] (pay) to perform the game and some were not. Those who ....[6] (pay) spent less free time performing than those for whom the only motivation was the pleasure of the game. Thus, motivation to play springs from within and the readiness to perform activities ....[7] (reduce) by external rewards.

C Read the notes for four sections of a report on a proposed Employee Incentive Scheme. Then write sentences, using the passive, to include in the report. For example, *Questionnaires were distributed to all departments.*

PROCEDURE

* Distribute questionnaires: all depts.
* Interview managers
* Canvass sample of workers

PRESENT PROBLEMS

* Not consult staff
* Not allow flexitime

MEASURES TO IMPROVE JOB SATISFACTION SINCE MARCH

* Consult staff properly
* Carry out research into flexitime

INCENTIVE RECOMMENDATIONS

* Introduce new scheme from 1 Nov
* Adopt system of team bonuses
* Carry out further research into share option scheme

Skills

Handling difficult situations

A For each of the situations 1–8 choose an appropriate response a)–h).

1 Someone asks about a colleague who's been fired.

2 You are invited out to dinner when you don't really want to go.

3 A colleague tells you some very bad news about themselves.

4 You arrive late for a meeting.

5 You recognise someone but you can't recall their name.

6 You want to end a conversation at a business reception.

7 You want someone to stop smoking in a no-smoking area.

8 You spill coffee over a client's desk at a meeting.

a) 'Excuse me. I'm afraid smoking isn't allowed here.'

b) 'I'm sorry but there's someone over there that I have to talk to.'

c) 'How clumsy of me. I'm really sorry.'

d) 'I'm terribly sorry to hear that.'

e) 'I'm so sorry. The traffic was a nightmare.'

f) 'I know we've met before but I'm afraid I can't remember the name.'

g) 'That's really kind of you but I'm exhausted after the flight.'

h) 'I'm afraid he left the company last month.'

B 🎧 5.3 Listen to these four conversations. In each case, match what the second speaker says to one of these headings.

- saying 'no' politely
- apologising
- showing sympathy
- ending a conversation

C 🎧 5.3 Listen again. Add one expression from each conversation under an appropriate heading in the Useful language box.

D Discuss what you would do and say in these difficult situations.

1 Your colleague applied for a promotion but didn't get it.

2 You invite a client for a meal and they ask if they can bring a friend. You see this as a business rather than a social occasion.

3 You're staying at a hotel that your host is paying for. It is not very comfortable and you would like to move.

Useful language

Saying 'no' politely
It's very kind / nice of you, but …
I'm very sorry, but …

Apologising
I must apologise …
I'm terribly sorry, but …

Showing sympathy
I quite understand …
I know how you feel …

Ending a conversation
Sorry, I really must be off …
Please excuse me, I really have to leave …

Raising a problem
Could I have a quick word with you?
I need to talk to you about something.

Office attraction

Background

Karl Jansen, Managing Director at London-based Crawford plc, has always believed that employees perform better in a relaxed working atmosphere. The staff rule book is slim and he'd like to keep it that way. However, recent events have made him wonder whether the company culture has become a little too casual. It could be because staff are working later at night and at weekends, or because fierce competition is causing more stress. Whatever the reason, close relationships between colleagues are definitely becoming more common. Look at Karl's e-mail to Jenny Cunningham, Human Resources Director.

To...	Jenny Cunningham
From...	Karl Jansen
Subject	Policy on office relationships
Date	30 June

I'm extremely concerned about the growing number of close relationships between staff. This is having a very bad effect on both performance and morale. As you know, there have been three cases recently where employees have developed personal relationships which seriously affected both their own performance and their colleagues'. Furthermore, I've heard this morning that one of the individuals concerned is threatening the company with legal action.

As a result, I'd like the Human Resources Department to review in detail each of the three cases and advise how to proceed. These are:
1   The appointment of Tania Jordan
2   The re-assignment of John Goodman
3   Complaints against Derek Hartman

The details

1 Appointment of Tania Jordan

A few months ago, Karl and two other directors, Marcus Ball and Julia Kovacs, appointed a new manager. There were three excellent candidates. Finally, Tania Jordan was selected – mainly because Marcus had argued strongly in her favour. Karl discovered later that she and Marcus had started living together. When Karl told him he should have withdrawn from the selection process, Marcus said angrily, 'Listen, I didn't know her so well at the time. In any case, it's my private life. I supported Tania because she was the best person for the job.'

Karl discussed the matter with Jenny. They decided to take no further action.

2 Re-assignment of John Goodman

A few weeks later, a problem arose in the Finance Department. The Financial Director and her ambitious deputy, John Goodman, had formed a very close relationship. Unfortunately, the relationship went sour and they had bitter rows in public. Because of these problems, serious mistakes were made in the annual report and the morale of the whole department was affected.

Karl and the other directors decided to move John to another department. However, John's new position is less challenging with little opportunity for promotion. He believes he's been very badly treated by the management and is threatening to take his case to an industrial tribunal.

3 Complaints against Derek Hartman

A week ago, a part-time employee in the General Office, Claudia Northcott, e-mailed Karl asking for a private meeting with him. When they met, he found out that she was representing all the part-time staff in the department. According to her, the Office Manager, Derek Hartman, is showing favouritism towards one of his staff, Petra Palmer, and this is upsetting everyone in the office. Karl asked for more details.

🎧 **5.4** Listen to an extract from their conversation.

Specific questions

Later on in his e-mail, Karl asked Jenny and her team to consider the following questions.

1 Did we make the right decisions concerning Marcus Ball and John Goodman? What further action, if any, should we take in each case?
2 If the accusation against Derek Hartman is true, what action should we take?
3 Should the company have a written policy on close relationships at work? If so, what should be the main guidelines for staff? What sanctions should there be for staff who don't follow the guidelines?
4 How can we avoid someone gaining an unfair advantage from having a close relationship with another member of staff? Are there any specific examples of bad practice that could be written into the policy document?

Task

You are members of the Human Resources Department at Crawford plc. Discuss the questions in Karl's e-mail and agree what action to take. One of you should take the role of Jenny and chair the meeting.

Writing

As a member of the Human Resources Department, write a set of guidelines on relationships at work for discussion at the next board meeting.

➡ *Writing file* page 142

> *You miss 100% of the shots you never take.*
> Wayne Gretzky, (b.1961) hockey player

OVERVIEW ▼

- [ ] **Vocabulary**
  Describing risk
- [ ] **Listening**
  Effective risk management
- [ ] **Reading**
  Planning for the future
- [ ] **Language review**
  Adverbs of degree
- [ ] **Skills**
  Reaching agreement
- [ ] **Case study**
  Suprema Cars

Starting up

A Which item in each of the categories below carries the most and the least risk? Explain why.

Travel	Lifestyle	Money	Shopping
car	drinking alcohol	property	on line
plane	poor diet	stocks and shares	mail order
train	smoking	savings account	private sales
ship	jogging	cash	auction

B Are you a risk-taker? What risks have you taken?

C What risks do businesses face? Note down three types.

→ *Vocabulary file* page 173

D 🎧 6.1 Listen to Allan Smith, who is an expert in risk management. Note down the risks he mentions.

Vocabulary
Describing risk

A The verbs in the box are used to describe risk. Check their meanings and put them under the appropriate heading.

calculate	eliminate	encounter	estimate	~~face~~
foresee	minimise	prioritise	reduce	spread

Predict	Meet	Assess	Manage
	face		

B Match these halves of sentences from newspaper extracts.

1 Internet businesses ...
2 We can reduce risk ...
3 Trying to minimise risk ...
4 It is impossible to ...
5 It is difficult to foresee the risks ...
6 Actuaries calculate risk ...
7 It's important to consider the ...

a) risks involved when sending staff to work in dangerous locations.
b) in order to advise insurance companies.
c) involved in setting up a new business.
d) eliminate all risk when entering a new market.
e) face increasing risks of running out of money.
f) by spreading our lending to more businesses.
g) is an important part of business strategy.

C The following adjectives can be used with the word *risk*. Which describe a high level of risk? Which describe a low level?

faint	great	huge	minuscule
negligible	remote	serious	significant
slight	substantial	terrible	tremendous

D In pairs, talk about the risks facing one of the following:

1 your company / institution
2 your city / town
3 your country.

Listening
Effective risk management

▲ Steve Fowler

A 6.2 Listen to the first part of the interview with Steve Fowler, Chief Executive of the Institute of Risk Management, London. What are the four main types of risk? Give two examples of each type.

B 6.3 Listen to the second part of the interview and note down the five key steps to effective risk management.

C 6.4 Listen to the final part of the interview. What three examples of effective risk management does he mention? What negative example does he mention?

D In pairs, discuss the following.

1 Give some examples of companies that have handled risk well or badly.
2 Choose a company and say what risk it faces.

Reading
Planning for the future

A In today's fast-changing world, how far ahead can companies realistically plan for the future?

B The following risks are of concern to senior executives. Where do you think they fit into the table below?

Changes in customer demand

Loss of productivity due to staff absence / staff turnover

Increased competition

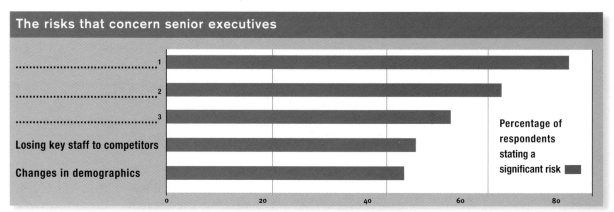

The risks that concern senior executives

..........................1
..........................2
..........................3
Losing key staff to competitors
Changes in demographics

Percentage of respondents stating a significant risk

0   20   40   60   80

C What types of risk are mentioned in the first three paragraphs?

D Why are companies paying more attention to risk management?

E According to the article, which of the people listed below believes the following?

Lord Levene   Ken Davey   Shivan Subramaniam   Neil Irwin

1 Businesses face greater risks because they are trying to expand in many different ways.

2 Businesses need to evaluate risks which can affect their profits.

3 Senior managers need to change their thinking in order to manage risk.

4 Many businesses concentrate too much on less important risks.

5 Businesses should check their exposure to risk often.

6 Businesses which have a well-thought-out approach to risk will increase their profits.

F Match the follow word partnerships as they appear in the article.

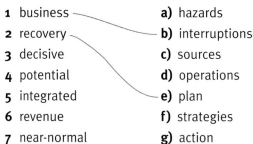

1 business — a) hazards
2 recovery — b) interruptions
3 decisive c) sources
4 potential d) operations
5 integrated e) plan
6 revenue f) strategies
7 near-normal g) action

G Match the word partnerships to the most appropriate verb below. For example: *develop* integrated strategies

take   protect   assess   ~~develop~~   implement   resume   prepare for

H Discussion.

1 Which types of risk do you think will **a)** become more significant in the next 50 years? **b)** become less significant in the next 50 years?

The dangers of not looking ahead

By Andrew Bolger

Risk management has undoubtedly moved up the corporate agenda in recent years with fears of war and terrorism being added to the usual list of business worries.

Shivan Subramaniam, the Chairman and Chief Executive of FM Global, a commercial and industrial property insurer, says: 'Corporations are operating in a turbulent world where businesses are seeking growth through globalisation, outsourcing, consolidation, just-in-time delivery and cross-border supply, further increasing their potential exposure to risk.'

'Add regulatory, legal and labour considerations, and you begin to understand the complex nature of business risk in the 21st century. While acts of terrorism receive the most coverage, it's the more traditional events such as fires, floods, explosions, power failures or natural disasters that have the biggest impact.'

FM Global believes the majority of all loss can be prevented or minimised and this should be the first part of any disaster recovery plan. It also argues that prevention is better than cure and says there is a lot companies can do to stop such events from becoming a disaster in the first place.

However, research shows that more than one-third of the world's leading companies are not sufficiently prepared to protect their main revenue sources and have room for improvement.

Ken Davey, a managing director with FM Global, says: 'To best protect cashflow, competitive position and profit, companies need to assess the potential hazards that can impact top revenue sources and make sure there is business continuity planning.'

Lord Levene, chairman of the Lloyd's insurance market, said recently that companies must be prepared for business interruptions, which accounted for 25 per cent of the $40bn lost as a result of the September 11 terrorist attacks. It was estimated that 90 per cent of medium to large companies that could not resume near-normal operations within five days of an emergency would go out of business.

'Looking ahead 10 years I firmly believe that the most successful, least crisis-prone businesses will be those whose boards have shown firm resolve and taken decisive action,' Lord Levene said. 'Effective, integrated strategies for dealing with tomorrow's risks require a change in culture at board level now.'

A new research report from Marsh, the world's biggest insurance broker, found that half of European companies did not know how to manage the most significant risks to their business.

Most of Europe's senior executives surveyed admitted that they did not have procedures in place to manage properly operational and strategic risks, which were responsible for most company failures in the twenty-first century.

The survey found that the three most significant risks, and those that businesses felt least able to manage, were:
- Increased competition
- Adverse changes in customer demand
- Reduced productivity because of staff absenteeism and turnover.

'While business leaders are aware that these risks are the most threatening to their future survival and growth they are scratching their heads when it comes to protecting their businesses against them,' says Neil Irwin, European development director of Marsh's corporate client practice. 'Management processes could easily help companies identify and address these risks. Instead, too many companies take a low-level approach to risk management preferring to focus on easy-to-solve risks, such as asset protection and health and safety.'

Mr Irwin says: 'Risk is dynamic, it changes with the environment. Unless businesses accept this and review risk regularly, they could eventually find themselves in a state of crisis, struggling to survive rather than focused on growth. Business leaders have an obligation to their employees, shareholders and other stakeholders to properly protect themselves against risk. Businesses that do attempt to manage these risks will boost their bottom lines.'

From the *Financial Times*

FINANCIAL TIMES

Language review
Adverbs of degree

- We can use adverbs to strengthen the meaning of adjectives:
  *International businesses believe they are not **fully prepared** to handle a growing number of threats in an **increasingly volatile** global marketplace.*
- We can also use them to soften the meaning:
  *The report was **slightly critical**.*

 page 132

A Which adverbs are the strongest and which are the weakest in the box below?

a bit	entirely	exceptionally	extremely	fairly
highly	increasingly	moderately	quite	rather
reasonably	slightly	somewhat	totally	very

B Complete these dialogues with a suitable adverb.

1 'What were your results like last year?'
'......................... good. We increased profits by over 5%.'

2 'How was the launch of your new product?'
'......................... successful. We've been flooded with orders ever since.'

3 'Do you really think we should try to enter that new market?'
'It's .... risky but on balance I think we should go ahead.'

4 'What did you think of the presentation?'
'It was .... useless. Most of the audience lost interest after five minutes.'

5 'Are you confident about those sales projections?'
'......................... confident, although it's going to be tough.'

C Write short dialogues using some of the phrases below.

fairly accurate	deeply disappointed
incredibly well-prepared	slightly damaged
absolutely awful	totally unrealistic
severely criticised	superbly presented
badly misjudged	thoroughly enjoyed

Skills
Reaching agreement

A 🎧 **6.5** Following the brainstorming meeting in Unit 2 International marketing (page 19), the team meets again to finalise plans for the launch of the website. Listen to the authentic meeting and complete the table.

Ideas	Approved Yes/No	Comments
Online promotion		
TV advertising		
Sponsorship		
Advertisements in journals		
Using established contacts		
Newspapers / magazines		

B Match the expressions below from the meeting to the appropriate heading in the Useful language box. (Some can be put under more than one heading.) Use the Audio script on page 163 to check the context of each expression.

1 ... I'm not sure if I agree with that.
2 I don't think we can ...
3 ... I would say it's really risky ...
4 OK.
5 Yes, I would agree with that.
6 Yeah. I think that's important ...
7 ... it's very important that we use the contacts ...
8 Could we combine the two maybe?
9 I just think ...
10 ... I think we've all agreed ...

C Work in groups of three. Read the information below. Then role play the meeting.

You are managers in a mobile phone company, Speakeasy Ltd., based in San Diego, California. The company wishes to send two executives to set up a branch office overseas. However, the location chosen is politically very unstable and there has been some terrorist activity in the area recently. Hold a meeting to decide:

a) whether to send the two executives to the area

b) if so, how to reduce the risks to which they will be exposed.

Manager A turn to page 146.
Manager B turn to page 151.
Manager C turn to page 155.

Useful language

Asking for opinions
Does anybody have any strong feelings about ...?

Giving opinions
Well, unfortunately, I think we'll probably have to ...

Agreeing
I think I'd agree with you there ...

Disagreeing
Well hold on ...

Adding a condition
I agree providing we can ...
We can do that if ...

Making suggestions
What about if we ...?

Emphasising
I keep going on about this, but ...

Summarising
So, we've agreed that ...

Suprema Cars

Background

'Our cars are for people who want something different.'

This has been the slogan for over 50 years of Suprema Cars, a manufacturer of a classic English sports car. The car is mostly handmade in the company's factory in northern England. Suprema Cars produces approximately 500 cars a year. About five years ago, the company began to lose sales and market share, and in the last two years, it has made a loss.

Recently, there have been problems with the labour force. The factory workers have demanded higher wages and better working conditions. They are also unhappy because the management is insisting that they increase production, but the workers think this will have a bad effect on the quality of the cars. In the last few months, there has been an increase in the number of Suprema cars that have broken down.

The company still has many loyal customers. People buy Suprema sports cars because they are handmade and have an image of quality and craftsmanship. Customers love the car's classic design and excellent performance. They are willing to pay the existing prices for the cars, but it is not certain that the company could increase prices significantly without losing more customers.

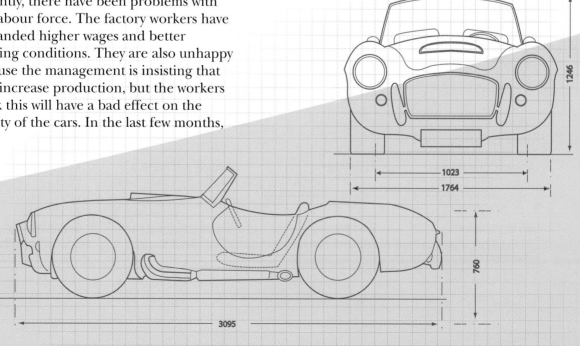

A time for taking risks

Jack Dexter, Managing Director, and his management team realise they must increase profitability or go out of business. A management consultant has advised them that they have the following options:

1 Cut the prices of the cars and accept a lower profit margin. Currently, the profit margin is 60%.

2 Cut production costs by installing automated machinery. Modernise the factory. In recent years, the roof of the factory has started to leak and could become hazardous. Raise prices by 20%.

3 Increase production substantially to approximately 4,000 cars a year. Subcontract some of the manufacture of the components to a low cost foreign manufacturer.

4 Try to get additional finance from an outside source then have a major launch of the cars in the United States.

5 Set up a joint venture with an overseas car manufacturer. An engine manufacturer in an unstable country in South East Asia has expressed interest in a joint venture to build all the engines for Suprema Cars. If they do this, Suprema would have to send out a team of engineers to the country to supervise production in the early stages.

6 Use the Suprema Cars brand name, and design and launch a sporty, environmentally friendly, dual fuel, small car.

7 Accept the approach of a major European manufacturer who is interested in providing finance and expertise to boost sales of Suprema Cars in return for a substantial stake in the company.

Type of risk	Option 1	Option 2	Option 3	Option 4	Option 5	Option 6	Option 7
Reputation							
Personal security							
Country / political							
Environmental							
Design and construction							
Financial							
Morale of workforce							
Legal							

Task

You are a member of Suprema Car's management team. Work in small groups.

1 Identify the types of risk in each option. Use the table above to help you.

2 Evaluate the levels of risk according to the following scale:

very high   high   medium   low   risk-free

3 Discuss the options. Consider the advantages and disadvantages of each one.

4 At this early stage, which option seems to be the best? Meet with other groups to discuss your ideas.

 6.6 Now listen to a conversation between Jack Dexter, Managing Director, and his Finance Director, Anita Taylor.

1 Which option(s) is Jack Dexter definitely not interested in?

2 Which option(s) is he quite interested in?

3 Which option(s) does he favour?

Do you agree with Jack? If not, give your reasons.

Writing

As members of the Suprema Cars management team, write a report for Jack Dexter analysing the options you considered. Make recommendations on what Suprema Cars should do.

➡ *Writing file pages 144 and 145*

e-commerce

❝ *Technology is the knack of so arranging the world that we don't have to experience it.* ❞

Max Frisch, (1911–1991)
Swiss architect, playwright and novelist

Starting up

Discuss these questions.

1 What goods or services do you buy over the Internet? What do you prefer not to buy?

2 What problems have you had buying on the Internet?

3 What kind of products or services are best sold on the Net?

4 Are there any things which could not or should not be sold on the Net?

5 What are the risks of e-commerce for **a)** the companies involved? **b)** their customers?

Listening
Success online

▲ Jeff Kimbell

A 🎧 **7.1 Listen to the first part of the interview with Jeff Kimbell, Marketing Director Europe, for Dell, and complete the sentences below.**

1 Dell has a .... with its customers.

2 They don't use .... to sell their goods.

3 They offer .... to customers to help customers make a
....

4 Customers can buy a system ....

B 🎧 **7.2 Listen to the second part of the interview and give four reasons why Dell has been successful doing business online.**

C 🎧 **7.3 Listen to the final part of the interview and say if the following statements are true or false.**

1 People will be less worried about security.

2 People will still want to go to shops to touch and feel products.

3 Advances in technology will encourage people to shop online.

D Do you agree with the statements in Exercise C above?

Vocabulary
Internet terms

A We often use the words and phrases below to talk about e-commerce. Check that you understand their meaning. Use a dictionary to help you.

browse	directories	hits	keyword	locate	Net
online	search	search engines	site	surfers	traffic

B *Topsite* is a service that helps companies improve their e-commerce business. Use the words and phrases above to complete this promotional page from its website.

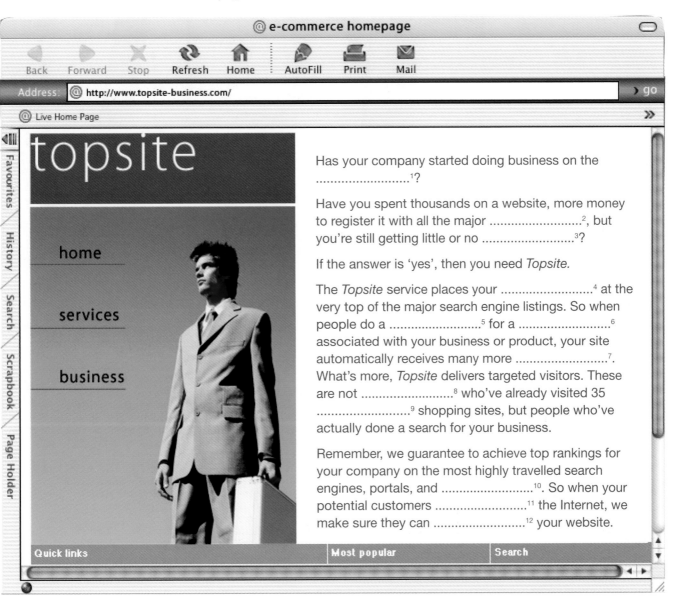

@ e-commerce homepage

Back   Forward   Stop   Refresh   Home   AutoFill   Print   Mail

Address: @ http://www.topsite-business.com/   › go

@ Live Home Page

Favourites / History / Search / Scrapbook / Page Holder

topsite

home

services

business

Has your company started doing business on the ....[1]?

Have you spent thousands on a website, more money to register it with all the major ....[2], but you're still getting little or no ....[3]?

If the answer is 'yes', then you need *Topsite*.

The *Topsite* service places your ....[4] at the very top of the major search engine listings. So when people do a ....[5] for a ....[6] associated with your business or product, your site automatically receives many more ....[7]. What's more, *Topsite* delivers targeted visitors. These are not ....[8] who've already visited 35 ....[9] shopping sites, but people who've actually done a search for your business.

Remember, we guarantee to achieve top rankings for your company on the most highly travelled search engines, portals, and ....[10]. So when your potential customers ....[11] the Internet, we make sure they can ....[12] your website.

Quick links   Most popular   Search

C Discuss these questions.

1 Which search engines do you use?
2 What makes a website easy or difficult to use? Why?
3 What do you like about the sites you visit regularly?
4 How much time do you spend browsing on the Net?
5 How can businesses make sure their websites receive more hits than their competitors?

Reading
Internet shopping

A What's the difference between a 'bricks and mortar' and an 'online' retailer? Can you give an example of each?

B What do you know about these companies: Amazon, eBay, Sears Roebuck?

Internet shopping – the sequel

By Neil Buckley

Pets.com; Webvan; Boo.com. The road to the online retailing future is littered with the wrecks of Internet start-ups once seen as the pioneers of a retailing revolution.

The shape of e-tail, however, is very different from what was predicted a few years ago. Apart from Amazon and eBay – the web's biggest forum for buying and selling, though it is an auction house not a retailer – most of the biggest online retailers are not Internet start-ups but traditional shop or mail-order groups. Retailers have brought their investment capacity and trusted brand names to bear on Internet shopping - thus boosting public confidence. Many have integrated online sales into a 'multichannel' strategy that may link a website, shops and a mail-order catalogue.

'There was a time when everybody said the Internet was going to steal purchases from shops. But the opposite is happening: multichannel retailing is the reality today,' says Darrell Rigby, head of the global retail practice at Bain & Co, the management consultants. 'Many classic bricks-and-mortar retailers actually started making money on their online operations long before Amazon did.'

A prime example of the fusion of the online and so-called 'offline' retail worlds is Amazon itself. The company has expanded well beyond its roots as a seller of books and CDs, acting as an online mall selling everything from gourmet foods to clothing. Evolving from pure retailer to 'retail platform', it now conducts its online commerce in partnership with bricks-and-mortar retailers such as Target, Nordstrom, Borders and Circuit City.

That blending of online and offline is offering consumers new ways to shop. They may research and order their purchase online, but have it delivered to a nearby shop - a service offered by retailers such as Sears Roebuck and Circuit City – so as to avoid delivery charges and allow them to see or try it on first.

Some of the biggest US retailers are developing integrated operations. JC Penney, the century-old department store chain, saw its Internet sales reach $600m last year. It offers 200,000 items that can be delivered to customers' homes or any of its 1,020 shops.

Steve Riordan, a consultant at AT Kearney, says traditional retailers that have not yet embraced the online world face heavy investment and some tough choices. Are they going to run online operations themselves or outsource them? Do they use the same sourcing model from the same factories? Do they have different distribution centres?

While the US still leads the way, it does not have a monopoly on successful Internet retailers. Tesco, the British supermarket chain, has the world's biggest online grocery business. It has helped Safeway, the third-largest US supermarket chain, set up its Internet operations.

The biggest e-commerce site in Japan is Rakuten, a home-grown online shopping mall that began life in 1997 with just 13 shops. Today, it has more than 10,000 and a share of the e-commerce market three times bigger than second-ranking Yahoo Japan, according to a report by JP Morgan.

Some pure Internet retailers are also continuing to grow. Yoox.com – which sells end-of-season and exclusive goods from designers such as Armani, Prada and Dolce & Gabbana - has proved that designer labels will sell online and that European e-tailers can succeed internationally.

It chose to launch in Europe first, close to the designers whose goods it sells. Yoox now sells in seven languages to 25 countries in Europe, North America and Japan. Its stylish site – which it calls an 'e-concept store' – enables shoppers to 'zoom' in on clothes and see them from different angles, and includes video and music.

Federico Marchetti, the Italian former investment banker who is Yoox's founder and chief executive, says that anyone selling online does not just have to get the technology and orders right. They also have to provide fun and entertainment. 'What we have been trying to do with Yoox is build a very nice customer experience,' he says. 'The online retailer always has to be doing something interesting and different.'

From the Financial Times

FINANCIAL TIMES

C **Match the summaries below to the first six paragraphs of the article.**

a) People mistakenly thought that Internet sales would take sales away from traditional stores.

b) A large number of Internet companies were unsuccessful.

c) A well-known American retailer is getting an increasing amount of revenue from online sales.

d) The largest online sellers are well-established businesses.

e) Consumers are taking advantage of the new partnerships by shopping online but using traditional retailers to collect their goods.

f) Some well-known Internet companies have joined with established companies to sell a wide range of products.

D **Now read the rest of the article and answer the questions below.**

1 What issues should traditional retailers consider before going online?

2 What facts show that a) Tesco and b) Rakuten have been highly successful in selling online?

3 According to Federico Marchetti, what do Internet businesses need to do to be successful?

E **Match the following word partnerships.**

1 distribution	a) labels	5 supermarket	e) catalogue
2 online	b) charge	6 shopping	f) houses
3 designer	c) retailing	7 auction	g) chains
4 delivery	d) centre	8 mail-order	h) mall

F **Check your answers in the article. Complete the following sentences with one of the word partnerships above.**

1 Unless you collect the goods from the retail store, there is an additional ....

2 Sotheby's and Christie's are probably the most famous .... in the world. Their sales of antiques and paintings are legendary.

3 In the US many people spend the whole day at their local .... because it is easy to park and you can buy everything there.

4 Some traditional businesses have found that they can make a lot of money from .... with a small investment in an easy-to-use website.

5 These days many .... sell not only food, but also services such as insurance and banking.

6 Goods with .... command premium prices in the shops.

7 From our .... just outside Paris we supply a network of wholesalers across Europe.

8 Many people like the convenience of ordering goods from home using a ....

G **Discuss these statements.**

1 All retailers will have to sell online.

2 There is no safe way of buying goods online.

3 Online businesses will never be able to guarantee delivery on time because they rely on postal services.

4 Some products and services cannot be sold online.

Language review
Conditionals

There are many different types of conditional sentence:
- First conditional: *If we get that designer, we'll have a winning team.*
- Second conditional: *If we relaunched our website, we'd get better results.*
- Third conditional: *If we'd prepared properly, we wouldn't have lost the contract.*
- 'Zero' conditional: *When markets crash, everyone suffers.*

The following are also examples of conditional sentences:
- *Lose that password and we'll never be able to access that file again.*
- *Tell us what you need to get the job done and you'll have it.*
- *Should you need any further information, please contact our helpline.*
- *Had the market conditions been better, the share offer would have been a success.*
- *Given time, our factory can meet all those orders.*

 → page 133

A Match sentences 1–12 to the six headings below.

| promise | invitation / request | speculating about the future |
| bargaining | reflecting on the past | advice / warning / threat |

1 They would've gone bust if they'd taken his advice.

2 If I were you, I'd redesign your website.

3 We'll deliver within 24 hours if you order online.

4 We'll be able to expand if they come up with the finance.

5 If you reduced your price by 8%, we'd increase our order substantially.

6 Your money back if not 100% satisfied.

7 If we go online our overheads will fall.

8 If you would like to apply, call Human Resources on 020 7753 3420.

9 If you order by the end of the month we can give you a discount.

10 I wouldn't do that if I were you.

11 If we'd had a better website, we'd have attracted more customers.

12 I would be grateful if you would advise your staff as soon as possible.

B Decide whether each of the situations below is a) *likely* or b) *unlikely* to happen to you. Then, tell your partner what you will or would do.

1 you get a pay rise next year   4 you travel abroad next year

2 you win a lot of money   5 you have to give a presentation in English

3 your computer gets a virus   6 your company is taken over by a competitor

C Discuss what went wrong in the following situation. Use the notes from the job list extract below. For example, *If they'd set up the site properly, they wouldn't have had so many complaints.*

ClickShop.com is in the Internet shopping business. In order to save money when it redesigned its website six months ago, it decided not to employ a specialist design company. Instead, the work was done by some of its own employees who had limited experience. Technical problems have now led to customer complaints, which have impacted on sales.

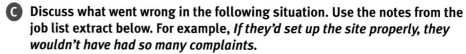

- set site up properly
- use an expert
- allocate a bigger budget
- listen to customer feedback
- plan carefully
- not try to cut corners
- recognise problems earlier
- do more research

Skills
Presentations

▲ Roger Marris

A 🎧 **7.4 Roger Marris, Head of Business Development at Smarterwork, gives a presentation to some customers. Listen to the first extract and answer these questions.**

1 What service does Smarterwork offer?

2 What do these figures refer to? **a)** 14 **b)** 60,000 **c)** 90

3 Who are its two types of users?

B 🎧 **7.5 Listen to the second extract and complete the stages in the process.**

- The client posts a project.
- Suppliers visit the site and make bids.
- ....
- ....
- The client transfers the fee to a holding account.
- ....
- The task gets completed and the client signs off the work.
- ....
- Smarterwork takes a commission.

C 🎧 **7.4 Listen again to the first extract.**

1 Which of the following does Roger do at the start of his presentation?
   a) introduce himself   **c)** tell a story
   b) greet the audience   **d)** ask a question

2 Complete what Roger says at the start of his presentation.

   This morning, ...¹ talk to you about Smarterwork. I'm going to ....² an overview of Smarterwork, then ....³ you about our two types of users and finally ....⁴ how it all works. Feel free to ask any questions you like as we go along.

D 🎧 **7.5 Listen again to the second extract. Note down the language Roger uses to introduce the stages in the process. For example, *Firstly ...***

E **Match these expressions from the presentation to headings in the Useful language box.**

1 Can you just raise your hands?

2 The great thing about the Internet is ...

3 What that means is ...

4 Right. The next thing I'd like to do is ...

5 As you can see, it outlines the steps involved.

Useful language

Commenting
I think that's interesting because ...
I think what this means is ...

Involving the audience
OK, what is Smarterwork?
How many of you have heard of ...?

Emphasising
I'd just like to highlight ...
I'd like to stress the importance of ...

Referring to visuals
Let's look at the chart.
Let me draw your attention to the table.

Changing subject
OK, I'll move on to ...
Turning now to ...

F **Prepare a three-minute presentation on a subject of your choice. For example, a product or service, your organisation or institution, or a city you know well.**

KGV Europe

Background

KGV is a traditional high-street music retailer. Based in Amsterdam, it has 12 stores in the Netherlands, three of which are megastores. Some years ago, it expanded into the rest of Europe and now owns 65 stores – eight of these are megastores.

The company is at present going through a difficult period. Over the last three years, profits have steadily fallen, from €450 million to €290 million. The megastores' sales have risen by 8%, accounting for 55% of the company's turnover, but the increased revenue has been achieved only by heavy expenditure on advertising and promotion. Fierce competition, a narrow product range and a lack of innovation are some of the reasons for KGV's poor performance. The management are concerned, especially, that they are not exploiting the opportunities offered by selling through the Internet.

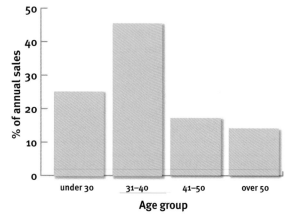

KGV CUSTOMER PROFILE

Market study

A study by KGV's Marketing Department was recently carried out and it produced the following findings:

1 It is estimated that, in five years' time, 70% of all music products will be bought via the Internet.

2 Sixty-five percent of consumers under the age of 30 prefer to do their shopping via the Internet.

3 KGV's customers would like stores to provide a wider product range (see chart 1).

4 Average spending per month in KGV's medium-sized stores is highest among the 41–60 age group (see chart 2).

5 Spending on music products by the over-60 age group will increase significantly in the next ten years in Europe.

6 The various age groups have clear preferences as to the type of music they enjoy and purchase (see chart 3).

🎧 **7.6** Listen to a conversation between Michael Johnson, a director of KGV, and Hanna Driessen, the recently appointed Financial Director of the company. They are discussing the company's strategy before a forthcoming management meeting about KGV's future. Make short notes on the opinions they express.

CHART 1: Preferences for additional products / services (% of respondents for each category)

	Age 18–40	Age 41 +
spoken word (talking books)	4	44
computer games	62	15
holiday information	35	48
computer software	58	32
banking services	25	12
concert tickets	70	75

CHART 2: Average spending per month in a medium-sized store

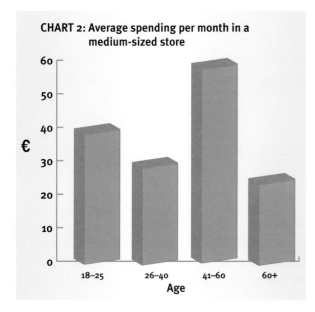

CHART 3: Preferences of consumers for music products

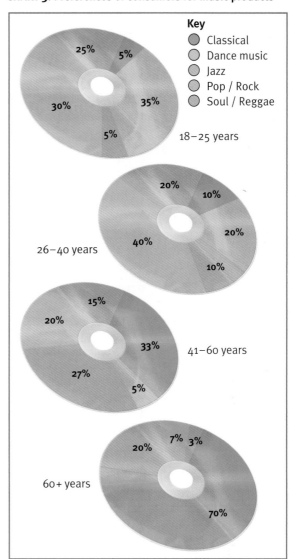

Key
- Classical
- Dance music
- Jazz
- Pop / Rock
- Soul / Reggae

Task

A You are a member of KGV's management. In small groups, prepare and give a presentation for your colleagues concerning KGV's future strategy. Your presentation should consider the following questions:

1 Should KGV keep some of their stores but sell at least 50% of their goods via the Internet?

2 Should they close all their stores and offer a total online service? If so:
   a) what risks would be involved?
   b) how would the costs of the business change?
   c) what organisational changes would the company have to make?

3 Should KGV stay as it is, but follow Hanna's advice:
   a) outsource advertising and promotion.
   b) introduce new products. If so, which ones?
   c) consider targeting new segments of the market.

4 What are the consequences of the chosen strategy? How can the problems be minimised?

B Meet as one group. One of you should lead the meeting. Decide what KGV's future strategy should be and work out an action plan for the next year.

Writing

You are the Managing Director of KGV. Write an e-mail to a director of the company who was unable to attend the management meeting. In the e-mail, summarise the discussion and decisions of the meeting and ask the director for his/her comments.

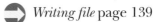 *Writing file* page 139

Revision

1 Communication

Vocabulary

A **Read the sentences and supply the missing vowels for each word.**

1 Our new manager is very p _ rs _ _ s _ v _. Everyone agrees to do what she wants us to do.

2 The CEO made an _ l _ qu _ nt speech, in which every single sentence had an impact on the audience.

3 They made an effort to keep their instructions s _cc _ nct so as not to confuse us.

4 It is very rewarding when people in a meeting are r _ sp _ ns _ v _ and ask lots of questions.

5 Our sales reps are good communicators, and they are all fl _ _ nt in two foreign languages.

6 He was a rather h _ s _ t _ nt speaker, who kept searching for his words.

B **Complete the definitions with a suitable adjective from the box.**

sensitive coherent extrovert focussed inhibited reserved articulate

1 If you do not easily show your feelings or express your opinions, you are ....

2 If you do not lose sight of the main message when you speak, you are ....

3 If you express your ideas in a clear and structured way, you are .... and ....

4 If you are happy and lively in social situations, you are ....

5 If you are .... , you are embarrassed and find it difficult to behave naturally.

6 If you are .... to other people's needs or feelings, you care about them and try not to cause offence.

C **Complete the sentences with the correct form of a word from the box.**

clarify confuse digress engage explain interrupt listen ramble

1 The presenter .... a little to give the audience some background information.

2 Despite your explanations, I'm not sure I understand, so I hope you .... your position soon.

3 Good communicators avoid complicated terminology and jargon so as not to .... their listeners.

4 Our discussion was .... by several phone calls, so I soon lost the thread.

5 The best sales reps are those who can .... with customers as well as with colleagues.

6 Practical examples, illustrations and graphs can all be more useful than words when you are trying to .... something complex.

7 The speaker tended to .... a lot, so that many in the audience forgot what the main topic was or stopped .... altogether.

Writing

Read the e-mail opposite from your company's HR manager. Then write a reply in approximately 200 words.

Hi,

It's great you were able to come to the meeting yesterday.

I realise you are quite concerned about those communication problems at your branch office.

It would be extremely useful if you could

• send us a summary of the current problems,

• and let us have your suggestions how they could be resolved.

Then we'll be in a better position to help.

Many thanks,

Alex

2 International marketing

Collocations and compounds

A Choose the correct items from the box to complete the pairs of synonyms below.

domestic	increasing	overseas	saturate	get a foothold in
expanding	launch	retreat from	withdraw	license

1 a growing market   = an .... market

2 to introduce a product   = to .... a product

3 international markets   = ... markets

4 to break into a market   = to .... a market

5 to pull out of a market   = to .... a market

B Add the appropriate items from the box to the nouns below to make compounds.

brand	leader	segment	consultancy	price
strategy	figures	product	targets	

1 marketing < .... / ....

2 market < .... / ....

3 sales < .... / ....

4 .... < range / design

5 .... < loyalty / image

6 .... < range / rise

Reading

Complete this text with the best word from each group on page 64.

Founded in 1985, Unigate has today become the country's leading company in the personal and domestic care industry. Its products ....[1] from soap and shampoo to disposable nappies and water purifying tablets. Three years ago, it ....[2] Thalassa, a revolutionary deodorant ....[3] on aromatherapy principles. Thalassa's therapeutic qualities, together with its unusual range of fragrances and its environment-friendly packaging, rapidly made it Unigate's cash ....[4]. In the last ....[5] year, Thalassa contributed 8.5 million euros to the company' s annual sales ....[6], accounting for 15% of its total ....[7].

As deodorants constitute a considerable ....[8] of the world hygiene product market, Unigate would like to get a ....[9] in overseas markets and make Thalassa a global ....[10]. The wonder deodorant is currently ....[11] as a health product. It is ....[12] through chemists' and select convenience stores and super-markets, and its price is in the top ....[13]. Media advertising is backed up by ....[14] contracts with well-known doctors, popular scientists, and film stars. The key question for Unigate is now whether they need to reposition Thalassa, and if so, how.

1 **a)** include	**b)** range	**c)** consist	**d)** provide
2 **a)** launched	**b)** ordered	**c)** threw out	**d)** put on
3 **a)** invented	**b)** developed	**c)** fabricated	**d)** manufactured
4 **a)** flow	**b)** card	**c)** cow	**d)** box
5 **a)** financial	**b)** accountancy	**c)** legal	**d)** book-keeping
6 **a)** expenditure	**b)** credit	**c)** profit	**d)** revenue
7 **a)** bonus	**b)** turnover	**c)** capital	**d)** equity
8 **a)** portion	**b)** division	**c)** area	**d)** segment
9 **a)** competition	**b)** shareholder	**c)** foothold	**d)** wholesale
10 **a)** mark	**b)** slogan	**c)** brand	**d)** sample
11 **a)** positioned	**b)** put out	**c)** situated	**d)** sold out
12 **a)** handed out	**b)** diversified	**c)** given away	**d)** distributed
13 **a)** class	**b)** range	**c)** section	**d)** sector
14 **a)** publicity	**b)** insurance	**c)** endorsement	**d)** fixed-term

3 Building relationships

Multi-word verbs

Match items from the boxes below to make the multi-word verbs which best complete the conversations. Note that each time, Speaker B paraphrases what Speaker A says.

A			
call	hand	hold	look
put	sound	tied	turn

B				
in	in	to	off	off
	on	out	up	up

1 A: I wonder when management is going to address our networking difficulties.

   B: So do I. They should .... the problem immediately, or it'll just get worse.

2 A: We've maintained our market share in Turkey, haven't we?

   B: That's right. We just managed to .... to it.

3 A: Is it true Nick is going to leave the company?

   B: I'm afraid so. He told me he was about to .... his resignation.

4 A: So the air traffic controllers have ended their strike.

   B: Not too soon! I thought they'd never .... it ....

5 A: It seems you'll be very busy this afternoon.

   B: Don't remind me! I'm going to be .... in meetings till 4.30.

6 A: Have you found out what our Brazilian contact thinks of the proposal?

   B: Not yet, but I'm going to Recife next week. So I'll .... her .... then.

7 A: How do you feel when someone comes to see you without an appointment?

   B: Well, in fact I usually don't mind at all when people .... unexpectedly.

8 A: I hear they've postponed the staff party.

   B: Oh no. This is the second time they've .... it ....

Writing

You are the Marketing Manager of Renova, a Belgian office furniture manufacturer. At a recent trade fair in Kraków, you met Marek Stawowy, the owner of a chain of furniture shops with outlets throughout Poland. Mr Stawowy showed interest in your products. You would like to have a distributor in Eastern Europe. Write a formal letter (in 200–250 words) to Mr Stawowy.

- referring to your meeting with him

- expressing your wish to do business with him, and explaining how this would be of mutual benefit

- inviting him over to Belgium to visit your production facility and head office.

4 Success

Prefixes

Add the prefix *de-*, *mis-*, *out-*, *over-*, *re-* or *under-* to the correct form of the verb in brackets to complete the following sentences.

1 The conference facilities were far from adequate. In addition, we were grossly .... (charge).

2 They have .... (regulate) the petrochemical industry in the hope of making it more competitive.

3 Crawley Engineering .... (bid) all its rivals and won the contract.

4 In some cultures, silence is sometimes .... (interpret). It can be seen as a sign of dissatisfaction or uncooperativeness.

5 The minister criticised the health authorities because they had .... (spend), but she did not try and understand the difficulties they face.

6 The organisation had been .... (manage) for years, so no wonder it was close to bankruptcy.

7 We withdrew the grinder because it had a design fault, but we think we can .... (launch) it before the festive season.

8 The five non-executive directors had .... (vote) the four executive directors to adjourn the AGM.

9 The city centre was far too expensive, so the company .... (locate) last summer.

10 We had .... (estimate) our competitors. They seem to be gaining market share day by day.

Reading

Read the text, then choose the best sentences to complete it.

Successful negotiations

In business negotiations, good people skills, mutual respect and trust are absolutely essential. One of the aims of the first meeting is therefore for the two parties to develop trust and sound each other out.

.... [1] Doing your homework means finding out as much as you can about the company you are dealing with, about its needs and expectations, and about its negotiating style. .... [2]

If you are clear about those points and generally feel well-prepared, you will be able to handle the bargaining stage much more effectively.

In this second phase, what you should be aiming for is a win-win situation. .... [3] Getting to a win-win situation clearly requires a number of special skills, such as making concessions. .... [4] Firstly, it may not be a good idea to start with your biggest one, as your prospect may then think you are desperate to strike a deal. On the other hand, starting small and making gradually bigger concessions is not recommended either, as this may arouse unrealistic expectations.

.... [5] And thirdly, make sure your prospect is fully aware of the value of every concession you make.

.... [6] The first pitfall to avoid is to allow the negotiation to drag on indefinitely. Agree on a schedule at the outset, and keep to it.

.... [7] Finally, never bow to pressure, and never exert undue pressure on your prospect either. Ultimatums, for instance, have no place in effective business negotiations.

a) It also means defining precisely what you want and what your conditions are, as well as deciding in advance what kind of concessions you are willing to make.

b) Let us now turn briefly to three serious dangers which often lurk behind negotiations.

c) Obviously, it is easier to reach an agreement if both parties take away something from the deal.

d) In addition, we need to remember that not all business negotiations end in a deal.

e) Secondly, resist the temptation to make a concession whenever your prospect grants you one.

f) The next one is the unwillingness to admit that your prospect's arguments may be right, and yours wrong.

g) There are three key issues to bear in mind when making concessions.

h) This phase can be made easier if you do your homework beforehand.

5 Job satisfaction

Passives

Complete the sentences with the correct passive form of the verb(s) in brackets.

1 He .... a substantial severance package when he left the company. *(give)*

2 Our remuneration policy .... currently .... *(revise)*

3 Burnout can ....if working hours .... *(avoid / reduce)*

4 Surprisingly, the sales staff .... only .... once in the past three years. *(appraise)*

5 If I .... more autonomy in my previous job, I don't think I'd have quit. *(give)*

6 Flexible hours .... in Accounts and HR next month. *(introduce)*

7 With a little goodwill, the amount of red tape we have to deal with could .... easily. *(reduce)*

8 She is preparing carefully for the interview. She knows that if she ...., she .... a competitive salary and excellent fringe benefits. *(select / offer)*

Writing

You and several other managers feel that your company's system of perks needs improving, or employee retention might become a critical issue. One of the directors has asked you to put forward your ideas in writing. Write an informal proposal (in 200–250 words) for the director.

Your proposal should:

• describe what are, in your views, the shortcomings of the present system of perks

• suggest a number of alternatives

• explain what kind of perks you think would work best, and why.

6 Risk

Adverbs of degree

Ⓐ Supply the missing vowels in these adjectives, which can all be used to describe risk(s).

small				big			
1 sl _ ght		3 f _ _ nt		1 h _ g _		3 s _ bst _ nt _ _ l	
2 n _ gl _ g _ bl _		4 r _ m _ t _		2 gr _ _ t		4 s _ gn _ f _ c _ nt	

Ⓑ Complete the sentences with a suitable phrase from the box.

badly misjudged	incredibly well-prepared	slightly damaged
deeply disappointed	severely criticised	superbly presented	thoroughly enjoyed

1 Fortunately we withdrew the product as soon as we heard the first complaints, so our reputation was only ....

2 Management had .... the staff mood on the new regulations and certainly did not expect a strike.

3 Our new briefing pack is .... and contains key information about the risks involved when working in certain locations.

4 The airline was .... for failing to respond to the needs of the victims' families.

5 The participants .... the promotional presentation and seemed mesmerised by the speaker.

6 The public was .... by the pharmaceutical company's arrogant attitude and its refusal to admit its fatal mistake.

7 We had foreseen all the risks involved and so felt .... when we moved our production plant to a region many consider dangerous.

Proof-reading

Read the passage below about risk.

- In most of the lines **1–10** there is **one extra word** which does not fit. Some lines, however, are correct.
- If a line is **correct**, put a tick on the appropriate line.
- If there is an **extra word** in the line, write that word in the space provided.

In its everyday sense, *risk* often has negative connotations, and is associated with danger, the loss, or accidents.	1 ......✓...... 2 .....*the*.....
In business, however, the concept is slightly more complex one. Risk is not only about threats, but also about opportunities. This is summarised as in the popular saying who 'nothing ventured, nothing gained' . Indeed, in order to grow, to become more profitable or competitive, businesses usually have to change direction, which it involves a certain amount of risk. Having said that, in business doing nothing is potentially more risky than moving forward and innovating. A company that plays it safe all the time and runs the risk of offering products which go unnoticed or which no longer meet up the needs of their customers.	3 .... 4 .... 5 .... 6 .... 7 .... 8 .... 9 .... 10 ....

7 e-commerce

Conditionals

A **Match these sentence halves.**

1 I'm sure that if we go online
2 I'm sure that if we went online
3 I'm sure that if we'd gone online
4 If we lose the password,
5 If we had a more attractive website,
6 If we'd hired a professional designer,

a) our overheads would decrease.
b) we won't be able to access those files ever again.
c) our overheads would have decreased.
d) we would get a lot more hits.
e) we'd have been able to relaunch our site sooner.
f) our overheads will decrease.

B **Complete the sentences with the correct form of the verb in brackets.**

1 The volume of e-commerce would increase rapidly if everyone .... a computer. *(own)*

2 If people weren't a bit technically-minded, the Internet .... so fast. *(take off)*

3 You .... much more traffic if you register your website with one of the top search engines. *(get)*

4 If I .... you, I would turn to a professional website designer. *(be)*

5 Had the economic climate been more favourable, our e-commerce industries .... massively. *(expand)*

6 If you .... online, you'll get a better discount. *(order)*

Proof-reading

Read the passage below about young Internet shoppers.

- In each line **1–10** there is **one wrong word**.
- For each line, underline the wrong word, and write the **correct word** in the space provided.

Consumers in the age range 15–22 like to shop online a lot more than adults. In the US, for example, a clear majority of young people now <u>shops</u> online. In addition, their online purchases generally include a much <u>wide</u> variety of products than adults'. The most popular products in there shopping carts include CDs, books, games, and clothing, with computer hardware follows close behind. Interestingly, statistics reveal that young consumers were often smarter and most sophisticated than adults. For example, many of them visit price-comparison websites, while very few adults are even awareness of the existence of such sites. Although young consumers had been very keen to adopt the Internet, they have not turned their back for offline stores. Indeed, a good experience in a retailer's offline store will often encourage him to visit its online branch, and the other way round.	1 ...*shop*... 2 ...*wider*.. 3 .... 4 .... 5 .... 6 .... 7 .... 8 .... 9 .... 10 ....

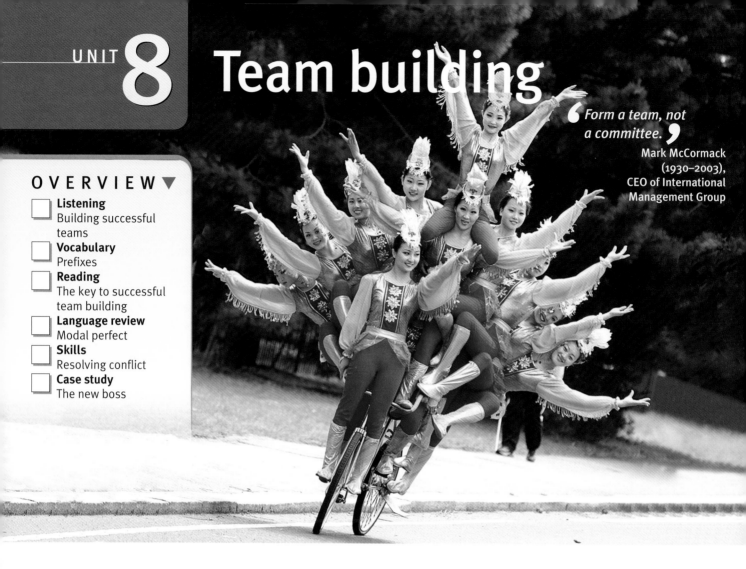

UNIT 8 Team building

'Form a team, not a committee.'

Mark McCormack
(1930–2003),
CEO of International
Management Group

Starting up

A Think of at least two advantages and disadvantages of working in teams.

B For each category in the quiz below, tick the three statements that most apply to you. Then read the explanations on page 152.

What sort of team player are you?

Doers vs Thinkers	Details vs Ideas	Mind vs Heart	Planners vs Improvisers
a) I consider what I say.	a) I often come up with unusual solutions.	a) I like to think logically.	a) Meetings have to be prepared for carefully.
b) I contribute a lot in discussions.	b) It's important to be realistic.	b) I keep emotions out of decision-making.	b) I like surprises.
c) Action is more important than reflection.	c) People see me as a creative person.	c) I avoid confrontation.	c) I hate time-wasting at meetings.
d) I listen to others before I say anything.	d) I like practical solutions.	d) I sometimes tread on people's toes.	d) Too much time can be spent on preparation.
e) Discussion gives me energy and ideas.	e) You shouldn't overlook details.	e) Understanding people is as important as being right.	e) People say I'm a punctual person.
f) I don't say a lot at meetings.	f) You shouldn't get lost in details.	f) I care about other people's feelings.	f) I need a deadline to get me going.

C Work in groups and compare your answers. Then discuss these questions.

1 How important are thinking styles in effective teamwork?

2 Do you think your group would make a good team, based on the results of the quiz? Explain why or why not.

Listening
Building successful teams

▲ Janet Greenfield

A 🎧 **8.1** Listen to the first part of an interview with Janet Greenfield, an American specialist in Human Resources. What are the three key points for effective team building that Janet mentions? Use these headings to help you: corporate culture, expectations and contributions.

B 🎧 **8.2** Listen to the second part of the interview. Work in pairs. Take notes on a) Vince Lombardi's ideas and b) how his ideas are applied to business.

C Discussion: describe a team you have been in that was either a) successful, b) unsuccesful and say why.

Vocabulary
Prefixes

A Match the prefixes of the words 1–10 to their meanings.

Prefix		Meaning of prefix		
1 *mis*manage	**a)** not	**b)** <u>do badly</u>	**c)** former
2 *pro*-European	**a)** opposite	**b)** in favour of	**c)** before
3 *pre*dict	**a)** not enough	**b)** against	**c)** before
4 *post*-merger	**a)** after	**b)** too much	**c)** not enough
5 *dis*honest	**a)** very	**b)** former	**c)** not
6 *ex*-boss	**a)** opposite	**b)** former	**c)** after
7 *bi*lateral	**a)** against	**b)** after	**c)** two
8 *re*consider	**a)** again	**b)** former	**c)** after
9 *ir*responsible	**a)** again	**b)** not	**c)** against
10 *hyper*critical	**a)** not enough	**b)** very	**c)** opposite

➡ *Vocabulary file* page 171

B Complete the text below using some of the words in Exercise A in the correct form.

Our company went through a difficult period a few years ago. Bad decisions were taken which caused us to lose a lot of money. Because the company had been ....¹, the chief executive had to resign. Last year, we merged with a much larger company. During the ....² period our future strategy was discussed. It was decided that we could consider becoming a more global organisation with a strong presence in Europe.

Most of us were ....³, we liked the idea of expanding into Europe. Indeed our ....⁴ had been strongly in favour of doing this. However the two new board members were strongly against the idea but never said so openly. I think this was very ....⁵. Instead, they behaved in an ....⁶ manner during meetings. For example, they would be ....⁷, raising stupid objections if someone came up with a good idea.

Because the meetings were so unproductive, the Board of Directors got cold feet and asked us to ....⁸ the decision to expand into Europe.

C Add prefixes to the words in the box to give their opposite meanings. Then use them to discuss the questions that follow.

> communicative   decisive   efficient   enthusiastic   flexible   focussed
> imaginative   loyal   organised   practical   sociable   stable   tolerant

1 Who is the best or worst person you have ever worked with? Explain why.

2 What qualities could you contribute to a team? What qualities would the other members need to have to create an effective team?

Reading

The key to successful team building

A *None of us is as smart as all of us.* **Do you agree? In what situations is it true or not true? Give examples.**

B **Read the article and answer these questions.**

1 What is the difference between the past and the present in terms of the key to success in a career?

2 What does the writer say about competition in the first paragraph?

3 In the second paragraph what does the writer say you need to be a good team player?

4 What three points does the writer make about effective teams in the third paragraph?

5 According to the writer which of the following attitudes should team members have?

a) We know exactly what we are trying to achieve.

b) I will lead when necessary.

c) People value my work.

d) I speak when invited by the team leader.

e) I am encouraged to be very critical of colleagues' opinions.

6 Why does the writer think that cultural differences do not have a big influence on teams?

7 What is the difference between Thai and Western team members?

C **Discuss the following statements.**

1 A team always needs a leader.

2 A team should change its leader regularly.

3 Tension between team members makes a team more effective.

4 Teams need people with similar personalities in order to succeed.

D **Complete the missing letters in the following words. Which of these qualities do you possess that would be useful when working in a team?**

1 p_t_ _ nc_

2 f_r_s_ght

3 cr_ _ t_v_ty

4 _ rg_ nis_t_ _n

5 _nt _ _t _ _ n

6 t _ _ghn _ss

7 st _m _n _

8 d _pl _m _cy

9 h _n _sty

E **Answer these questions.**

1 Do you have any other qualities which would be useful for a team?

2 What would you find difficult about working in a team?

3 If you were a team leader, how would you get your team members to co-operate?

THE KEY TO SUCCESS

None of us is as smart as all of us

By Howard Cant

A good team player has the key to success. Being the smartest, being the brightest, being the hardest; all of these attributes that worked so well in
5 business in years gone by, now will not push you up the ladder quickly. How good a team player you are and how well you share your knowledge with your colleagues is the all-important factor in
10 growing your career today. If you can build a company culture that does not worry about who gets the credit for something, think about what you could achieve! To survive in the big bad tough working environment of today you don't need to
15 have your own people competing with each other. It is the commercial 'enemy' against whom all their energy should be focussed.

It's not always easy to be a good team member and compromise your own views for the good of
20 the whole, but it works for the betterment of the company. You have to believe in the workings and power of the team and recognise where your own strengths and contribution fit in. You have to be honest, both with yourself and with your team
25 members. You will have conflict within the team and as long as this is controlled then it can be a very healthy element for both the team and the development of the business. Research into high-performing teams shows that each member cares
30 for the development of his team mates. This appreciation of each other's learning and development is key to the success of a team and the commitment of each member to the other.

Over 70% of a manager's time is spent in some
35 form of group activity, often in meetings with others; relatively little time is spent in the supervising of single individuals or on one-to-one discussions, thus the need for team building. Indeed, the success of individual managers
40 depends on how well that manager's team or teams improve in quality and productivity on a continuous basis. In reality, group productivity is more important than individual task accomplishment. The most effective teams are
45 able to solve complex problems more easily than one person can, for many capable minds are brought to bear on an issue. However, all teams must be managed well by a capable facilitator who understands that every team is unique, dynamic
50 and ever-changing. Moreover, teams have behaviour patterns, just as individuals do and, just as children develop into adults, teams have developmental stages, being more productive and efficient at one stage than another.

55 It is also extremely desirable for team members to have the following attitudes; 'I know what I have to do and the team's goals are clear', 'I am willing to share some responsibility for leadership', 'I am an active participant', 'I feel
60 appreciated and supported by others', 'Other team members listen when I speak and I respect the opinions of others', 'Communication is open, new ideas are encouraged and we are having fun working together'.

65 Teams soon develop a clear problem-solving approach that can be applied time and again as long as their leader initially creates a common purpose and vision, pointing the team in the right direction.

70 Cross-cultural issues can assail and impact the working of teams, but it is well to remember that, despite culture, most team members have similar objectives in life. Objectives that relate to happiness and health, to success and recognition,
75 to love and being well-accepted by others. The clever team leader recognises and plays upon these similarities while moulding the cultural differences to benefit the team. For example, Thai team members place a greater focus on personal
80 relationships in everything they do while Western team members are looking more for personal achievement.

From *Benjarong Magazine, Thailand*

Language review
Modal perfect

- The modal perfect is formed using **modal verb + *have* + past participle**.
  *We **might have won** the contract.*
- Two uses of the modal perfect are:
  a) criticising or commenting on past actions.
  *You **should have told** me the meeting was cancelled.*
  *She got there very early. She **needn't have allowed** so much time to find the place.*

  b) speculating about the past or present.
  *He **may have moved** to another department.*
  *He **must have finished** now.*

 page 133

A Answer *yes, no* or *not sure* to each of the questions below.

1 *You should have chosen her for the team.*
   Was she chosen for the team?

2 *He must have made over 30 changes to the project.*
   Did he make over 30 changes to the project?

3 *They needn't have spent so much time on the report.*
   Did they spend too much time on the report?

4 *They could have prepared better if they'd had more time.*
   Did they prepare as well as they wanted to?

5 *The team would have been stronger without him.*
   Was the team as strong as it could be?

6 *Sylvia may have arrived by now.*
   Has Sylvia arrived yet?

7 *Thomas should have reached Barcelona by now.*
   Has Thomas reached Barcelona?

8 *They couldn't have done enough research as the launch was a failure.*
   Did the team do enough research?

B Which of these statements uses the modal perfect correctly? Suggest alternative modals for the incorrect statements.

1 It's too late to apply for the job now. You must have applied last month.

2 It was silly to leave your wallet in the hotel room. It would have been stolen.

3 The fire in our showroom last night could have destroyed all our merchandise.

4 He bought the land cheaply and sold it at a higher price to developers, so he needn't have made a lot of money.

5 Gerry wasn't at the meeting. He might have been delayed in traffic.

6 You couldn't have seen Mr Lebeau at the conference because he was in Hong Kong at the time.

7 He looked exhausted when he arrived. He should have had a bad flight.

8 He was charismatic and decisive. We must have made him team leader.

C Role play this situation in pairs.

A sales rep went on a three-day business trip. He/She:

- stayed in a five-star hotel
- phoned home from their room
- ordered breakfast in their room
- hired a top-of-the-range car
- drank most of the mini-bar
- had clothes dry-cleaned by the hotel.

After the trip, the Finance Director thinks the rep's expenses are excessive and refuses to pay them. The sales rep defends their actions. Use as many of the following structures as possible: *should have / shouldn't have / could have / needn't have / + past participle.*

Skills
Resolving conflict

A Read the suggestions below about ways of dealing with conflict. Put each of them under one of the following headings: either *Do* or *Don't*.

1 Delay taking action, if possible.
2 Get angry from time to time with difficult members.
3 Try to see the problem from the point of view of the team.
4 Be truthful about how you see the situation.
5 Encourage open and frank discussion.
6 Try to ignore tensions within the team.
7 Bring potential conflict and disagreement into the open.
8 Give special attention to team members who are creating problems.
9 Persist with 'impossible people' – you may win them over.
10 Try to find 'win–win' solutions.

B 8.3 Listen to the conversation between Karen, Head of Department, and Larissa. Which suggestions, listed above, does Karen use to deal with the conflict between Larissa and her colleague, Sophie?

C Read the transcript of the conversation on page 164. Underline the phrases she uses to deal with the conflict. Add them to the Useful language box.

Useful language

Expressing your feelings
My main concern is …

Making suggestions
One thing you could do is …

Expressing satisfaction
Yes, that would be very helpful …

Expressing dissatisfaction
I don't think that would do much good.

Showing sympathy
I know how you feel.

Identifying the real problem
What's really bothering you?

Resolving the conflict
How do you think we should deal with this?

Reviewing the situation
Let's meet next week and see how things are going.

D Work in pairs. Role play the following situation. Use phrases from the Useful language box above to discuss the problems.

A team of six multinational staff is managing a number of apartment blocks in Nice, France. However, one of the team is unhappy. The employee is difficult to work with and uncooperative.

Team leader turn to page 146.
Team member turn to page 155.

The new boss

Background

Business Equipment and Systems (BES), based in Birmingham, England, sells fax machines, data projectors and slim plasma screens. Eighteen months ago, its national Sales Manager, Vanessa Bryant, moved to a senior management position. Her replacement, Nigel Fraser, has been told to increase turnover by at least 10% and to create a high-performing sales team.

However, since Nigel's appointment the team has not been working effectively and morale is low. Last year's sales were over 20% below target. The sales team has a mix of nationalities because BES intends to enter other European markets in the near future.

Nigel Fraser is well aware that his sales team is not working well together. Before considering what action to take to improve its performance, he made some notes on the team. Read about Nigel and then read the notes on the sales team (on page 75).

🎧 8.4 Listen to the meeting chaired by Nigel Fraser. What do you learn about the team's problems?

Additional problems in the sales team

1 When the sales staff miss their targets or when customers complain, the staff blame each other or other departments. No one takes responsibility for mistakes.

2 Members of the team do not help each other enough, for example by passing on information about customers. Some members dislike each other.

3 Staff become aggressive when Nigel criticises them for poor performance.

4 Morale in the department is poor. Nigel felt happier in his previous job, and he has heard people talking about the 'good old days' when Vanessa Bryant was running the department.

NIGEL FRASER

A 'whiz kid'. Previously worked for a business equipment chain. Ambitious and creative with a direct, 'no-nonsense' approach. Task-oriented, he sees his main objective as meeting sales targets. Very disappointed with current sales performance. Believes the team needs to be controlled more tightly and is underperforming because of bad habits acquired under Vanessa Bryant.

Task

You are directors of BES. Work in groups of four. Choose a role card (see pages 146, 149, 150, 151). Director 1 leads the meetings.
1 Read your role cards and prepare for a meeting to resolve your company's team building problems.
2 Identify all the problems which are affecting the performance of the sales team.
3 Discuss how to improve the performance of the sales team.
4 Work out an action plan for the next six months.
5 If there is more than one group of directors, compare your action plans.

JOHN
Fax machines   Aged 42

Personality: Calm, relaxed, reliable. A good influence on the team.

Performance: Missed his sales targets five times last year. Ranked sixth in department (value of sales). Competition very strong in the fax machine market. Steady worker.

Good/bad points: supports Nigel, good team player.

Other: Very popular with everyone.

The sales team

ELIANA
Data projectors,
new products   Aged 25

Personality: Very ambitious, hard-working, creative

Performance: Excellent. Ranked second in department (value of sales).

Good points/bad points: Feels demotivated. Wants to move to plasma screens.

Other: Some people are envious of her success. They don't accept her ideas.

MARTIN
Plasma screens   Aged 35

Personality: Extrovert, dominating, charismatic

Performance: Top sales person last three years (value of sales).

Good points/bad points: Popular with customers. Unpopular with some colleagues. Typical comments:'arrogant', 'boastful', 'doesn't listen'. Often late for meetings or makes excuses and doesn't come.

ANNA
Fax machines   Aged 26

Personality: Reliable, quiet, hard-working

Performance: Missed her sales targets three times last year. Ranked seventh in the department (value of sales).

Good points/bad points: Some good ideas but colleagues don't listen to her. Very helpful to her colleagues.

Other: Martin and Markus often 'put her down' in meetings.

DENISE
Fax machines   Aged 35

Personality: Dynamic, moody, outspoken

Performance: Excellent. Ranked fourth. Usually meets her sales targets.

Good points/bad points: Gets on well with John and Robert. Argues a lot with Markus in meetings. Becomes very aggressive.

Other: Used to have a personal relationship with Markus.

ROBERT
Data projectors,
new products   Aged 46

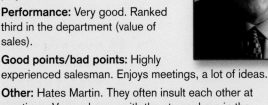

Personality: Strong, sociable, team player

Performance: Very good. Ranked third in the department (value of sales).

Good points/bad points: Highly experienced salesman. Enjoys meetings, a lot of ideas.

Other: Hates Martin. They often insult each other at meetings. Very unhappy with the atmosphere in the department. Is considering leaving the company.

MARKUS
Plasma screens   Aged 30

Personality: friendly, charming, volatile

Performance: Needs to improve. Ranked fifth (value of sales).

Good points/bad points: Talented salesman, but inconsistent. Works hard when he's in the mood. Popular with most colleagues. Always makes his final call close to home (not good for the company).

Other: Dislikes Denise and shows it!

Writing

Either:
Write a letter to the Managing Director of BES outlining your solution to the problems.

Or:
You are a sales manager. The behaviour of one of your salespeople is upsetting the others in the team. Write a letter warning them about their conduct and indicating where improvements should be made.

 Writing file page 138

UNIT 9 Raising finance

> *Lend only that which
> you can afford to lose.*
> Proverb

Starting up (A) **What are the advantages and disadvantages for a private individual of borrowing money from the following sources?**

a) a bank

b) a friend or colleague

c) a member of your family

d) a loan shark

e) a credit card company

f) another source

(B) **If you needed to raise money for the following, which source of finance would you use?**

- to buy a car
- to buy an apartment or house
- to go on an exotic holiday
- to finance your children's education
- to buy your partner an expensive present

(C) **What do you think these sayings mean? Do you agree with them?**

a) The love of money is the root of all evil.

b) Time is money.

c) Money talks.

d) Money can't buy you love.

e) Don't throw good money after bad.

Listening

Getting a bank loan

▲ Patrick Grant

A What do you think you would need to offer a bank to get a loan?

B 🎧 **9.1 Listen to the first part of the interview with Patrick Grant, a specialist in finance. He is talking about how to get a loan from a financial organisation.**

1 What four things does Patrick say about the question in Exercise A?
2 What different types of security for a loan does Patrick mention?
3 Fill in the chart below.

TYPE OF LOAN	PURPOSE OF LOAN	LENGTH OF LOAN
....	....	....
....	....	....
....	....	....

C 🎧 **9.2 Listen to the second part of the interview and answer these questions.**

1 What action does Patrick recommend if a request for a loan is turned down?
2 After getting the loan what kinds of things could you negotiate?
3 What is Patrick's final piece of advice?

Vocabulary

Idioms

A Complete the idioms below with the following words.

trees	fool	muck	rope	object	licence

1 You really can sell anything on these Internet auction sites. *It's money for old* ....
2 We're way over budget on this. We'll have to make some cutbacks. Someone needs to tell the marketing department that *money doesn't grow on* ....
3 Every great industrialist will tell you that where *there's* .... , *there's money*.
4 Charging people to park their cars at airports is *a* .... *to print money*.
5 He's always investing in businesses which have no hope of being successful. I don't know much about business angels but it seems to me that *a* .... *and his money are soon parted*.
6 Their new headquarters cost millions and millions. They are making so much profit that *money is no* ....

B Match the idioms in Exercise A with these definitions.

a) Be careful with money as there is only a limited amount.
b) Money earned easily by doing something which is not difficult. (two idioms)
c) Where you find dirt you also find money.
d) Stupid people spend money quickly without thinking about it.
e) You can spend as much as you like on something.

C Comment on each statement using one of the idioms in Exercise A.

Example: They pay me a fortune and the work is really easy.

> *It's money for old rope, then.*

1 He inherited two million dollars and spent it all in less than a year.
2 Gloria can afford to spend huge sums of money each week.
3 Mario set up a garbage collecting company. It was so successful that he was able to retire at 40.
4 My son expects me to buy him anything he wants.

Reading
Raising finance

A **Before you read the article choose the correct word for each sentence.**

1 The group's .... of twelve stores in Bordeaux was successful.

   a) acquisition   **b)** property   **c)** overdraft

2 They are financing the acquisition through .... rather than debt.

   a) cash flow   **b)** equity   **c)** assets

3 Our state-of-the art machinery is our major ....

   a) possession   **b)** asset   **c)** equity

4 The .... rate on the loan was 12%.

   a) fee   **b)** charge   **c)** interest

5 They could not pay their debts and faced ....

   a) bankruptcy   **b)** warranty   **c)** overpayment

6 Sorbat has gone into .... with debts of about £20 million.

   a) indemnity   **b)** investment   **c)** administration

B **Read lines 1–64 of the article and answer these questions.**

1 What does the article say about cash flow?

2 What is really important when looking at raising new business finance?

3 What are the key differences between equity and debt?

4 What is the main aim when raising finance?

C **Read lines 65–133 of the article and match the words 1–7 and phrases to their meanings a)–g).**

1	venture capital	**a)**	Lending a business a sum of money equal to that owed to the business by its suppliers or customers
2	grant	**b)**	Buying expensive goods by making regular payments over a period of time
3	invoice discounting	**c)**	Money lent to start a new business
4	hire purchase	**d)**	Allowing customers to take out more money from their bank than they had in it
5	leasing	**e)**	Money borrowed on which interest is paid
6	loan	**f)**	Giving someone the right to use something for a period of time in return for payment
7	overdraft	**g)**	Money given to an organisation for a particular purpose, often by a government.

D **Which source of finance described in the second part of the article is most appropriate for each of the following situations? Explain your decisions.**

1 a company in a high-technology industry which does not wish to purchase all the expensive equipment it needs

2 a new company in a depressed area which will create a lot of new jobs

3 a company that has already borrowed a lot of money but cannot pay its costs until slow-paying customers pay their bills

4 a successful company wishing to engage in a high risk but potentially profitable new enterprise where the owners are willing to give up part of their equity in order to expand

E **Do you agree with the following. Why? Why not?**

1 People with overdrafts are bad money managers.

2 It is good business practice for a company to pay its bills late.

Raising finance

When a company is growing rapidly, for example when contemplating investment in capital equipment or an acquisition, its current financial
5 resources may be inadequate. Few growing companies are able to finance their expansion plans from cash flow alone. They will therefore need to consider raising finance from other
10 external sources. In addition, managers who are looking to buy-in to a business ('management buy-in' or 'MBI') or buy-out ('management buy-out' or 'MBO') a business from its owners, may not have
15 the resources to acquire the company. They will need to raise finance to achieve their objectives.

There are a number of potential sources of finance to meet the needs of
20 a growing business or to finance an MBI or MBO:
   - Existing shareholders' and directors' funds
   - Family and friends
25 - Business angels
   - Clearing banks (overdrafts, short or medium term loans)
   - Invoice discounting
   - Hire purchase and leasing
30 - Merchant banks (medium to longer term loans)
   - Venture capital

A key consideration in choosing the source of new business finance is to
35 strike a balance between equity and debt to ensure the funding structure suits the business.

The main differences between borrowed money (debt) and equity are
40 that, with debt, bankers request interest payments and capital repayments, and the borrowed money is usually secured on business assets or the personal assets of shareholders and/or directors.
45 A bank also has the power to place a business into administration or bankruptcy if it defaults on debt interest or repayments or its prospects decline.

In contrast, equity investors take the
50 risk of failure like other shareholders, whilst they will benefit from participation in increasing levels of profits and on the eventual sale of their equity stake.

The overall objective in raising finance
55 for a company is to avoid exposing the business to excessively high borrowings, but without unnecessarily diluting the share capital. This will ensure that the financial risk of the
60 company is kept at an optimal level.

Raising finance is dependent on a good business plan which demonstrates that the management is aware of all the risks involved.

65 ## TYPES OF FINANCE
Venture Capital
Venture capital is a general term to describe a range of ordinary and preference shares where the investing
70 institution acquires a share in the business. Venture capital is intended for higher risks such as start-up situations and development capital for more mature investments. There are also
75 certain large industrial companies which have funds available to invest in growing businesses and this 'corporate venturing' is an additional source of equity finance.

80 ### Grants
Government, local authorities and local development agencies are the major sources of grants. Grants are normally made to facilitate the purchase
85 of assets and either the generation of jobs or the training of employees.

Invoice Discounting
Finance can be raised against debts due from customers via invoice
90 discounting, thus improving cash flow. Debtors are used as the prime security for the lender and the borrower may obtain up to about 80 percent of approved debts.

95 ### Hire Purchase and Leasing
Hire purchase agreements and leasing provide finance for the acquisition of specific assets such as cars, equipment and machinery
100 involving a deposit and repayments over, typically, three to ten years.

Loans
Medium term loans (up to seven years) and long term loans (including
105 commercial mortgages) are provided for specific purposes such as acquiring an asset, business or shares. The loan is normally secured on the asset or assets and the interest rate may be variable or
110 fixed.

Bank Overdraft
An overdraft is an agreed sum by which a customer can overdraw their current account. It is normally secured
115 on current assets, repayable on demand and used for short term working capital fluctuations. The interest cost is normally variable and linked to the bank base rate.

120 ### Completing the finance-raising
Raising finance is often a complex process. Business management needs to assess several alternatives and then negotiate terms which are acceptable to
125 the finance provider. The main negotiating points are often as follows:
   - Whether equity investors take a seat on the board
   - Votes ascribed to equity investors
130 - Level of warranties and indemnities provided by the directors
   - Financier's fees and costs
   - Who bears costs of due diligence.

From *2005 Tutor2u Limited (www.tutor2u.net/business/finance _raising_intro.htm)*

Language review

Dependent prepositions

Prepositions commonly occur after certain verbs, adjectives and nouns. Look at these examples from the article.

Verbs	Adjectives	Nouns
● Venture capital is **intended <u>for</u>** higher risks.	● negotiate terms which are **acceptable <u>to</u>** the finance provider	● **investment <u>in</u>** capital equipment
● The interest cost is **linked <u>to</u>** the bank base rate.	● management is **aware <u>of</u>** all the risks involved	● a **share <u>in</u>** the business

➔ page 134

A Read the article again then complete these sentences with suitable words and dependent prepositions from the article.

1 A key .... choosing the source of new business finance is to strike a .... equity and debt.

2 A bank has the power to place a business into administration or bankruptcy if it .... debt interest or repayments.

3 Equity investors take the .... failure like other shareholders, whilst they will .... participation in increasing levels of profits.

B Join the halves of sentences below. They are all from newspaper articles.

1 She had a sound business specialising	a) on my investment.
2 Self-employment may be the only alternative	b) of the risks facing European companies.
3 Researchers say this results	c) of finance, beyond his grasp.
4 Why do women still have limited access	d) in lower failure rates.
5 Once you understand the mind set of your investors, you can profit	e) from their suggestions.
6 He can see opportunities which lie, through lack	f) in renovating and refurbishing buildings.
7 The document contained an assessment	g) to starvation in poorer countries.
8 I want a return	h) to venture capital?
9 We are very focussed	i) to any further investment.
10 They are strongly opposed	j) on transferring ideas from the hard world of industrial economics to the dot-coms.

Skills

Negotiating

A Which of these negotiating tips do you agree with? Explain why or why not.

1 In the early stages, you need to ask the other side a lot of questions.

2 Always interrupt if you don't understand something.

3 Never make a concession for free. Always get something in return.

4 Use simple, direct language and be open about your aims.

5 Signal what you are going to do. For example, say, 'I'd just like to clarify that.'

6 Summarise often so that everyone is clear when you reach agreement.

7 Adapt your language so that you don't appear aggressive.

8 Talk about your emotions and how you are feeling.

B Research shows that skilled negotiators often use techniques 1–5 below to achieve their negotiating objective. Match the techniques to their definitions.

1	Open questions	**a)**	say what you are going to do before you do it.
2	Closed questions	**b)**	modify language so that it does not appear too aggressive.
3	Softening phrases	**c)**	go over the points covered to highlight when agreement is reached.
4	Signalling phrases	**d)**	gather information and explore the opposite number's views.
5	Summarising	**e)**	check understanding and ask for precise information.

C 9.3 Listen to the five expressions and match each one to the correct technique listed in Exercise B.

D 9.4 Listen to the dialogue and complete these expressions. Then place each expression under the correct heading in the Useful language box.

1 .... what other people are providing finance for you?

2 Have you approached any other bank, if ....?

3 I'd like .... Why don't you revise your business plan?

4 Good. .... what sort of repayment terms do you have in mind?

5 Let me .... The 250 thousand would be for working capital.

6 We seem to be getting somewhere now. .... what we've agreed so far.

Useful language

Open questions
Why do you need a loan?
What other sources of finance do you have?

Closed questions
Do you have any other backers?
Can you transfer the money by next week?

Summarising
Let's see what we've got so far.
Let's recap before we go on to ...

Signalling phrases
I'd like to make a proposal. I think we should ...
Could I make a suggestion, why don't we ...?

Softening phrases
I'm sorry, we can't go that high.
We were hoping to pay a little less.

E Work in pairs. Role play the following situation.

The creator of an exciting range of fashion jewellery (necklaces, earrings and bracelets), sold under the brand name Eternity, meets a business angel to get additional investment to develop their business. The owner of the business has already borrowed 100,000 euros from a family member, and in return has given that person a 20% stake in the business.

Owner of business: turn to page 151.
Business angel: turn to page 152.

Vision Film Company

Background

Vision Film Company (VFC) was founded fifteen years ago by two Polish expatriates. Now based in Kraków, Poland, it has produced numerous television commercials and documentaries, some of which have won international awards for originality and creativity. It has a small, highly experienced production staff and depends on an extensive freelance staff for its projects.

The Director and Executive Producer of VFC now want to make a feature film. The film is a drama set in post-war Europe. VFC have presented their business plan to a film finance company, European Finance Associates (EFA).

EFA have provisionally agreed to finance the project with a budget limit of $10 million. They have asked for a second meeting next month (April) to negotiate the details of the finance package. Industry practice is for film finance companies to be repaid their investment, usually with interest, and receive a share of the film's net profits.

Here are some extracts from the VFC Business Plan.

Executive Summary

The extraordinary success of independent films in recent Academy Awards shows that there is a huge demand for dramatic human interest films, whether they are performed by unknown actors or by stars. This proposal is for an independent feature film with a budget of $5.5 million.

The Polish Affair is a romantic thriller about Alicia, a young Polish interpreter, and a British intelligence officer, Justin, who meet and fall in love in the chaos of Vienna at the end of the Second World War. Without warning Alicia disappears, and their brief, passionate relationship ends. When, ten years later, they meet again by chance in Berlin their feelings for each other are as strong as ever. However, as the mystery behind Alicia's disappearance unfolds it threatens to destroy them both. This story will have great appeal to all age groups, but especially to film-goers in the 25–40 age group, who form a large segment of most countries' film-going audience.

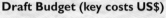

Target audience

25–40 year olds; well-educated, frequent film-goers. The film will also appeal to older people.

Target market

Worldwide distribution.

Main markets: USA, Canada, Europe.

Promotion

To help the producer make deals with major film distributors, the film will be shown at key film festivals (e.g. Cannes and Berlin).

Production Schedule

This year
July — Complete financing and casting
December — Complete pre-production

Next year
March–June — Carry out principal photography
July — Complete studio editing

Final year
January–June — Sundance Film Festival
(US distribution deals)
Berlin Film Festival
Cannes Film Festival
(European distribution deals)
Publicity campaign
July — Release film in the United States and Europe

Draft Budget (key costs US$)

Story and script	400,000	
Producer's fee / costs	370,000	
Director's fee	120,000	
Principal artistes	140,000	
Total		**1,030,000**
Production unit	1,500,000	
Camera crews / equipment	290,000	
Artistes (other than principals)	280,000	
Music	450,000	
Travel and transport	230,000	
Hotel and living expenses	950,000	
Completion bond*	290,000	
Total		**3,990,000**
Other expenses	480,000	480,000
TOTAL COST		**5,500,000**

Three-year income projection summary: Gross revenues

Low: $15million   Medium: $25million   High: $40million

(*A *completion bond* is like an insurance policy. If a producer runs out of money or exceeds his/her budget, the completion bond provides the finance to finish the film.)

Task

Work in groups.

Group A: Director and Executive Producer of Vision Film Company (turn to page 153).
Group B: Directors of European Finance Associates (turn to page 150).

Read your role cards and prepare for the negotiation. Then hold a meeting and negotiate a suitable agreement.

Writing

As Executive Producer of Vision Film Company or as a Director of European Finance Associates, write an e-mail to all senior staff informing them of the results of the negotiation and indicating how the project will proceed.

 Writing file page 139

Reasons why *The Polish Affair* will appeal to audiences worldwide

- Outstanding script
- Romantic interest
- Exciting locations: Warsaw, Vienna, Berlin
- Dramatic tension

OVERVIEW ▼

- [ ] **Listening**
  Customer service
- [ ] **Discussion**
  Customer complaints
- [ ] **Vocabulary**
  Handling complaints
- [ ] **Reading**
  Customers first
- [ ] **Language review**
  Gerunds
- [ ] **Skills**
  Active listening
- [ ] **Case study**
  Hermes
  Communications

They usually have two tellers in my local bank. Except when it's very busy, when they have one.
Rita Rudner, American actress

Starting up

A Which of the following irritate you the most when dealing with customer service departments?

On the phone	Face-to-face	Repairs and refunds
• Being put on hold • Speaking to a disinterested person • Choosing a series of options during your call • Finding the Customer Service number is continuously engaged • Being cut off	• Unhelpful customer service personnel • Stressed or indifferent staff • Salespeople with poor product knowledge • Too few staff at peak times • No company policy on customer service or complaints	• Delays on repairs • Delays in getting money back • No replacement equipment while repairs are carried out

B How important to a company's success is customer care? Is it possible to have too much customer care?

Listening
Customer service

▲ Sarah Andrews

A Sarah Andrews is Retail Sales Director at Harrods. What do you know about Harrods?

B 🎧 **10.1** Listen to the first part of the interview and decide if the statements below are True / False / Not given.

1 Good customer service at Harrods is about meeting customer expectations.

2 Harrods customers expect a level of service as good as other retailers.

3 Harrods employees are trained in a seven step customer service programme.

4 Harrods employs people to test the customer service in different departments.

5 Harrods employees are given feedback on their performance once a month.

6 Employees receive champagne if they score 100% in the mystery shop tests.

C 🎧 **10.2 Listen to the second part of the interview and complete the sentences according to Sarah Andrews.**

1 Good customer service helps retailers to ....

2 The problem retailers face these days is that products ....

3 Companies which don't take customer service seriously will ....

D How does Sarah think new technology can help improve customer service? Does she think this is useful for Harrods?

E 🎧 **10.3 Listen to the third part of the interview and fill in the missing verbs to create the *Seven Steps to Exceptional Service.***

1 .... customers within one minute of arrival

2 .... customers at an appropriate time and .... a conversation

3 .... questions to .... customers' needs

4 .... product knowledge to .... items to .... customer needs

5 .... the features and benefits of products to customers

6 .... related products to .... the service

7 .... customers and .... them to return

F Work in pairs. Using the above seven step programme as a guide, write a dialogue between a Harrods employee and a customer in one of the following departments: a) luggage, b) cosmetics, c) TV and Hi-fi. Role play the conversation.

Discussion	Work in two groups, A and B. Choose the five best suggestions from your group's advice sheet. Then form new groups. Negotiate a single list of the six best suggestions from both sheets.
Customer complaints	

Group A Dealing with customer complaints

1 Show the customer you are listening by checking that you understand.
2 Allow the customer to show their emotions if they are upset or angry.
3 Say you are sorry that the customer is upset.
4 Admit that the problem was your fault as soon as possible.
5 Make sure you get full details of the problem.
6 Summarise and make sure that the customer understands what you have said.
7 Ask the customer to put the complaint in writing.
8 Be firm if you are sure of your facts.

Group B Dealing with customer complaints

1 Keep an open mind at all times.
2 Do not end up arguing with the customer.
3 Do not be defensive.
4 Concentrate on the situation not the personalities.
5 Don't force your solution on the customer.
6 Try to find out what result the customer wants.
7 Tell the customer what you can and cannot do.
8 Offer compensation of greater value than the goods or service complained about.

Vocabulary
Handling complaints

A Complete the beginnings of sentences 1–5 with words from the box. Then finish each sentence with a sentence ending a)–e).

standards	products	rapport	complaints	reassure

1 When you handle .... it is important ...

2 You can establish a .... with a customer if ...

3 A key element in customer care is to .... people ...

4 Companies which do not meet their .... of service ...

5 Many companies will replace .... free of charge if ...

a) ... when they are worried.

b) ... will lose customers.

c) ... they are faulty.

d) ... you know about their buying habits.

e) ... to be diplomatic.

B Match the idiomatic expressions 1–7 to their meanings a)–g).

1 pass the buck
2 get to the bottom of the problem
3 it was the last straw
4 got straight to the point
5 slipped my mind
6 ripped off
7 talking at cross purposes

a) forgot to do something
b) paid far too much for something
c) avoid responsibility
d) find the real cause of something
e) talked about the subject directly
f) the last in a series of irritating events
g) misunderstanding what someone else is referring to

C Use the idiomatic expressions to complete the sentences appropriately.

1 She was very helpful. She promised to .... and find a solution.

2 He's the person responsible. He shouldn't try to .... and blame others for his mistakes.

3 Several customers have complained about our service contract. They say they're paying far too much and feel they have been ....

4 I meant to send him a brochure but we were very busy and it ....

5 They wanted to place a larger order. I thought they wanted a bigger discount. We were ....

6 They ignored my complaints, but .... when they refused to refund my money.

7 I saw no point in arguing with him. I .... and said I wanted my money back.

Reading
Customers first

A Read the article and answer these questions.

1 What customer service problems did the author have?

2 What examples are given of poor customer service by British utilities?

3 What answer does the author give to the question: 'Why is customer service important?'

4 Why is customer service difficult to implement? Give three reasons.

Customers first: the message for this or any other year

By Michael Skapinker

What, the caller from Hewlett-Packard wanted to know, did I think the big business issues would be this year? Well, I replied, in Hewlett-Packard's case, I thought the issues should be that my new HP printer-scanner-copier refused to scan when I bought it and it took me weeks to sort it out. Also the machine could not print on lightweight card, as it was supposed to, without jamming.

The man from HP laughed nervously. Were there any other big business issues I would like to mention? No, I said. If HP took care of those small ones, the big ones would take care of themselves.

I could have talked for longer, but I had to call Powergen. I should not have been using the FT's time to sort out my electricity difficulties but no one had answered the 24-hour Powergen helpline the previous evening. This time I got through and, after a few false starts, they sorted out my problem.

Why is it so hard for companies to get things right?

The British utilities seem to have surrendered all their post-privatisation customer-service improvements. Some have gone back to their tricks of 20 years ago, including not turning up at the appointed time and then claiming to have rung the doorbell and found no one home.

Many banks, retailers and the rest are no better. Some seem to have cut back on the essentials of customer service training: please, thank you – that sort of thing.

I know this is not just a British phenomenon: every time I write about deteriorating customer service, many of you e-mail from elsewhere with the same complaints.

What is the problem? Some of it is industry-specific: either there is insufficient competition or dissatisfied customers cannot be bothered to change because they doubt they will find anything better. But I sense a deeper problem: many companies seem to have forgotten what business is about.

They think it is about cutting costs: hence the mania for outsourcing. I am not attacking outsourcing as such; it is not, on its own, responsible for deteriorating customer service. Rather, the problem is the mindset that so much outsourcing represents: the idea that a startling reduction in employment costs is all you need to succeed.

Costs do matter. If they exceed revenues, you have no profit – and no company, or individual, can carry on for long without profits.

But making a profit, essential though it is, is not the purpose of business either. It is its consequence. As Peter Drucker wrote: 'Profit is not the explanation, cause or rationale of business behaviour and business decisions, but rather the test of their validity.'

The purpose of a business is to provide something that a customer wants at a price he or she is prepared to pay. In Prof Drucker's words: 'It is the customer who determines what a business is. It is the customer alone whose willingness to pay for a good or for a service converts economic resources into wealth, things into goods.'

It is a simple idea. You provide goods or services that customers are pleased with – so pleased that they come back, and tell all their friends to buy from you too. You then sell more. Result: happiness.

Carrying this out, of course, is less simple. Others may have found a way of providing the same goods at far lower prices, in which case costs will have to be looked at again and you may have to move jobs to low-wage countries.

There is also the difficulty of execution: the bigger your business becomes and the more widespread your suppliers and customers, the harder it is to deliver. You may need information technology systems to keep track of supplies and to ensure that when your customers call, it takes you no more than a few seconds to call up the information you need.

But when the new IT system has been installed, or the foreign factory built, or this or that activity put out to contract, there is only one test of whether it was worth it: are the customers happy?

It is with the customer that all business decisions should start and end.

From the Financial Times

FINANCIAL TIMES

B **Now read the article again. Which of the following points does the author make?**

1 The British utilities are improving their customer service.

2 Some companies need to spend much more on customer service training.

3 Outsourcing often has a negative effect on customer service.

4 The key to business success is reducing costs.

5 Many companies do not have the right objectives.

C **Give an example of good and bad customer service you have experienced.**

Language review
Gerunds

- A gerund is formed from a verb but behaves like a noun.
- It can be the subject of a sentence or clause: *Aiming for customer delight is all very well ...*
- It can be the object of a sentence or clause: *Many people do not like **talking** to machines ...*
- It often follows a preposition: *Customers receiving good service will stimulate new business **by telling** up to 12 other people ...*
- A useful way to use gerunds is in lists. (See Starting up Exercise A 'On the phone'.)
- Most gerunds are formed by adding *-ing* to the base form of the verb: *answer, answer**ing** handle, handl**ing** get, gett**ing***

→ page 134

A The article on page 87 has many examples of the gerund used. Find:

a) one example as the subject of a sentence

b) one example as the object of a sentence or clause

c) three examples following a preposition.

B Some verbs can be followed by either a gerund or infinitive, but the choice can lead to a change in meaning. Match the sentences with their meanings: For example: a) *He remembered to reply to the complaint – he didn't forget* b) *He remembered replying to the complaint – he has a clear memory of this.*

1 I'm too tired to deal with this complaint

2 I'm tired of dealing with this complaint

3 They stopped producing the customer service manual

4 They stopped to produce the customer service manual

5 We tried to explain the reasons for the fault

6 We tried explaining the reasons for the fault

a) I'm fed up with the complaint and don't want to deal with it anymore.

b) I may deal with this complaint later when I have more energy.

c) They stopped the production of something else in order to produce the manual.

d) They stopped the production of the manual.

e) We made an effort to explain.

f) We did the explaining as an experiment to see if it was effective.

C Complete the guidelines for improving customer service with suitable gerunds. Add some tips of your own.

Improving customer service
Recommended ways of improving customer service include:

1 ....*returning*.... calls promptly.

2 .... key customers special discounts.

3 .... research to find out what customers need.

4 .... staff training programmes in customer care.

5 .... procedures so they are customer-focussed.

6 .... clear performance targets.

7 .... results in order to review progress.

8 .... quickly with complaints.

9 .... the customer is happy with the outcome.

10 .... from complaints.

Skills
Active listening

A How do you know if someone is not listening to you? How does it make you feel?

B Which of the following do you do to show people that you are listening to them? Can you add any other suggestions?
- look people directly in the eye at all times
- nod your head often to show interest
- repeat what the speaker has said in your own words
- be aware of the speaker's body language
- interrupt the speaker often to show you are listening
- think about what you are going to say while the speaker is talking
- use body language to show you are attentive
- try to predict what they are going to say next
- ask questions if you do not understand
- say nothing until you are absolutely sure that the speaker has finished

C 🎧 **10.4** Listen to three conversations in which people are talking about customer service.

1 Make notes under the following headings:
   a) Product or service
   b) Reasons why service was good or bad

2 Listen again. Tick the words and phrases in the Useful language box that you hear. Then add other words and phrases of your own.

D Work in pairs. Describe two examples from your own experience where the service you received was:
a) excellent   b) poor.

When your partner is speaking, make an effort to listen actively. Use some of the language from the Useful language box.

Useful language

Showing interest
Really?
That's interesting.
Right / OK / Mmm /
Yes / No

Showing empathy
I know what you mean.
How awful!

Asking for details
So what happened?
What did you do?

Clarifying
Are you saying ... ?
What (exactly) do you mean by ... ?
Could you be more specific, please?

Summarising
(So) you think ...
(So) what you're saying is ...

Repetition / Question tags
A We've reduced customer complaints by 30%.
B 30%? / Have you?

Background

You are members of the Customer Services Department of Hermes Communications, a telecommunications company based in Switzerland. You sometimes receive correspondence, telephone calls and voicemail messages from customers who are unhappy with the products or service of your company. You have to deal diplomatically and effectively with these dissatisfied customers and to come up with solutions to their problems.

Task

1 Work in pairs. One of you is the Customer Service Manager and the other is the Assistant Customer Service Manager. Read the written correspondence.

🎧 10.5 Then listen to the telephone conversation and the recorded message and make notes. Because you are so busy, decide which complaints you will handle now as a priority, and which you will leave until later.

2 Discuss how you are going to deal with the complaints that you have prioritised.

3 As one group, discuss how you could improve the service you offer to your customers.

Writing

Write a short report for the Director of Customer Services summarising the problems that customers have experienced and make recommendations for improving the service to customers.

 Writing file page 144

Complaint 1

To...	email@uspemail.co.uk
From...	cust.serv.@hermes.co.uk
Subject:	complaint

I'm writing to you because I've been trying to get through to your helpline unsuccessfully for the past three days. I've called at various times of the day and night and <u>never</u> get through. I wish to query something on my monthly bill. Is there any point having a helpline if it's always busy?

I intend to visit you next week to discuss this in person at your regional office.

Complaint 2

To...	**Customer Services Department**
From...	**Cindy Chu**
Date:	**24 November**

I'm writing to complain about the mobile phone I bought from you a month ago. I chose it because it had a big screen, much bigger than most models. Unfortunately, the battery loses power very quickly. I think this is due to the large screen size and I have heard about other people with the same model and the same problem. There is clearly a design fault.

I would like to know what you are going to do about this situation. I paid a lot of money for the phone, but it's causing me a lot of problems.

Complaint 3

To...	Customer Services Department
From...	Simon Reed
Date:	5th October

I'm writing to complain about your terrible customer service. I topped up my phone using my credit card on two occasions (£20 each time), however the amount wasn't credited to my account. It's not so much the loss of £40 which upsets me. I'm sure I'll get it back. But my phone didn't work when I needed it to make an urgent call to an important client. This is not the sort of service I expected from a company as well known as yours. I'd like to know how you're going to compensate me.

Complaint 4

FAX
TRANSMISSION

I became a subscriber to your service because you promised six months of cheap-rate calls to the US, where my daughter lives at present. So imagine my horror to find this service withdrawn, with no explanation from you, after only three months.

Then you wrote to me asking for an extra £30 a month to maintain the previous level of service. I find this absolutely outrageous.

Complaint 5

As a mobile phone user and subscriber with your network for the past five years, I have been very pleased with the level of service provided.

However, recently, I've been experiencing headaches. After visiting my doctor, he informed me that this could be due to mobile phone use. As I am in sales and travel a lot, I am on the phone up to three hours per day. I was not previously aware of any health risk associated with mobile phones and am now very concerned about the long-term health risks of prolonged exposure to microwave radiation.

I've heard of other cases like mine and therefore I would like to know what your company is doing about this problem.

I look forward to hearing your comments with interest.

Yours sincerely,

Katherine Sands

UNIT **11** # Crisis management

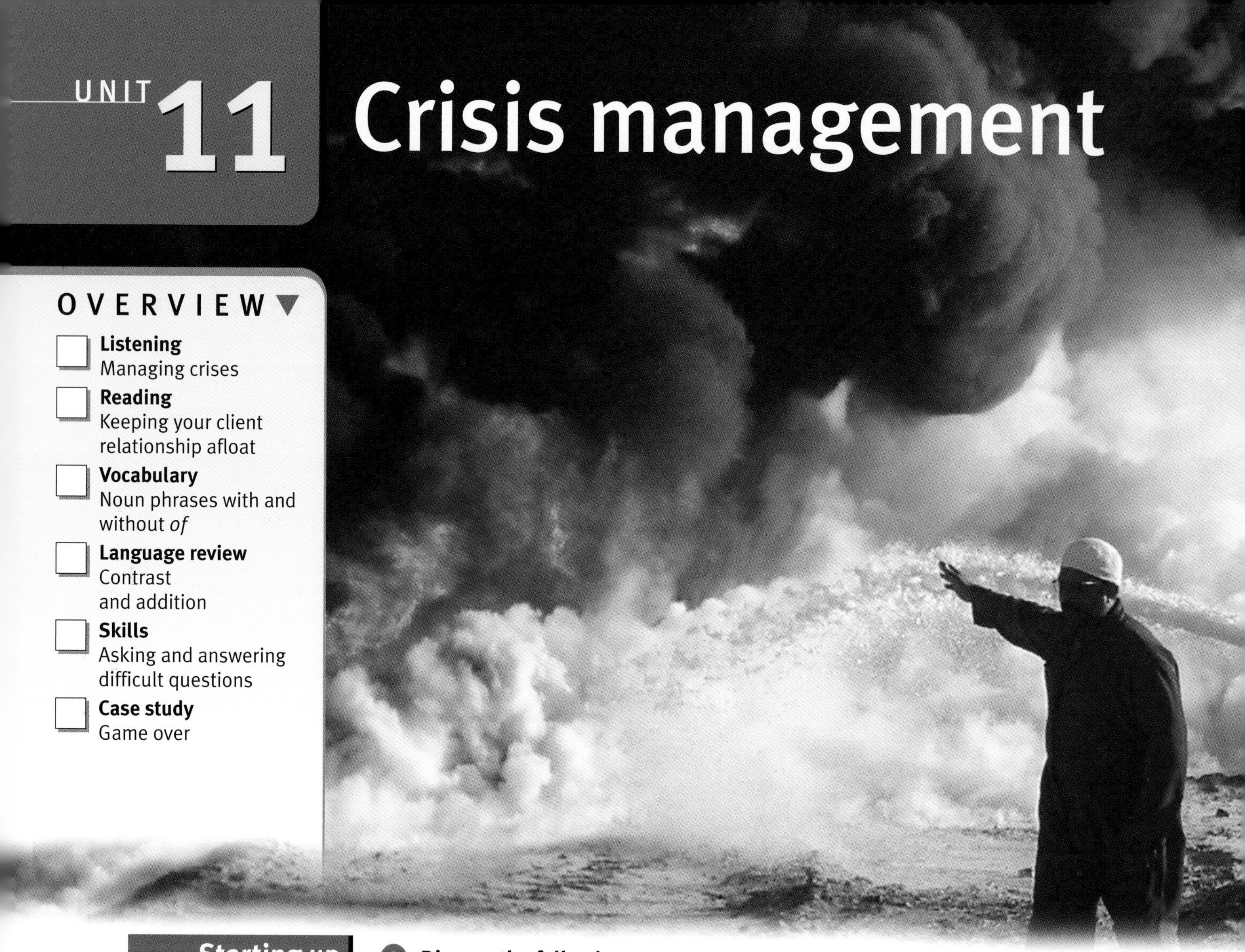

OVERVIEW

- **Listening** Managing crises
- **Reading** Keeping your client relationship afloat
- **Vocabulary** Noun phrases with and without *of*
- **Language review** Contrast and addition
- **Skills** Asking and answering difficult questions
- **Case study** Game over

Starting up

A Discuss the following.

1 What crises do business managers have to face?

2 When, in your opinion, does a business problem become a crisis?

3 Think of a crisis you have experienced. Say what happened and how it was handled.

B Crisis management experts have identified the following key steps for companies in a crisis. Use them to complete the chart below. Then discuss your answers.

1 Set up a crisis management team.

2 Try to predict what crises could occur.

3 Role play a potential crisis.

4 Inform the directors.

5 Disclose as much information as you can.

6 Analyse the actions you took to deal with the situation.

7 Write down and circulate your crisis management programme.

8 Practise making decisions under stress.

9 Work out an action plan to ensure the crisis does not happen again.

10 Find out what happened and how it happened.

Before the crisis	During the crisis	After the crisis

危机

❝ *When written in Chinese, the word* crisis *is compounded of two characters – one represents danger, and the other represents opportunity.* ❞

John F Kennedy (1917–1963), 35th US President

Listening

Managing crises

▲ Mike Seymour

A 🎧 11.1 Listen to the first part of the interview with Mike Seymour, an expert on crisis management. What three crisis areas does he mention?

B 🎧 11.2 Listen to the second part. Mike mentions three things that companies should do to prepare themselves to manage crises. What are they?

C 🎧 11.3 Listen to the third part and describe the crises in the following companies.

1 Johnson and Johnson
2 Heineken
3 Union Carbide
4 Mercedes

D 🎧 11.3 Listen to the third part again. What are the characteristics of a) good crisis management, b) bad crisis management?

Reading

Keeping
your client
relationship afloat

A Imagine you are going for a holiday on a ship around the world.
What problems could arise?

B Read the article and answer these questions.

1 What went wrong with the ship?

2 How did the passengers feel and why?

3 What can happen if you do not deal effectively with a service failure?

4 What interesting statistic highlights the consequences of poor service?

Keeping your client relationship afloat

by Morgan Witzel

The passengers of the Aurora had every right to be angry. The round-the-world cruise for which they had paid thousands of pounds was cancelled after persistent engine problems.

Yet there was little anger among the passengers. While the ship was held off the south coast of England, the passengers remained calm and even cheerful. Though many expressed regret as they finally disembarked, they were not hostile towards the ship's operators, P&O. This may have been due to the company's management of the crisis.

Dealing with a service failure is a formidable task for any marketing manager. If poorly handled, the consequences can be bad public relations, desertion by customers and even lawsuits. The Aurora story shows how managers, if they move quickly, can avoid some of the worst effects of service failures.

While high-profile cases are still relatively rare, companies everywhere may regularly suffer small service failures. Plumbers fail to fix leaking drains, restaurant meals are often undercooked or holidaymakers find their hotel room is directly above an all-night disco. Every failure is bound to create a dissatisfied customer, which in turn creates other problems for the company.

Unhappy customers tend to tell others of their experience. Studies in the US have shown that dissatisfied customers tend to tell around ten other people of their bad experience; even worse, they can take their stories to the press.

Dissatisfied customers also defect to rival businesses. Although every service failure will be different, some basic principles can assist in recovery. The first is early recognition of the problem. In P&O's case this was easy: everyone involved knew that the large ship was not going anywhere. Other failures are harder to detect, especially when management is asleep at the wheel.

The second principle is accepting responsibility. Many companies prefer to argue with customers over where responsibility lies, without realising that damage is being done regardless of who is at fault. Although there are limits to the responsibilities companies should accept – such as accidents and injuries that were not the company's fault – there is usually little profit in scoring moral victories over customers. Hence clothing retailers often have a no-questions-asked policy on returned goods, believing that the harm done by the occasional dishonest customer is more than outweighed by the satisfaction created among the rest.

Once responsibility is accepted, the two most urgent needs for the company to address are communication and compensation. Transparency is vital. Academic studies have shown that when faced with product or service failure, companies that communicate truthfully and promptly with their customers receive a favourable response. These customers feel that their concerns are actually being addressed and taken seriously. In the Aurora case, senior P&O managers were often on hand to provide information to passengers, who regarded this as a positive feature.

Compensation must be carefully matched to the customer's dissatisfaction. Too small an amount trivialises the customer's experience and can give offence, but it is also possible to go too far the other way. Researchers in the US found an example of a hotel chain that had a policy of instantly refunding the full room rate to any guest with a genuine complaint, no matter how trivial. Yet many customers – against expectations – found it embarrassing to be given hundreds of dollars in compensation when they had merely complained about a faulty light fixture or a dripping tap.

Service industries often have their compensation benchmarks. In the holiday sector, the standard was set by the 19th-century inventor of the package holiday, Thomas Cook, who made it his policy to refund in full the money paid by any customer whose holiday was curtailed or cancelled, and offer a discount on their next booking. P&O's policy would have pleased Cook – the company reportedly offered the same level of compensation to the passengers of the Aurora. Not every package holiday company follows this example.

Following these simple principles should please most customers most of the time. Research across a wide variety of service industries over the past 20 years confirms that a successful service recovery operation reduces or even eliminates any consumer dissatisfaction.

The aborted cruise of the Aurora was disappointing for P&O passengers. But the consequences could have been far worse. Many of the passengers said they planned to travel on a P&O cruise in the future.

From the *Financial Times*

FINANCIAL TIMES

5 What are the four basic principles you must consider when dealing with a crisis?

6 What do P&O and Thomas Cook have in common?

7 What is the surprising fact in the last paragraph?

C The writer provides guidelines for dealing with a crisis. Read the article again and complete the guidelines with words from the following box.

encourage	deal	compensate	communicate
ensure	concede	listen	take

1 .... that monitoring systems are efficient

2 .... customers to complain

3 .... with complaints

4 .... failures seriously

5 .... to customer views

6 .... responsibility where necessary and appropriate

7 .... quickly and effectively

8 .... customers fairly

D Now give some examples of crises which were either well or badly managed. Which of the guidelines in Exercise C were or were not followed?

Vocabulary

Noun phrases with and without *of*

A Match words from each box to make word partnerships, adding the word *of* if necessary. For example, *action plan, admission of liability.*

~~action~~ ~~admission~~ contingency
damage flow legal loss
press press speed

action conference confidence
information ~~liability~~ limitation
plan ~~plan~~ release response

B Complete these sentences with the word partnerships above.

1 How quickly management react to a crisis is known as the ....

2 In a breaking crisis, a manager may speak to the media at a(n) ....

3 Alternatively, they may have a written statement which is given to the media in the form of a ....

4 During the crisis, management may choose to keep customers, employees and shareholders up to date with a regular ....

5 A strategy for dealing with a crisis is a(n) ....

6 A backup strategy is a(n) ....

7 The risk of being taken to court is the threat of ....

8 An acceptance of responsibility in a crisis is a(n) ....

9 Following a crisis, a company may suffer a decline in loyalty from its customers, or a(n) .... in its product or service.

10 Minimising the negative effects of a crisis is known as ....

C Answer these questions.

1 Which of the above would you expect to happen or be needed
   a) before a crisis? **b)** during a crisis? **c)** after a crisis?

2 Which of the above, in your opinion, should exist all the time?

Language review
Contrast and addition

We can use *while*, *although* and *whereas* to make a contrast.

Although your business may not need to prepare in advance for a crisis, you must at least know who to call when a crisis occurs.

Despite and *In spite of* are like *although*, but they are followed by a noun, gerund or noun phrase.

Despite being new to the job, she handled the crisis well.

We use *however* to link together two sentences which are in contrast to each other.

*The report on the crisis had many recommendations. **However**, some of them were not implemented.*

We use *furthermore*, *moreover* and *in addition* to show addition (extra information)

*We've set up workshops. We've ensured that all staff know what to do in a crisis. **In addition**, we've written a manual.*

 see page 135

A Look at the article on page 94 and find examples of addition and contrast.

B Underline the correct words.

1 The crisis was badly managed. *However / While*, we learned a lot from it.

2 *Although / Despite* we set off in good time, we still arrived late.

3 *Although / In spite of* the delay, he still arrived at the start of the meeting.

4 The Japanese office has crisis management meetings, *whereas / in addition* the Hong Kong office has none.

5 We are likely to meet our financial targets this year. *Moreover, / However,* the new product lines are performing much better than we anticipated.

C Complete the article below with a suitable word from the box.

however	while / although	despite	moreover / furthermore

Is the hotel and tourism industry in crisis?

The hotel and tourism industry has been suffering in the last few years due to world events. The general economic downturn has reduced the industry's growth rate. .... [1] changes in the world's weather have had a negative on the industry.

.... [2] some journalists have suggested that the tourism industry is in crisis, other commentators have been more positive in their analysis.

Promotional campaigns undertaken by the tourism industry to reduce the negative effects of the crisis have worked. .... [3], they have had a much greater effect on leisure tourism than on business travel. .... [4] business travellers accounting for no more than one fifth of travellers, they contribute nearly half of the industry's revenue.

.... [5] the revenue from this source could be even greater in the future as many airlines are targeting this segment of the market.

From the *Financial Times*

FINANCIAL TIMES

Skills

Asking and answering difficult questions

A The Chief Executive of a pharmaceutical company is answering questions at a press conference. The company is accused of offering bribes to doctors and medical staff in order to increase sales.

Read the questions and statements from journalists. In each case decide whether it is: a) neutral / polite b) forceful / aggressive.

1 Could you answer my question?
2 Would you mind answering my question? What is your policy about gifts to customers?
3 Could you please tell me how many sales staff you employ?
4 Could you tell me how many sales staff you employ?
5 Do you deny that bribery is a common sales strategy of your company?
6 Could I ask why you're replacing your Sales Director?
7 Do you mind if I ask how many letters of complaint you have had from doctors?
8 I'm interested in knowing whether you consider yourself an ethical company.
9 Isn't it true that you don't care how your staff behave as long as they meet their sales targets?
10 May I ask why you didn't investigate the allegations more quickly?
11 Surely you're not saying that no payments were made?
12 Could you clarify what gifts can be offered to customers?

B 🎧 11.4 Now listen to the questions above being spoken. Have you changed any of your answers to Exercise A?

C The responses below are from a speaker at a press conference. Decide whether the speaker is answering a question which is:

a) neutral / polite – one which helps them to explain their message.
b) forceful / aggressive – one which they can't or don't want to answer.

1 I'm afraid I'm not in a position to comment on that.
2 That's a very good question. Let me explain.
3 I'm sorry, I can't possibly comment on that.
4 I'm afraid I don't know the answer to that one.
5 Sorry, I don't have any information on that at the moment.
6 No comment.
7 I'll be happy to answer that.
8 I've no idea off the top of my head.
9 I'm pleased you raised that point.
10 I'm glad you asked me that.
11 Sorry, I'm not prepared to answer that at the moment.
12 Can I get back to you on that one?

D Role play the following situation.

A mobile phone company has been attacked in several newspapers for using 'dishonest' methods to sell its phones. The managers arrange a press conference to defend their company's reputation and answer questions.

Managers turn to page 148.
Journalists turn to page 153.
Read your role cards, then hold the press conference.

CASE STUDY

Background

The article below appeared in today's edition of *Euronews*, a weekly newspaper published in English throughout Europe.

High Street Retailer in Pirated Goods Row

Retailing chain Titan Stores was accused last night in a TV documentary of selling illegal software products. The documentary claimed that pirated copies of the best selling computer game *Race against Time* were flooding the market in Europe.

According to the programme, in the last three months Titan Stores have sold approximately 50,000 packs of the game, said to be illegal copies from a supplier based in the Netherlands. It was alleged that the copies had been bought at a heavily discounted price and were 'selling like hot cakes' because the price was so low.

Titan's chief executive, Penny Taylor, insisted the accusation could not be true, saying 'Titan Stores is known for its integrity and high ethical standards. We price our products competitively and offer top quality goods. We have a skilled and committed workforce in whom we have great confidence.'

A company employee who does not wish to be named said that Titan Stores have had problems in their buying department recently. Staff turnover in the department has been high. This has affected employees' morale and efficiency.

🎧 **11.5** Listen to part of a conversation between Carla Davis, Director of Public Relations for Titan Stores, and Hugo Stern, an independent crisis management consultant.

Discuss what information you receive about the following:

- The supplier of *Race against Time*
- The manufacturer of the game
- Stocks of *Race against Time*

What advice does Hugo Stern give to Carla Davis?

Company profile

TITAN STORES

Based in Dublin, Ireland, Titan Stores is a major retailer with stores in most European cities. The company started by selling stationery, books and greeting cards, later branching out into magazines and music products. Because of fierce competition it has repositioned itself, concentrating on computer products, especially computer games.

Its merchandise appeals particularly to teenagers and young adults. The chain prides itself on providing quality products at affordable prices. It is known for its high ethical standards, with its advertising slogan, 'We put people first'.

Key figures	
Workforce	8,000
Sales	€ 720m
Pre-tax profits	€ 90m

Key
- ■ Computer software / games
- ■ Stationery and cards
- ■ Books and music
- ■ Office equipment
- ■ Other

Task

Because of the serious allegations and the effect on the company's image and share price, Titan Stores decide to hold a press conference. This will enable them to defend the company, explain how they are dealing with the crisis and answer questions from journalists.

You are either:
a director of Titan Stores (turn to page 146)
or a newspaper journalist (turn to page 149).

Read your role card and prepare for the press conference. Then hold the press conference.

Writing

One of the objectives of the Society for the Prevention of Software Fraud (SPSF) is to eliminate software piracy. Its members include over 1,000 UK companies, some of them leading software publishers. It is highly respected and has the power to impose large fines in cases of extreme malpractice. Any warnings or sanctions it issues in such cases can damage a company's reputation.

Journalists

The head of the SPSF has asked you for a report on the Titan Stores crisis. It should include the following information:

- the background to the crisis
- an analysis of the actions the company took to deal with it
- recommendations about what action you think the SPSF should take, if any.

Titan Stores Directors

The head of the SPSF has asked you for a report on the recent crisis. It should include the following information:

- the background to the crisis
- an explanation of the actions you have taken to deal with it.

You need to put up a good defence as a strong sanction from the SPSF will further damage your company's reputation.

 Writing file pages 144 and 145

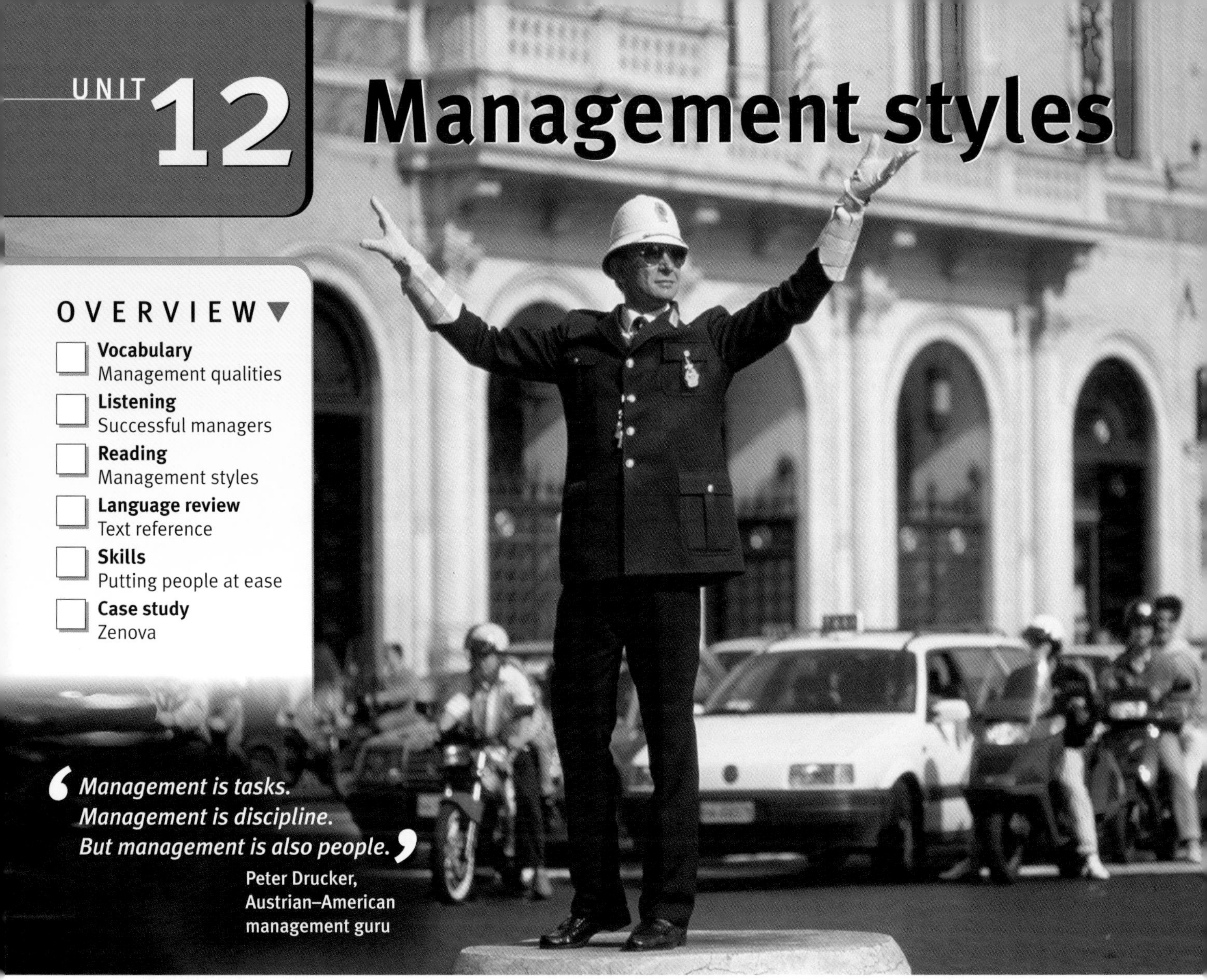

UNIT 12 Management styles

OVERVIEW

- **Vocabulary** Management qualities
- **Listening** Successful managers
- **Reading** Management styles
- **Language review** Text reference
- **Skills** Putting people at ease
- **Case study** Zenova

'Management is tasks. Management is discipline. But management is also people.'

Peter Drucker, Austrian–American management guru

Starting up

A Which of these statements do you agree with? Explain your reasons.

A manager should:

1. know when your birthday is.
2. know where you are and what you're doing at all times during working hours.
3. not criticise or praise.
4. not interfere in disagreements between members of staff.
5. not ask people to do things they're not prepared to do themselves.
6. be available at all times to give staff advice and support.
7. keep their distance from staff and not get involved in socialising outside work.
8. use polite language at all times.
9. work longer hours than their staff.
10. comment on the personal appearance of their staff.

B What is the role of a manager? Choose your top three roles from the following:

- coach/motivator
- mediator
- problem-solver
- instigator
- dictator
- organiser
- facilitator
- leader
- mentor
- decision-maker

Vocabulary
Management qualities

A Complete column 2 of the table with opposite meanings. Use the prefixes *in-*, *ir-*, *un-*, *il-* or *dis-*. Then complete column 3 with the noun forms.

1 Adjective	2 Opposite adjective	3 Noun form
considerate	*inconsiderate*	*consideration*
creative		
decisive		
diplomatic		
efficient		
flexible		
inspiring		
interested		
logical		
organised		
rational		
responsible		
sociable		
supportive		

B Choose the four best qualities of a manager from the list above and rank them in order of importance. Then choose the four worst qualities and rank them (1 = worst).

C Discuss your answers to Exercise B. What other management qualities or weaknesses can you add?

D Match these pairs of contrasting management styles.

1	autocratic	**a)**	collaborative
2	centralising	**b)**	controlling
3	directive	**c)**	delegating
4	empowering	**d)**	democratic
5	hands on	**e)**	people-orientated
6	task-orientated	**f)**	laissez-faire

E Different business situations call for different management styles. Which kinds of situation need to be tightly managed and which loosely managed?

F Which management styles have you experienced? Which do you prefer? If you are a manager, how would you describe your own management style?

Listening
Successful managers

▲ Niall Foster

A What do you think are the key qualities for a successful manager today?

B 🎧 12.1 Listen to the first part of an interview with Niall Foster, an expert on management styles, and answer the following questions:

1 What does Niall say a successful manager must do?

2 What does Niall do before he makes contact with people in other countries?

C In pairs, think of five ways managers can get the best out of people.

D 🎧 12.2 Listen to the second part of the interview and note down Niall's five key points on ways managers can get the best out of people.

Reading

Management styles

A Before you read the article answer one of these questions.

1 If you are a manager, what sort of style do you have?

2 If you were a manager, what sort of style do you think you would have?

B Work in groups of three. Each of you read about <u>one</u> of the management styles – *Directing*, *Discussing* or *Delegating* – and decide which of the following statements are true for your style.

1 It is up to employees to keep the manager up to date on progress.

2 Managers set strict time limits.

3 Managers encourage staff to put forward their ideas.

4 Managers and employees decide together what needs to be achieved.

5 Decisions are made by managers and their staff.

6 Employees get precise instructions.

7 Managers do not want employees to avoid making decisions which employees should make.

8 Managers have tight control of employees' movements and work schedules.

9 When employees are given tasks, they decide how to complete them.

C Meet as one group and summarise the main features of the style you read about to the others in your group.

D Which of the three management styles would you prefer to: a) use as a manager? b) experience as an employee?

E Match the word partnerships in groups 1 and 2, then check your answers in the article.

Group 1

1 establish	a) feedback	
2 monitor	b) goals	
3 provide	c) decisions	
4 set	d) performance	
5 make	e) roles	
6 assign	f) standards	

Group 2

1 present	a) action
2 achieve	b) employees
3 direct	c) ideas
4 take	d) performance
5 improve	e) goals

F Check the following word partnerships. Find the odd one out in each group.

1 check / assess / look   performance

2 make / achieve / establish   goals

3 reach / do / implement   decisions

4 meet / set / get   standards

5 establish / assign / make   roles

6 reach / deliver / achieve   goals

7 come up with / make / present ideas

8 achieve / direct / guide   employees

The Big Three Management Styles

by Paul B. Thornton

Management literature describes numerous management styles, including assertive, autocratic, coaching, country club, directing, delegating, laissez-faire, participatory, supportive, task-oriented and team-based. Are there really that many styles? I believe there are three basic styles – directing, discussing and delegating, the 3-Ds of Management Style.

DIRECTING STYLE

Managers using this style tell people what to do, how to do it and when to have it completed. They assign roles and responsibilities, set standards and define expectations.

Communicating - The manager speaks, employees listen and react. Managers provide detailed instructions so employees know exactly what to do. The ability to communicate in a clear, concise and complete fashion is critical. The only feedback managers ask for is, 'Do you understand what needs to be done?'

Goal-Setting - 'Your goal is to sell 15 cars per month.' The manager establishes short-term goals. When goals are specific and time bounded, employees are clear on what is expected of them. Goals and deadlines often motivate people.

Decision-Making - 'I want you to stop what you are currently doing and help Sue set up the room for the seminar.' The manager makes most if not all decisions. When problems arise the manager evaluates options, makes decisions and directs employees as to what actions to take.

Monitoring Performance and Providing Feedback - Managers establish specific control points to monitor performance. 'Get back to me at 11:00 a.m. to brief me on what you have accomplished.' Managers provide frequent feedback including specific instructions on how to improve performance.

DISCUSSING STYLE

Managers using this style take time to discuss relevant business issues. What happens in a good discussion? People present ideas, ask questions, listen, provide feedback, challenge certain assumptions and coach as needed. It's important to make sure ideas are fully discussed and debated. Managers often perform the role of facilitator, making sure the discussion stays on track and everyone has a chance to contribute.

Communicating - Two-way communication is the norm. 'Let's go around the table and give everyone a chance to discuss their ideas.' Managers spend as much time asking questions and listening as they do talking and sharing their ideas. The right question focuses the discussion and draws out people's ideas.

Goal-Setting - 'Ingrid, what do you think our sales target should be for the fourth quarter?' After adequate discussion, goals are then established. Utilising a participatory style generally helps to increase employees' commitment to achieve their goals.

Decision-Making - 'We have a problem with the amount of inventory we're currently carrying. What action do you think we should take?' Decisions are made collaboratively. Both manager and employee play an active role in defining problems, evaluating options, and making decisions.

Monitoring Performance and Providing Feedback - The manager and employee monitor performance and discuss what actions need to be taken. This works best when both parties are open and make adjustments as needed.

DELEGATING STYLE

Managers using this style usually explain or get agreement on what has to be accomplished and when it must be completed. The how-to-do-it part of the equation is left up to the employee. Responsibility and authority are given to employees to get the job done.

Communicating - Regarding what has to be accomplished, communications may be one-way: 'I want you to deliver a 15-minute presentation on our new compensation program at Tuesday's meeting.' In other situations it may be two-way: 'Let's discuss what needs to be accomplished in the marketing brochure you're designing.' Additional communication takes place to review what has been accomplished and obstacles preventing progress.

Goal-Setting - As stated above, specific goals may be established by the manager or may evolve after a discussion between manager and employee. Failures in delegation can often be traced back to a lack of understanding of the desired output or deliverable. 'I thought you only wanted recommendations, not an implementation plan.'

Decision-Making - 'Barbara, that's your decision to make.' Decisions as to how the task will be accomplished are left to the employee. Employees have the power to take appropriate actions to achieve the desired goals. Managers must avoid 'reverse delegation' when employees try to give back decisions that they should be making.

Monitoring Performance and Providing Feedback - 'I want a weekly update on plan accomplishments.' Managers decide how much monitoring is necessary. The amount of monitoring depends on the priority of the task and the person doing it. Providing feedback is the responsibility of the employee. Keeping the manager informed, especially when the plan is off track, is critical.

From The CEO Refresher (www.refresher.com/!bigthree.html)

Language review
Text reference

- In written English, we often use pronouns to avoid repeating words and phrases when it is already clear what we are talking about. For example, *We need the report urgently — **it's** got to be sent to head office*.
- Writers sometimes use *we* to refer to themselves and the readers together. For example, *As **we** saw in Chapter 2 ...*
- We sometimes use *it* as an 'empty' subject with no real meaning. For example, ***It's** raining*.
- We can use *it, this, that, these* and *those* to refer back or forward to something in a text, or outside the text itself.
- We can use *they* to avoid saying *he* or *she*, especially after indefinite words like *anyone, no one, somebody*, etc. For example, *Someone's been trying to send us a fax but **they** can't get through*.

➡ page 135

A **Look at the article on page 103 and answer these questions.**

1 What do the following words refer to?

a) they (line 4) *in Directing style*

b) this (line 1) *in Discussing style*

c) they (line 22) *in Discussing style*

d) their (line 35) *in Discussing style*

e) this (line 51) *in Discussing style*

2 Find an example of *it* as an empty subject.

B **The following paragraphs are from the same article. Look at the paragraphs and do the following.**

1 Find all references to the writer.

2 Find all references to the first highly competent person mentioned.

3 Find all references to the second highly competent person mentioned.

4 Find an example of *it* as an empty subject.

I once had two highly competent people working in similar roles who needed very different styles.

5 One did her thing and kept me informed. She used me to bounce ideas off, but never waited for or expected approval before proceeding. 10 She gave me reports and I rarely checked on progress. The other person, who was equally competent but less experienced, felt that I didn't 15 care about his work unless I checked on progress 20 frequently and provided feedback on how he was proceeding.

At first I didn't know my delegating style with him was ineffective because he was meeting objectives. On the other hand, he always 25 seemed to want to stop by and give me verbal updates that I felt were unnecessary.

Finally I asked him how our relationship was working for 30 him and he told me how he felt about my lack of apparent interest. He thought what he was doing was not important unless I was asking about the 35 progress on a regular basis. What I thought was a vote of confidence was actually eroding his confidence.

When using each style it's 40 important to pay attention to both project results and the behaviour/morale of the people.

C **Write a short article agreeing or disagreeing with the following statement.**

'Female managers are generally better managers than male managers.'

Skills
Putting people at ease

A **Discuss these questions.**

1 What is *small talk*?

2 What are your five favourite topics for small talk?

3 What topics are definitely not suitable?

B **Someone is visiting your country. To which questions might the following be answers?**

1 Terrible. There was a lot of turbulence and several people were sick.

2 Yes, several times.

3 Right in the centre.

4 Very comfortable, and the service is first class.

5 We're doing very well, thanks.

6 I enjoy tennis, when I get the time.

7 I'm really impressed. The architecture is fascinating. I hope I have time to take it all in.

8 I'd love to.

C 🎧 **12.3** **Now listen to the conversation. Were your questions the same as on the recording?**

D **Discuss these questions.**

1 What ways could you use to put people at ease in the following situations?

a) entertaining socially with friends

b) business entertaining with colleagues

c) entertaining foreign visitors

2 Do you feel comfortable when there is silence in a group?

3 Do you feel more comfortable:

a) in a small group or a large group?

b) with members of your own sex or with the opposite sex?

c) in a formal situation or an informal one?

E **The Managing Director of a large American company made the suggestions on the left for putting people at ease. Match them to the comments on the right.**

1 Use informal greetings when you meet people.

2 Show you know something about somebody you meet.

3 Share something of a personal nature.

4 Pick a topic which isn't work-related.

5 Use open questions rather than statements.

a) 'I'm a bit stressed - we've got the builders in our house!'

b) 'Did you see the football last night?'

c) 'Hi, I'm John.'

d) 'How are you finding the conference?'

e) 'You must be Dan Jervis. Weren't you with Datacom?'

F **Which would be appropriate in your culture? What other things do you say to put people at ease?**

G **You are about to meet a foreign business contact socially for the first time. Choose four of the topics below and prepare to talk about them.**

- places of interest in your town / country
- the building you are in
- the stock market
- the weather
- cars
- families
- food and restaurants
- hobbies
- holidays
- how you travelled here
- IT topics
- jobs

CASE STUDY

Zenova

Background

Zenova is based in Hanover, Germany. It is a multinational group which makes health and beauty products. Four months ago, it assembled a project team of 16 members drawn from subsidiaries in Europe, America, Asia and the Middle East. The working language was English.

The team, managed by Ryan Douglas, was instructed to carry out a major survey of job satisfaction in all the subsidiaries. This would involve travelling to subsidiary companies, interviewing staff, administering surveys, analysing results and producing a final report in 18 months' time. The team would have to work to tight deadlines, under constant pressure to complete the various stages of the work.

Four months later, it became clear that the project was being badly managed. The morale of team members was low and progress on the project had been much too slow.

The management of Zenova decided to replace Ryan Douglas, the current Project Manager. The problem was to decide who to put in his place. Who would have the right management style to lead this multinational team?

Management style of Ryan Douglas

🎧 **12.4** You are directors of Zenova. You interviewed three members of the project team about Ryan's style of management. Work in small groups. Listen to the comments. Note down the strengths and weaknesses of his style, using these categories: Personality; Communication; Goal-setting; Decision-making; Monitoring performance and giving feedback.

Task

1 Work in small groups. You are directors of Zenova. Discuss each of the candidates' management style. Analyse their strengths and weaknesses.

2 Rank the management styles of the four candidates in terms of their suitability for the position of project manager. Number 1 would be your first choice, number 4 your least suitable candidate.

3 Working as one group, compare your decisions and choose one candidate to be the Project Manager.

Writing

As one of the directors, write a summary of the meeting you have just attended. This summary will be sent to the Chief Executive of Zenova, who was unable to attend. Your summary should contain the following:

● an analysis of each candidate's management style.

● your choice of candidate for Project Manager, together with your reasons.

Replacing the Project Manager

The directors of Zenova have talked informally to several candidates who would be interested in taking over from Ryan Douglas. The candidates were asked to note down their management style. Read the descriptions of their style.

Manager 1 Elliot
NEW BUSINESS MANAGER

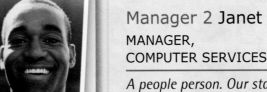

I'm a strong, confident person.

My job: *To give instructions and see they're carried out. Not interested in excuses if the work isn't done. Essential to give staff clear goals. Check often to make sure they're meeting deadlines. Don't like staff arguing, if they do, I listen then tell them what to do. I'm decisive, sometimes I get it wrong. Who doesn't? My staff are multinational - I'm trying to adapt my management style.*

Appraisal interviews: *Once a year with staff - always friendly and productive.*

My strengths: *Leadership, achieving targets.*

My personality: *tough, fair, loyal to staff. Bit impatient at times.*

Manager 2 Janet
MANAGER, COMPUTER SERVICES

A people person. Our staff are our biggest asset.

My job: *To try and make sure everyone's happy in the department. Enjoy meetings. Decide everything in discussions with all staff. Talk about our goals with them - we decide them together. Once I've made up my mind, I don't change it - very decisive. Spend lots of time sorting out staff problems. It's a priority.*

Appraisal interviews: *Every six months. Check each week to see if they're OK.*

My strengths: *Good listener; well-organised; get the details right.*

My personality: *Warm; friendly; understanding. Wonderful atmosphere in the department.*

Manager 3 Anna
TRANSPORT MANAGER

Ambitious, hardworking and responsible.

My job: *Organising people so that they get the work done. I'm tough, I have to be with my staff - truck drivers, warehouse men. Always set goals. Then let them get on with it. Their job? To carry out my instructions - to the letter. Like to offer them incentives, e.g. Bonuses, prizes, free holidays. Competition is good, it brings out the best in staff.*

Appraisal interviews: *Once a year. Usually a waste of time.*

My strengths: *Organising; motivating, getting job done.*

My personality: *Strong, bossy, successful. Tough outside, soft inside!*

Manager 4 Koichi
SALES DIRECTOR, EUROPE

Hardworking, democratic and loyal.

My job: *To meet the targets set by my superior. Essential not to let the company down. Hold lots of meetings with staff. No time limit. Discuss our goals with staff. Never take decisions without consulting staff. Do not allow arguments at work - bad for team morale. Discuss sales targets with each member of staff. Set realistic targets. Work six days a week, often at the weekends. Expect staff to do the same. Want staff to feel ashamed if they do not meet targets.*

Appraisal interviews: *Every quarter.*

My strengths: *Hardworking, sociable, never get angry.*

My personality: *Serious; polite; professional. Very important for staff to respect me.*

Takeovers and mergers

You cannot buy a company merely by buying its shares.
Sir James Goldsmith (1933–1997)
Anglo–French financier

Starting up

A **What do you understand by the following expressions?**

a) a takeover **b)** a merger **c)** a joint venture

B **Think of three reasons why one company might wish to take over another company.**

C **Think of a takeover or merger. What kinds of businesses were involved? Were both companies successful before it happened? What about now?**

Vocabulary

Describing takeovers and mergers

A **Match the terms on the left to the definitions on the right.**

1 joint venture
2 MBO (management buyout)
3 merger
4 takeover / acquisition
5 bid
6 stake

a) money risked or invested in a company
b) two or more companies joining to form a larger company
c) offer money for shares in a company
d) when a company's top executives buy the company they work for
e) a business activity in which two or more companies have invested together
f) getting control of a company by buying over 50% of its shares

B **Circle the noun which forms a word partnership with the verb.**

1 take   a stake / a bid / an acquisition
2 make   a merger / a stake / a bid
3 launch   a bid / an alliance / a stake
4 target   a company / a bid / a takeover
5 set up   a share / a joint venture / a stake
6 make   a merger / a joint venture / an acquisition

C Use the following words or phrases to complete the extracts.

merger	takeover bid	stake	joint venture

1 Banco Popolare Italiana has finally received agreement from the Bank of Italy to launch a .... for Banca Antonveneta, in competition with ABN Amro of the Netherlands. ABN Amro's offer is worth more than Banco Popolare's, but some analysts think that Banco Popolare may already control more than 50% of Antonveneta's shares.

2 PC-Ware, the German IT services specialist, has increased its .... in its domestic competitor Senas from 50% to 100%.

4 The Swiss bank, UBS, is in talks with Beijing Securities to set up a China-based .... By working together on a number of projects, the two banks will be able to compete more effectively against western rivals such as Goldman Sachs and Merrill Lynch.

From the *Financial Times*

FINANCIAL TIMES

3 Japan yesterday confirmed the creation of the world's biggest bank when shareholders approved the .... of Mitsubishi Tokyo Financial Group and UFJ Holdings. The new bank will be headed by MTFG's Nobuo Kuroyanagi, aged 63.

Listening
Making acquisitions

▲ Susan Barratt

A 🎧 13.1 Susan Barratt, a Financial Director, talks about the process of acquiring another company. Listen to the first part of the interview and answer these questions.

1 What three preparatory steps does Susan mention?
2 After taking the preparatory steps what do companies need to do next?

B 🎧 13.1 Listen to the first part of the interview again and complete the examples of strategic goals:

1 market ....
2 economic ....
3 vertical ....
4 international ....

C 🎧 13.2 In the second part of the interview Susan Barratt talks about the successful integration of a new business. She mentions two sides of success. What are they? Give an example of each.

D 🎧 13.2 Listen to the second part again and choose the best ending to the following sentence. *According to Susan Barratt an acquisition has been successful when:* a) you improve efficiency, b) open up new markets, c) add value to your business.

E 🎧 13.3 Listen to the third part of the interview. Susan Barratt gives an example of a successful merger. What reasons does she give for its success?

Reading
Making a corporate marriage work

A **Before you read the article discuss these questions.**

1 What are the secrets of: **a)** a successful marriage? **b)** a successful merger?

2 In what ways are a marriage and a business merger similar?

B **Read the article and complete the guidelines for a successful merger. Find at least three DOs and three DON'Ts.**

DOs	DON'Ts
1 *Prepare early before the merger is announced publicly*	1 *Relax once the deal is signed*
2	2 ....
3	3 ....
4	4 ....

C **Match the experts quoted in the article to their opinions about mergers.**

1 Michelle Bligh

2 Charles Hampden-Turner

3 Roger Pudney

a) 'Respect the other company even if your company is stronger.'

b) 'You need to pay special attention to the different ways that companies do things.'

c) 'You need to act quickly in the post-merger period.'

D **Complete the definition with the most suitable answer.**

1 *big-picture* questions (lines 3–4) are:

  a) very important   **b)** very difficult   **c)** very expensive

2 *ground rules* (line 118) are:

  a) complicated rules   **b)** strict rules   **c)** basic rules

3 *the nitty-gritty* (line 132) is:

  a) problems   **b)** details   **c)** advantages

4 *buy-in* (line 132) is:

  a) acceptance   **b)** disagreement   **c)** enthusiasm

5 *shop floor* (line 146) is:

  a) where the goods are stored   **b)** where the goods are made   **c)** where the goods are delivered

6 *steam-rollered* (line 172) is:

  a) invited to do something   **b)** paid to do something   **c)** forced to do something

E **Answer these questions.**

1 Have you ever been *steam-rollered* into something? What was it? How did you feel?

2 Do you know any *shop floor* workers? How do they feel about their jobs?

3 If you have a problem to solve are you better at seeing the *big-picture* or are you better at *the nitty-gritty*?

4 What are the *ground rules* of your favourite sport? Explain them to your partner.

5 How can you get employees to *buy in* to a new company policy, e.g. a strict new dress code following a takeover?

F **In pairs, discuss these questions.**

1 What do you think are the most difficult problems following a takeover for **a)** management? **b)** employees?

2 How can they be solved?

Making a corporate marriage work

By Stefan Stern

Bringing two companies together is an enormous task. There are grand, big-picture questions that need to be resolved, such as the new group's strategy and direction. There are also administrative, logistical and technical challenges. Will new contracts of employment be required? Where should the headquarters of the combined operation be located? How can the companies' information technology systems be integrated?

'It takes a certain humility to make a merger work,' says Charles Hampden-Turner, co-author of Building Cross-cultural Competence. 'It doesn't follow that your company is a better one simply because it has taken another company over. It just means that you've got more money and have been prepared to pay,' he says.

Work on bringing the partners together should start well before the deal becomes public knowledge. But how can executives start planning integration without the news leaking out? Some use a so-called 'clean room', where both sides to a deal can meet and discuss future plans confidentially. Computer manufacturers Hewlett-Packard and Compaq, for example, adopted this approach in their $25bn (£13.3bn) merger.

Speed is of the essence. Roger Pudney of the UK's Ashridge business school says: 'There is often a tendency for companies to relax once the deal is signed, but this is precisely the point at which speed of implementation becomes crucial. Successful Mergers & Acquisitions companies stress the importance of quick wins as a way of demonstrating that the new combination is already producing added value.'

HP and Compaq ran a series of 'Fast Start' seminars for their staff as soon as the deal was announced, to provide reassurance and a sense of direction - seminars that had been planned in advance in the clean room. Offering employees detailed information is essential at the early stage. An internal human resources website set up for HP and Compaq staff received 2m hits on the day the merger was unveiled.

Managers will inevitably be occupied with practical, administrative changes, such as establishing new terms and conditions and pushing through any redundancies. Yet dealing with the cultural issues in a merger is more subtle and challenging. And when things go wrong in this context they can go wrong very quickly.

Michelle Bligh, a professor at Claremont Graduate University, California, has suggested measures leaders should take to avoid the worst consequences of mergers. After studying a merger of health organisations in the US, Prof Bligh advised leaders to avoid taking a dictatorial, top-down approach or micro-managing the transition.

They need to respond as the new situation demands, she says, and must 'help followers negotiate, modify and even manipulate cultural similarities and differences in the post-merger environment'.

Prof Bligh identifies a few simple ground rules. Managers should recognise cultural differences between the companies, for example, by learning about the history of the new partner. They should give employees reasons why change is necessary, and find practical ways of communicating. As one manager told her: 'When you sit down and start showing employees the nitty-gritty, you get buy-in a lot quicker.'

Symbolism matters too. 'Instead of making great speeches,' Dr Hampden-Turner suggests, 'why not start acting differently and providing a lead that way? Words are too easy, but actions will be noticed.' Even apparently simple gestures can count. Discussing employees' new working conditions and being visible on the 'shop floor', for example, may reassure staff that management has an interest in their well-being. One manager in Prof Bligh's study said: 'We have to start with the little things: they really matter to people.'

How do the most successful acquirers handle the process of merger integration? General Electric, the US engineering conglomerate, has made more than 400 acquisitions in the past 20 years. But it is still learning how to make these deals work better. When GE bought Amersham, the UK bioscience company, for $9bn, it made a big effort to reassure the acquired business that it would not be steam-rollered.

Talk of a revival in merger and acquisitions activity is on the rise. Investment bankers and management consultants are once again seeking out potential deals and making flattering noises as they lead candidates to the altar. But marriages succeed or fail in the years following the wedding. Even before the hangover has worn off, the hard work has to begin.

From the *Financial Times*

FINANCIAL TIMES

Language review
Headlines

Newspaper headlines are often written in a special style which can make them difficult to understand. They often:
1 contain groups of several nouns: *pharmaceutical company takeover battle*
2 leave out articles and the verb *to be*: *Coke and Danone close to deal*
3 contain simple tenses instead of progressive or perfect forms, and use the present simple is used for both present and past events: *Shell confirms China stake*
4 contain words used both as nouns and verbs: *French company targets UK media group; UK media group becomes takeover target*
5 refer to the future with infinitives: *Japan's Bandai to acquire Namco*

see page 136

A Look at these headlines. Which of the features described in the Language box do they show? (Some headlines show more than one feature.)

1 Renault on brink of two alliances
2 US law firms agree merger deal
3 Austin Reed rejects offer as unwelcome
4 Gazprom and Rosneft agree merger
5 Titan in £9.3bn bid for US store group
6 Chromogenex to raise £2m
7 Sara Lee to dispose of 60 smallest units
8 AOL deal calls rivals' web plans into question

B Write out the headlines above in full. For example: *1 Renault is on the brink of two alliances.*

C Certain words are used more commonly in headlines, often because they are shorter or more dramatic than their alternatives. Match the italicised words in the headlines on the left to their meanings on the right.

1 ANZ mulls further *link* in China
2 Blockbuster drops hostile *bid* for Hollywood
3 EU wrong to *block* US merger
4 TomOnline *seeks* merger for growth
5 Boeing scores victory over Airbus with AirCanada *deal*
6 Lodi deals ABN big *blow* in Italy takeover fight
7 Golman chairman under fire *over* NYSE deal
8 Coors and Molson *unveil* $6bn merger
9 Mannesmann investors *split* over bid
10 Treasury seeks peace deal in takeovers *row*
11 Takeover *backing* for Union Fenosa

a) offer to buy a company
b) connection
c) about, concerning
d) announce
e) disagree
f) agreement
g) support
h) look for
i) disagreement
j) obstruct
k) bad news

Skills
Summarising in presentations

A Jeremy Keeley, an independent management consultant, is giving a presentation to a board of directors involved in a takeover. Before you listen match the words 1–8 that he uses to their meanings a)–h).

1	pitfalls	a)	things that limit your action
2	rigorous	b)	thorough
3	constraints	c)	to work together to produce something
4	confidential	d)	unexpected difficulties
5	hamstrung	e)	those who try to please important people
6	sycophants	f)	competing for
7	vying (for jobs)	g)	intended to be kept secret
8	collaborate	h)	prevented from doing something

B 🎧 13.4 **You will hear part of the final section of Jeremy's presentation. He is giving a summary of common mistakes that managers make. Which of the four points in his presentation notes below does he *not* make?**

> ## Avoiding the pitfalls
> - Recognise the constraints
> - Pay attention to the cultural differences
> - Beware of the sycophants
> - Refer to core meaning / purpose

C 🎧 13.4 **Study the Useful language box. Then listen again and tick the phrases that you hear.**

Useful language

Referring back
As I mentioned earlier in my presentation ...
So as you were saying a few minutes ago ...

Making points in threes
You really have to plan carefully, be rigorous in your analysis and be flexible ...
It's a long process. It's expensive. It can also be very profitable.

Asking rhetorical questions
What are the advantages of the merger?
But what are the sort of things that the experts forget generally?

Ordering
Firstly ..., then ..., finally ...
There are three things in my mind and the first thing is ...

Using emotive language
Beware of the sycophants in your organisation ...
It is commercial suicide ...

Repetition
They're going to be saying Yes! Yes! Yes!
It won't work. It just won't work.

Exemplifying
For instance ...
... for example, caring as their primary task.

Asking for feedback
Is there any area I haven't covered?
What's missing?

D Work in two groups, A and B. Group A discuss some of the advantages of takeovers and mergers. Group B discuss the problems associated with them.

Then form pairs – one from Group A and one from Group B. Give a short presentation summarising the points you discussed in your group.

Bon Appetit PLC

Background

Bon Appetit plc is a chain of restaurants in the UK offering top class cuisine to higher-income groups. It has been extremely successful since it was founded in the late 1970s, and is now at a point where it can see no further opportunities for expansion. The management have decided therefore to grow the business by acquiring an already established company in the food industry, either in the UK or overseas. The main objectives of the acquisition are:

• to increase Bon Appetit's profits

• to enhance its image

• to buy a company which will continue to grow and contribute to the group's success

• to buy a company which will not take up too much of the present management's time and energy.

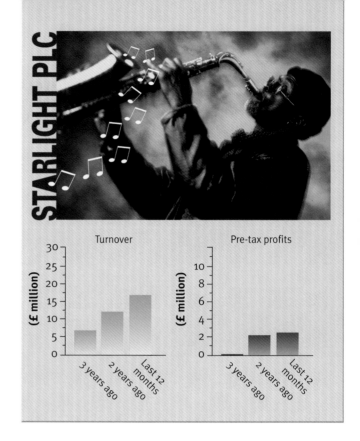

The Corporate Strategy department of Bon Appetit was given the task of looking for suitable acquisitions. They worked in three groups and carried out a great deal of research. Each group finally came up with a possible takeover target. The three companies they have researched are:

a) Coffee Ground plc (UK) – a chain of coffee shops

b) Starlight plc – a chain of nightclubs/restaurants (UK)

c) Mario Ferrino – a chain of delicatessens (Italy).

Key financial information

The past financial performance of the three companies is given in the charts on the right. All figures are in millions of pounds.

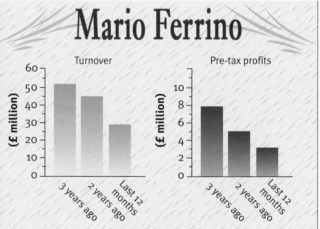

Reports from business magazines

Read the reports about Coffee Ground plc and Starlight plc. Note the key points.

Coffee Ground grinding to a halt

Disappointing results for the first half of the year.

Turnover down by £1.8 million. New stores cut back. Only five opened. The figures reflect stiff competition in the UK from giant chain Starbucks and dynamic small groups like Café Nero and Costa.

Experts question whether there are further opportunities for growth in the UK market. Is Coffee Ground running out of steam? Or can the management team come up with new products and ideas to take away market share from its rivals?

Starlight still rocketing

Good news from Starlight. They have produced the goods once again.

Chairman and CEO Lisa Martin has announced an increase in turnover of just under £3.9 million for the first six months of the year.

The increased revenue has come from four new night clubs in the North of England. These have performed well.

In spite of the excellent results, experts wonder whether it's moving too fast. Starlight has a small, inexperienced management team – can they handle this level of growth in the future?

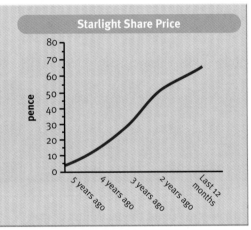

Starlight Share Price

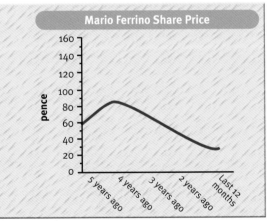

Mario Ferrino Share Price

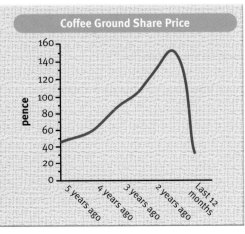

Coffee Ground Share Price

Debt ratio*

Coffee Ground plc	35%
Starlight	72%
Mario Ferrino	44%

(*Debt ratio: a company's debt in relation to the amount of share capital it has.)

 13.5 Listen to the news broadcast from the television programme *European Business*. Make notes.

Task

1 Form three groups: A, B and C. Analyse the information you have gained from the charts, the magazine reports and the television programme. Discuss what the data tells you about the three companies. What conclusions can you reach?

2 Each group has made notes on one of the companies.
   Group A (role card, page 148)
   Group B (role card, page 154)
   Group C (role card, page 152)
Prepare a **presentation** of the results of your research. Use the notes on your role card and include any conclusions you have reached so far about the company you have studied.

3 Listen to each other's presentations. Note down key information about the companies researched by the other groups.

4 In your groups, consider the three possible acquisitions. Decide which company would be a suitable acquisition for Bon Appetit. Give your reasons.

5 Meet as one group. Decide which company, at this stage, seems to be the most suitable as an acquisition.

Writing

Write a report to the board of directors on the possible takeover targets. Give your recommendations for acquisition.

➡ *Writing file pages 144 and 145*

6 If I had asked people what they wanted, they would have said faster horses. 9

Henry Ford (1863–1947),
US Industrialist

OVERVIEW ▼

Starting up

(A) **The business world has changed dramatically in recent times. Which of the following do you think could happen in the next 50 years? Explain why.**

1 People will have more leisure time.
2 Few people will have full time jobs.
3 There will be cities of 100 million people.
4 There will be a world stock market.
5 Cash won't be used any more.
6 People will live and work in space.
7 Trade unions will disappear.
8 There will be no retirement age.
9 Countries will be run by big businesses rather than governments.
10 Fresh water will be more valuable than oil.

(B) **What other changes do you think are likely?**

(C) **How do you think your career will develop in the future?**

(D) **How optimistic are you about the future of business in your own country? Explain your answer.**

Listening
The future of business

▲ Tamar Kasriel

A 🎧 **14.1** Tamar Kasriel, Head of Knowledge Venturing at the Henley Centre, is talking about business opportunities in the future. Listen to the first part of the interview and complete the chart below.

New business opportunities

1 A development in .... and in ....

2 Targeting a particular .... of ...., for example, older people who are going to be an important .... of the market.

Expanding business sectors

1 Areas where companies are very ...., for example, the growth of .... in Europe and the United States.

2 Companies where they can .... a .... and offer something a bit special.

B 🎧 **14.2** Listen to the second part of the interview and answer these questions.

1 What is Tamar Kasriel's opinion about technology and efficiency?

2 **a)** How did companies try to become more efficient in the 1980s?

   b) How will they try to be more efficient in the future?

Vocabulary
Describing the future

A Complete the expressions below with words from the box.

art	date (2)	edge	fashioned	time	forward	minute	past	times

1 up-to- *date* ....

2 a thing of the ....

3 ahead of its ....

4 old- ....

5 state-of-the-..........................

6 the way ....

7 out of ....

8 up to the ....

9 at the cutting ....

10 behind the ....

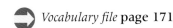

Vocabulary file page 171

B Use some of the expressions above to comment on products or companies that you are familiar with. For example, *Using cash could become a thing of the past.*

C The adjectives in the box can be used to talk about the future. Use them to complete the table below.

bleak	bright	brilliant	depressing	dire	doubtful
dreadful	great	magnificent	marvellous	promising	
prosperous	rosy	terrible	uncertain	worrying	

very bad	⇒	bad	⇒	good	⇒	very good
bleak						

D Discuss the short- and long-term futures for some key industries in your country. Combine adjectives from the table with words like: *possibly, potentially, probably, certainly, undoubtedly*. For example, *The future for shipbuilding is potentially very bright.*

Reading
New working model

A What do you think will happen in your country during the next five years with regard to the following?

- population
- unemployment
- inflation
- universities
- wages
- leisure time
- information technology
- market regulation

B Read the article and answer these questions.

1 According to the writer, what are the two greatest changes in the world affecting business?
2 According to the writer, what lessons can be learned from previous attempts to predict the future of work?
3 What have been the effects of outsourcing on global business?
4 What is the point which the writer makes about capital and labour?
5 What example of problem-solving does the writer give?

C What key point(s) does the writer make about the following countries?

Germany   France   the UK   Japan   India   China   the US

D Put the following words in the correct order. Then check your answer in the article. For example: *excessive labour market regulation*

1 regulation   labour market   excessive
2 leadership   economic   world
3 in-house   think-tank   economic
4 markets   potentially   huge
5 vehicle   lower   development costs
6 niche   new   markets
7 world-class   centres   research

E Now put the following words in the correct order. For example: *increasingly difficult market conditions*

1 difficult   conditions   market   increasingly
2 gifted   researchers   university   exceptionally
3 increasingly   rate   high   unemployment
4 developing   rapidly   information   technology

F Discuss these questions.

1 How do you think the way people work will change in the future?
2 Which five countries do you think will dominate the world economy in twenty years' time? Rank them in order of importance and give reasons. Compare your ideas with your partner.

New working model

By Michael Skapinker

As we embark on this new investigation of the future of work, there are several lessons we can draw by looking back. First, time, and our own adaptability, may solve some of our deepest problems. There are still developed countries worried about large-scale unemployment, France and Germany among them. But their problems are now widely seen as the result of excessive labour market regulation. Far from telling employees to enjoy more leisure, French and German companies are trying to find ways to ensure their staff work more hours. And in the UK, employers and policy-makers now worry about a shortage of workers, not of work.

Second, the countries that seem poised to assume world economic leadership - Japan in the past; India and, especially, China now - may face obstacles that are barely visible today. And third, there is nothing new about our sense that we are at a turning point. People have often felt that work was changing in ways they had not seen before. Is it different this time? Is the way we work really changing fundamentally?

In one sense yes, simply because the countries that are playing a fuller part in the world economy, particularly China and India, have such large populations. 'We simply have not comprehended yet the full impact of 2.5bn people coming into the world economy who were not part of it before,' says Kim Clark, dean of Harvard Business School.

The second change is the technology affecting work today. The internet and broadband connections have made it far easier for companies to distribute their work around the world and to remain open 24 hours a day, seven days a week.

The trend towards both outsourcing and offshoring have offered India and China huge opportunities to develop their people's skills. They have also provided companies around the world with enticements that are difficult to resist. Diana Farrell, director of the McKinsey Global Institute, the consultancy's in-house economic think-tank, says that 70 per cent of the costs of a typical company in the developed world come from labour and 30 per cent from capital. Capital is expensive and labour cheap in countries such as India and China. Companies that benefit from the cost savings involved in employing Indian or Chinese labour are at a significant advantage.

The problem is, Ms Farrell says, that competitor companies can achieve the same benefits by moving some of their operations to India or China too. Competitive advantage can only be retained if companies understand that there is more to be gained from India or China than cost-cutting. The two countries are potentially huge markets too. Lower vehicle development costs in India, for example, mean cheap cars can be produced for the local market. New niche markets can be found for these products in developed countries too.

Companies can address business problems in India and China that they could not solve in their home markets. For example, Ms Farrell cites an airline that used to find it uneconomic to chase debts of less than $200. By using Indian accountants, they were able to chase debts of $50. This is good for western companies, but what of western workers?

A common question heard in the US and Western Europe today is: 'What are we all going to do?' Prof Clark says: 'First of all we have to recognise something that's lost in a lot of these conversations: most of us don't work in places that are competing with the Chinese.' Or the Indians.

Technology is likely to continue to allow more jobs to be done remotely, but, Prof Clark argues, there will be an opposing trend too: companies offering a more personal service at close quarters. Ms Farrell argues that demographic changes mean there are going to be fewer Americans and western Europeans to do the jobs available anyway.

Japan and Western Europe are ageing societies. Even the US, still a relatively young country by comparison, will have 5 per cent fewer people of working age by 2015 than it does today.

Faced with these projections, western societies can either export the jobs or import the workers.

Will China and India become as dominant as Japan once looked like becoming? Prof Clark says the most significant obstacle they face is the quality of the universities. Few of them show signs of becoming the world-class research centres they need to be if China and India are to become world economic leaders.

From the *Financial Times*

FINANCIAL TIMES

Language review
Prediction and probability

There are many ways to talk about prediction and probability:
We can use *will* or *going to*.
There **are going to** be fewer Americans and Europeans to do the jobs available.
Even the US **will** have 5% fewer people of working age by 2015.
We can use modals.
*The economic situation **may** improve.*
We can use lexical phrases.
Certain: *There's **certain** to be more outsourcing of production in the next 10 years.*
Probable: *It's quite **probable** that Russia will join the European Union.*
Possible: ***Maybe** we'll have to hire a new CEO.*
Unlikely: *It's **unlikely** that Coke will lose its position.*
Impossible: *It's just **not possible** to meet that deadline.*   see page 136

A **Look at the following examples and say whether the lexical phrases suggest they are: *certain, probable, possible, unlikely* or *impossible*.**

1 *There's no chance of* us entering the European Union.
2 *There's bound* to be an increase in interest rates soon.
3 *I doubt whether* there will be a stock market crash next year.
4 They *probably* won't call off the strike.
5 Our CEO's taking a salary cut. *It's out of the question*.
6 *It's possible that* the retirement age will be increased to 70.
7 *Perhaps* the majority of managers will be women in the future.
8 *It's highly likely that* China will become the dominant world power.
9 *There's a good chance that* the World Wide Web will have serious problems.
10 Poor infrastructure will *definitely* undermine economic growth.

B **In pairs say what you really think about the likelihood of a stock market crash next year, the retirement age being increased to 70, the majority of women being managers, China becoming the dominant world power, and the World Wide Web having serious problems.**

C **Work in pairs. Make predictions about your company, your country or yourself. Use as many forms from the Language review box and Exercise A as possible. You may also find the phrases in the box below useful:**

In my lifetime …	Over the next decade …
Before long …	By this time next year …
In the near future …	By the end of this century …
In the next … years	Sometime in the next decade / century

Skills
Getting the right information

A 🎧 **14.3 Listen to each dialogue and answer the questions. Then listen again and tick the expressions in the Useful language box that you hear.**

Dialogue 1
1 Why does Carla have difficulties contacting Li Wang?
2 Who helps her with her enquiry?

Dialogue 2
1 Why is Michael Bishop angry?
2 How does the person he calls deal with the situation?

Dialogue 3
1 What caused the breakdown in communication?
2 What do the two speakers do to understand each other?

Dialogue 4
1 Why does the caller telephone the supplier?
2 How did the problem arise?

Useful language

Making contact
Could you put me through to Mr Li Wang please?
You seem to have got the wrong extension.
Can you transfer me to his extension?

Asking for information
Could you give me a few details?
When did you give us the order?
Can you tell me what the order number is?

Asking for repetition
Sorry, I didn't hear what you said.
I'm sorry, I didn't catch that.
What did you say the reference number was?

Checking information
Fine. Shall I just read that back to you?
Let me just check. What you need is ... Is that right?
Could you spell that, please?

Clarifying
What exactly do you mean by ... ?
Sorry, I don't follow you.
Are you saying that ...?

Confirming understanding
Right, I've got that.
Fine / OK / Right.

Confirming action
I'll check it out right away.
I'll get on to it immediately.
I'll call you back as soon as I can.

B Role play these situations in pairs.

1 A Marketing Director is due to attend a meeting with an overseas customer. He/She phones to confirm the arrangements.

Marketing Director
You are phoning to confirm details of a meeting which was arranged by a colleague two weeks ago. You want to meet half an hour earlier, if possible. Also, check the date, time, day and venue of the meeting. Your colleague left you a message with these details:

Time   14:30
Date   Tuesday, 13 November
Venue   Metropolitan
Contact at hotel Karen

If you cannot agree on a suitable time and date, suggest alternatives.

Overseas customer
You receive a call from the Marketing Director who wishes to confirm details of a meeting arranged by his/her colleague. You have the following information in your diary.

Time   16:30pm
Date   Thursday, 30 November
Venue   Metropole
Contact at hotel Kieran

• Confirm the arrangement for the meeting.
• Ask the Marketing Director to bring samples of his / her company's latest products.
• If you cannot agree a suitable time and date, suggest alternatives.

2 A customer telephones the Sales Manager of a German kitchen equipment manufacturer. The customer has ordered some microwave ovens which are more than a month overdue.

Customer turn to page 147. Sales Manager turn to page 151.
Read your role cards, then role play the telephone conversation.

Yedo Department Stores

FACT FILE

Yedo Department Stores

Founded	1895
Staff	Approximately 3,200 (mostly full-time)
Opening hours	7 days 10am – 6pm (Fridays 7pm)
Location	Usually near major railway stations
Core customers	Well-off, brand-conscious; over 80% female
Discount policy	Discounts only available during regular January and July sales
Décor	Traditional / Old-fashioned
Parking	Very limited
Special services	Classes in foreign languages and leisure activities; Travel service

Background

Yedo is a successful Tokyo-based department store chain with six outlets in Japan and two more in London and New York. It has an excellent reputation for high-quality goods. Yedo also offers outstanding service and a large number of sales staff. Many lifts have uniformed attendants.

Yedo's strategy – to offer a wide choice of products and personalised service – has worked well until recently. Last year however,

profits fell sharply and results for the first six months of this year have been disappointing. Furthermore, several similar famous store groups are now heavily in debt.

Market research

Yedo's management has asked an international marketing agency, TWCB, for advice on how to maintain and increase profitability.

Yedo Department Stores: extract from TWCB's market report

3 COMPETITION

3.1 CONVENIENCE STORES

These appeal to all groups, including housewives. They offer a much wider range of goods and services than they used to, and respond quickly to demand. Conveniently located, they often operate round the clock.

3.2 DISCOUNT STORES

Prices in these stores are 20%–30% below the manufacturers' recommended level. Also, stores which price all products at ¥100 have become popular in Japan.

3.3 SPECIALITY STORES

Stores such as Muji and Fast Retailers sell good quality, 'no-brand' products at low prices, backed up by sharp advertising. Fast Retailers has opened 430 stores in Japan and plans another 80 to 100 each year. Muji has 251 stores in Japan, and appeals mostly to young shoppers.

3.4 FOREIGN RETAIL CHAINS

Following deregulation in the retail industry Carrefour from France, and the American chain Wal-Mart, plan to open in Tokyo.

🎧 **14.4** The Head of TWCB, Susan Lam, talks about Japanese social and consumer trends with Kazuo Yamashiro, CEO of Yedo Department Stores. Note down the five trends. Discuss which you think will have most influence on Yedo Department Stores.

Discussion questions

1 Should Yedo continue to position itself as an up-market store selling exclusive products?

2 Should Yedo try to appeal more to older or younger people? What products and services should it offer to appeal to these target customers?

3 What are the advantages and disadvantages of renting parts of the store to other businesses? Should Yedo be doing this?

4 Should Yedo expand overseas, with more stores abroad? If so, what countries would be suitable for overseas expansion?

5 Should Yedo use the Internet? If so, how can it use the Internet effectively?

6 How can Yedo compete against the convenience stores?

7 How do you see the Yedo Department Store group developing in the future?

Task

You are members of the marketing agency, TWCB. An informal meeting has been arranged to discuss ways of maintaining and increasing Yedo's profitability. Yedo's CEO has prepared some discussion questions for you to consider. Hold the meeting and note down your best ideas, which will be incorporated into a report.

Writing

As head of TWCB, write a report for the CEO of Yedo, Kazuo Yamashiro, on your agency's ideas.

➡ *Writing file* pages 144 and 145

Revision

8 Team building

Negative prefixes

Complete the sentences with the negative form of a word from the box.

communicative honestly loyal practical responsible tolerant

1 I had flu, so it would have been .... to attend the meeting and spread my germs around.

2 In a brainstorming session, you should listen to all suggestions, even if some of them seem .... at first sight.

3 It transpired that the project manager had acted .... , tampering with the statistics in order to mislead the public.

4 Just because someone applies for a job with one of our competitors does not mean that they are .... to our company.

5 The workshop participants were rather .... , interacting very little even during the coffee breaks.

6 They resented their ex-boss for being .... and never even listening to differing points of view.

Modal perfect

Complete the modal perfect forms in these sentences.

1 The team leader was great, but I think she could .... spent more time on simulations.

2 You might have .... to my letter sooner. I thought you were no longer interested in my proposal!

3 Alex and Sam .... have had an argument. They aren't talking to each other any more.

4 I'm afraid you .... have brought some form of identification. We can't let you in without that.

5 You ......'.... have reached me on my mobile because I'd left it at the office.

6 They needn't .... into the office – there was no work for them to do when they got there.

7 If your application had been successful, we .... informed you in writing.

8 It .... a stormy meeting! We could hear people arguing and shouting.

Writing

You are one of the most senior members of a sales team. The team is not functioning very well at the moment, and morale is low. The sales manager is concerned, and has asked all senior members to express their views in writing.

Use the notes below and your own ideas to write an informal report (in 200–250 words)

• explaining why you think the team is not functioning properly

• putting forward one or two ideas how the situation could be improved.

Problems	*Solutions*
team members competing with each other *too focussed on personal achievement* *no responsibility for mistakes*	*clarify team's goals* *focus more on group results, less on individual success*

9 Raising finance

Dependent prepositions

Complete the sentences with a suitable preposition.

1 What would happen if you defaulted .... your loan repayments?

2 How much did that consultant charge you .... her services?

3 Borrowed money is often secured .... business assets.

4 Our shareholders will soon expect a higher return .... investment.

5 It is essential .... bank managers to have the time and the ability to engage .... their customers.

6 Equity investors benefit .... participation .... increasing levels of profits.

7 Their financial problems stemmed .... customers failing to pay their invoices on time.

8 The current economic climate is not conducive .... risk-taking.

9 There is a need .... greater transparency in our selection procedure.

10 Delays .... redesigning our main product account .... our disappointing sales figures.

Negotiating phrases

A **Put the expressions 1–8 under the correct heading in the table below.**

1 Could I just make a suggestion? How about looking for another backer?

2 When could you revise your business plan?

3 I'm very sorry, but we can't possibly invest in a project of this kind.

4 Right. Let's recap on the main points, then.

5 We were hoping the money could be transferred before the 15th.

6 Have you ever had a cash flow problem?

7 Why haven't you repaid the overdraft yet?

8 Let me explain. What I meant was, if you repay in six instalments instead of four, we'll have to revise the interest rate.

a) Fine. So we can see what we've agreed so far.

b) We should be able to find one, but it might take some time.

c) Only very temporarily when a number of customers defaulted on their payments.

d) Since we are talking only about minor modifications, say by the end of next week.

e) Thanks for clarifying that. We'll go by what we agreed on earlier, then.

f) That could be done, but it would certainly raise the costs a great deal.

g) Then I don't suppose we have any other option but to look elsewhere for support ...

h) Unfortunately an important customer has just let us down.

Open questions	Closed questions	Softening phrases	Signalling phrases	Summarising
No. ..... and	No.	No. ..... and	No. ..... and	No. .....

B **Now match the expressions 1–8 in Exercise A to the responses a)–h).**

1 =	2 =	3 =	4 =	5 =	6 =	7 =	8 =

10 Customer service

Gerunds and infinitives

Complete the second sentence in each pair so that it means about the same as the first sentence. Use between two and five words, including the word given.

1 We managed to attract a lot of new customers.

successful

We .... attracting a lot of new customers.

2 Having to wait so long for a replacement was a bit of a disappointment.
expect
I .... to wait so long for a replacement.

3 Don't bother to argue with them. You'll never get a refund.
point
There .... with them. You'll never get a refund.

4 Make sure you explain the reasons for the fault as soon as you can.
put off
Don't .... the reasons for the fault.

5 That's no problem. I'll wait for a replacement.
mind
I .... for a replacement.

6 If you work in our customer services department, you'll have to deal with a lot of complaints.
involve
Working in our customer services department will .... with a lot of complaints.

7 At first I disliked working in the customer services department, but it's alright now.
used
I have .... in the customer services department.

8 Please don't interrupt the speaker all the time.
mind
Would .... the speaker all the time?

9 Getting through to the right person isn't always easy.
difficult
It is .... through to the right person.

10 They say it's not true they fiddled their expenses.
deny
They .... their expenses.

Writing

A **Put the sentences of this letter of complaint in the correct order.**

Secondly, Invoice No. TG/573 for €75 has been debited twice. ☐

We have checked our records and we are certain that we never ordered or received such paper. ☐

Thank you for your February statement for €1,350, which we have just received. ☐

We have deducted the sum of €195 from your statement and will send you a draft for €1,155 as soon as you confirm this amount. ☐

Firstly, you have charged us for a delivery of A3 photocopying paper, Invoice No. TG/507 for €120. ☐

We would like to bring to your attention two accounting errors that have been made. ☐

B **Write a reply to the letter in Exercise A.**

Use the following structure: apologise for the mistake; explain how it occurred; explain what you have done to put it right; end on an upbeat note.

11 Crisis management

Linking ideas

Link the following pairs of contrasting ideas using *although*, *despite* / *in spite of*, and *however*.

1 they managed the crisis badly / their reputation was not damaged
2 the airline reacted quickly to the crisis / it was accused of incompetence
3 the rescue team showed efficiency and compassion / it was criticised by the media
4 the cruise was cancelled after just a few hours / the passengers were not angry
5 every service failure is different / some basic principles can assist in recovery

Reading

Complete the text with the best words from each group below.

One of the main crises facing companies today is that of loss of reputation. Damage to reputation almost always has a snowball effect and entails damages to share ....[1] as well as to public confidence. Some business people say that their company's reputation is their main ....[2]. Consequently, it is necessary not only to preserve it, but also to ....[3] in it, because once you have lost some of it, not only is it extremely difficult to regain it, but it also costs huge amounts of money. When ....[4] a crisis, management must react as quickly as possible. Speed of ....[5] is particularly crucial when human lives are in question. The next step is to enter into dialogue with all your ....[6], and to make sure that you maintain a steady ....[7] of information. You have to explain to the public what went wrong, and accept responsibility for any mistake you have made. If you are indeed responsible for what happened, an admission of ....[8] is your only viable course of action. Denying responsibility will inevitably damage your reputation in the long term, and increase the chances of ....[9] action being taken against you.

1	a) cost	b) fee	c) bonus	d) price
2	a) profit	b) asset	c) benefit	d) value
3	a) pay	b) stake	c) secure	d) invest
4	a) dealing	b) foreseeing	c) handling	d) prioritising
5	a) response	b) responding	c) reaction	d) reacting
6	a) stakeholders	b) suppliers	c) buyers	d) consumers
7	a) conference	b) flow	c) release	d) press
8	a) credibility	b) illegality	c) liability	d) criminality
9	a) legal	b) lawful	c) court	d) tribunal

12 Management styles

Opposites

A **Use the prefixes in the box to form the opposites of the adjectives below.**

dis-	il-	in-	ir-	un-

1 decisive ....

2 efficient ....

3 inspiring ....

4 logical ....

5 organised ....

6 rational ....

B **Complete the nouns related to the six adjectives in Exercise A.**

1 decisi.........

2 effici.........

3 inspir.........

4 logi..........

5 organis........

6 rational........

C **Complete the sentences with the correct form of an adjective from Exercise A.**

1 Our new manager seems to have an .... fear of technology. He wouldn't even touch a mobile phone!

2 I found the CEO's opening address rather ...., if not altogether boring.

3 If there is a delay in production, then the .... conclusion is that we won't be able to launch the new model this year.

4 The conference was extremely well .... All the delegates knew what was on, where and when.

5 The designer was a bit .... about how to modify the prototype.

6 Our recruitment procedure is extremely ...., so why would you want to change it?

Text reference

Put the sentences of the following biographical passage in the correct order. The words in *italics* will help you.

After *that*, he went on to Brentford Business School to deliver a lecture on career management, which has been one of his passions since 2002. ☐

He has been senior honorary visiting fellow at *the college* ever since. ☐

Alex Magee, Chairman of Logonet, attended a meeting of the non-executive directors to discuss their draft interim results. ☐

All those lectures eventually led to 'Human Capital', published last week by Omega Books. ☐

In addition to those *European academic activities*, Alex has also delivered lectures on career management at Harvard. ☐

It is in the summer of *that year* that he was asked to design and deliver a course on *that topic* at Mannheim College of International Management. ☐

13 Takeovers and mergers

Reading

Complete the text with the best words.

Premier Foods announced half-year results in line with expectations, and said it was acquiring FW Gedney, a fresh foods company, in a ....[1] to boost its struggling potato business.

Robert Schofield, Chief Executive, said: 'The outlook for the remainder of the year is for our core convenience foods arm to remain on track, with groceries compensating for our disappointing potatoes business.'

Mr Schofield also signalled that the group, which makes Branston Pickle and Cadbury's Hot Chocolate, would boost its portfolio through ....[2]. He said the group is looking to buy non-core businesses from multinational groups and planned to make one acquisition per year.

'Our brands, scale and efficiency mean we are well ....[3] to deliver profitable growth and strong cash flow ....[4] to support progressive dividends and further acquisitions in the future,' Mr Schofield added.

The group's recent acquisition of Marlow Foods, the maker of the alternative meat product Quorn, was ....[5] 'to expectation' with double digit ....[6] and 60 per cent of the market. It plans to increase marketing for Quorn by £2m in the second half of 2005, ...[7] 'health conscious' households in a bid to ....[8] to a wider audience and not just the traditional vegetarian consumer.

Premier Foods agreed an interim dividend of 4.75p per ordinary share while earnings per share were 5.4p.

1	**a)** bid	**b)** purchase	**c)** merger	**d)** stake
2	**a)** joint ventures	**b)** buyouts	**c)** acquisitions	**d)** alliances
3	**a)** positioned	**b)** situated	**c)** located	**d)** established
4	**a)** production	**b)** generation	**c)** reaction	**d)** competition
5	**a)** exporting	**b)** importing	**c)** evaluating	**d)** performing
6	**a)** increase	**b)** growth	**c)** rise	**d)** raise
7	**a)** advertising	**b)** supplying	**c)** targeting	**d)** delivering
8	**a)** attract	**b)** persuade	**c)** reach	**d)** appeal

Headlines

In each headline, replace the word in *italics* with the correct original word from the box.

split	seek	backing	unveil	deal	probe

1 Chunghwa *agreement* boosted

2 Renova to *look for* merger for growth

3 Sonelca and Nori *announce* $13bn merger

4 Chemotex investors *disagree* over bid

5 Takeover *support* for Kantotrade

6 Norton & Meyer *investigate* fraud allegations

14 The future of business

Vocabulary

Supply the missing vowels in the following adjectives, which can all be used to describe the future.

The future looks …

good	bad
1 br _ ght	5 d _ r _
2 r _ s _	6 dr _ _ df _ l
3 pr _ m _ s _ ng	7 w _ rr _ _ ng
4 br _ ll _ _ nt	8 _ nc _ rt _ _ n

Telephoning

Complete the conversation with the items from the box.

a) Are you saying	e) I'll sort it out right away
b) And what seems to be the problem?	f) I'm calling about
c) I'll put you through	g) please accept our apologies
d) Hold on a second	h) What did you say the reference number was?

Customer: Good morning. Sam Brunswick here. ………………[1] an invoice I've just received from you …

Reception: ………………[2] please Mr Brunswick. ………………[3] to our Accounts department.

Accounts: Accounts good morning. How can I help you?

Customer: I've just received this invoice from you, reference number TG/343, for €375 for a DVD recorder.

Accounts: Sorry. ………………[4]

Customer: TG/343

Accounts: Right, I've got that. Just one moment, please. Let me get it up on the screen. There we are. ………………[5]

Customer: Well, the problem is, I never received a DVD recorder, and I don't want one. I've never even bought anything from your company, although I've heard about Sobeltronics, of course.

Accounts: Let me just get that right. ………………[6] that you did not order a DVD recorder from us?

Customer: That's absolutely right, yeah.

Accounts: That's most peculiar! I've been in this department for 40 years and I've never heard of anything like that.

Customer: Oh well. There's always a first time, they say.

Accounts: Obviously there's been a mix-up somewhere. ………………[7], and make sure the order is cancelled. Meanwhile just destroy the invoice, Mr Brunswick, and ………………[8].

Customer: Alright then. Well, goodbye for now.

Grammar reference

1 Idioms

In the language of business, idioms and metaphors are often used with reference to the domains of sport, war and gambling.

Sport

*I don't know the exact price but $500 is a good **ballpark figure**. (= estimate).*
*She's smart and really **on the ball**. (= quick to understand).*
*Follow his advice and it'll be **plain sailing**. (= easy to do or achieve).*
*You don't know where you stand, they keep **moving the goalposts**. (= changing their aims or decisions).*
*There must be no unfair competition in the EU and we shall continue to stress the need **for a level playing field**. (= a situation that gives no one an advantage)*

War

*Bill's **on the warpath** again (= very angry) – there are mistakes in the publicity material we sent out.*
*You may have to **do battle with** (= fight it out) the insurers because they won't want to pay up.*
*Manufacturers often feel they are **fighting a losing battle** (= making no progress) against counterfeiting.*
*If you can convince the commercial attaché here, that's **half the battle** (= the rest is easy).*
*I've been **fighting a running battle** (= having a series of arguments) with the financial department but they won't give us the money.*
*She may want to convince you otherwise but you should **stick to your guns** (= maintain your point of view).*
*She's **up in arms** (= very angry and ready to fight) about the lack of safety procedures.*

Gambling

*We are trying to **hedge our bets** (= reduce our chances of failure) and not put all our eggs in one basket.*
***The odds are stacked against us** (= there are many difficulties) but we're determined to succeed.*
*It **makes no odds** (= makes no difference) whether we get permission or not, we'll go ahead anyway.*
*They're paying **over the odds** (= more than it's worth) for the site but it's a prime location.*
*We had our doubts about Susan but she has really **come up trumps** (= produced good, unexpected results).*
*If you **play your cards right** (= do the right thing) you'll get the promotion.*

2 Noun compounds and noun phrases

1 When two nouns occur together, the first noun is used as an adjective and describes the second noun. The first noun answers the question 'what kind of?'

   a manufacturing subsidiary
   a draft agenda
   a phone conversation
   a network operator

2 Noun + noun compounds can often be transformed into structures where the second noun becomes the subject:

   an oil refinery (= a refinery that produces oil)
   company executives (= executives that work for the company*
   a travel agency (= an agency that sells travel)

3 They may also be reformulated using a preposition:

   market research (= research **into** markets)
   rail transport (= transport **by** rail)
   leisure activities (= activities **for** leisure)
   a web page (= a page **on** the web)
   their Paris store (= their store **in** Paris)
   income distribution (= distribution **of** income)

4 The first noun is usually singular:

   five-star hotel (*not* five stars)
   consumer-purchasing behaviour (*not* consumers)
   risk assessment (*not* risks)
   brand names (*not* brands)

   However, some words retain the plural form:
   sales policy
   newsletter
   needs analysis

5 Sometimes three or more nouns occur together:

   line management system
   production research centre
   travel insurance claim form
   Motorola's software development establishments

6 Noun compounds can be modified by adjectives and adverbs:

   ***inspiring** team leadership*
   ***international** business development directors*
   ***extremely boring** conference presentation*
   ***increasingly volatile** mobile phone market*

3 Multi-word verbs

Multi-word verbs are formed when a verb is followed by one or more particles. Particles can be prepositions or adverbs.

The meaning of a multi-word verb is sometimes very different from the meanings of the two words taken separately.

*How are you **getting on**? (get on is not the same as get + on).*

There are two different types of multi-word verbs.

1 Intransitive: without an object
*The plane has just **taken off**.*
*She **turned up** unexpectedly.*
*What time did you **set off**?*

2 Transitive: with an object
*We will **set up** a new subsidiary.*
*They have **called off** the strike.*
*She has **handed in** her resignation.*

- With two particles:
*I'm **looking forward to** seeing you.*
*She's trying to **catch up with** her work.*
*We need to **make up for** lost time.*

- Multi-word verbs are either separable or inseparable.
An adverb particle can come before or after the object if the object is a noun.
*We've **put by** some money.*
*We've **put** some money **by**.*

- But you cannot put a pronoun after the particle:
*She's **switched off** the computer.*
*She's **switched** the computer **off**.*
*She's **switched** it **off**.*
*(NOT *She's switched off it.)*

- If the particle is a preposition, the verb and particle are inseparable:
*Can you **cope with** your work?*
*(NOT *Can you cope your work with?).*

- We do not normally separate multi-word verbs with two particles. However, there are some transitive three-word combinations that allow separation. For example:
*Multinationals can **play** individual markets **off against** each other.*
*She **puts** her success **down to** hard work.*
*I'll **take** you **up on** that suggestion.*

4 Present and past tenses

1 The **present simple** is used to make true, factual statements.
*Established customers **tend** to buy more.*
*Nokia **sells** mobile telephones.*

2 Verbs relating to beliefs, being, knowledge, liking, perception and appearance are normally only used in the simple form.
*I **understand** what you **mean**.*
*It **depends** on what the chairman **wants**.*
*I **appreciate** your concern.*

3 The **present continuous** is used to refer to events in progress and temporary or changing situations.
*'I'll be back late, I**'m sitting** in a traffic jam'.*
*They**'re installing** a new switchboard.*
*The world **is getting** smaller.*

4 The **past simple** is used to refer to events completed in the past. We frequently use a time expression to say when the event took place.
*In the late 1940s Ford **decided** it needed a medium price model to compete with General Motors.*
*2001 **was** a good year for our company.*

5 The **past perfect** sequences two or more past events.
*Before he joined this company **he had** worked for two competitors abroad.*

6 The **present perfect** is used to say that a finished past action is relevant now. There cannot be any specific reference to past time.
*They **have changed** the address of their website.* (it's new)
*The share price has **plummeted**.* (it is lower than before)

7 The present perfect covers a period of time starting in the past and continuing up to the present. An appropriate time expression takes us up to now.
*So far, the company **has defied** predictions that its rivals will catch up.*
*Stella McCartney **has been** one of the leading fashion designers since the mid-1990s.*
*He**'s been** acting strange lately.*
*Over the last few years e-commerce **has become** fashionable.*

5 Passives

We use the passive when the person who performs the action is unknown, unimportant or obvious.

*The file **was stolen**.*
*The roof **was damaged** during the storm.*
*She**'s been given** the sack.*

1 The passive can be used in all tenses and with modal auxiliaries.

*A new fitness centre **is being built**.*
*The job **was going to be done** on Friday.*
*He **had been asked** to do it twice before.*
*She **may be required** to work on Sunday.*
*The best employees **should be given** a performance bonus.*
*He **would have been told** eventually.*

2 If we know who performed the action (the agent) we use 'by':

*The file was stolen **by** a secret agent.*

3 In a passive sentence, the grammatical subject receives the focus:

a) *Giovanni Agnelli **founded** Fiat in 1899.*

b) *Fiat **was founded** by Giovanni Agnelli in 1899.*

In a) our attention is on the agent – Giovanni Agnelli. In b) it is Fiat rather than Agnelli that is the topic of the sentence.

4 The subject of the sentence can be a pronoun.

*We **were informed** that the firm was going to be taken over.*

5 Passive constructions are common in formal contexts, for example in reports or minutes, and help to create an impersonal style. Using 'it' as a subject enables us to avoid mentioning the person responsible for saying or doing something.

*It **was felt** that the system needed to be changed.*
*It **was decided** that expenditure would be limited to $250,000.*
*It **was suggested** that staff be given stock options.*
*It **was agreed** that the proposal should be rejected.*

6 Adverbs of degree

1 If we want to amplify the quality an adjective describes we use an intensifying adverb. These are some of the most common:

*The presentation was **really** /**very** good.*
*She's **dead** certain to get the job.*
*The new design looks **pretty** good.*
*I was **extremely** surprised by her reaction.*
*She's a **thoroughly** efficient organiser.*

2 The relative strength of adverbs is shown on this scale:

Strong: *absolutely, altogether, awfully, completely, greatly, highly, quite, terribly, totally, very*
Moderate: *fairly, mildly, moderately, partly, quite, reasonably, somewhat*
Weak: *a bit, a little, marginally, poorly, slightly.*

*The whole thing is **quite** amazing.*
Note that quite also means fairly:
*The restaurant is **quite** cheap but the food isn't wonderful.*

*The goods are **reasonably** cheap.*
*I was **slightly** surprised by what she said.*

3 Intensifying adverbs modify adjectives that are **gradable** – that is, they can signify degrees of a given quality. Adjectives that are not gradable or identify the particular class that something belongs to are not normally used with intensifying adverbs. We cannot say:

(NOT * a very unique idea)
(NOT * a fairly free gift)
(NOT * a very impossible solution)
(NOT * some slightly financial news)

4 However, you can use an adverb such as *absolutely* or *utterly* with an ungradable or classifying adjective to show that you feel strongly:

*It doesn't cost anything – it's **absolutely** free.*
*The task is **utterly** impossible.*

7 Conditionals

1 We use conditional sentences to make hypothetical statements and questions.

We'll deliver within 24 hours if you order online.
If we order now, will you give us a discount?

The use of *it* + *will* + verb suggests that these arrangements are feasible.

2 If the proposal is more tentative and possibly less feasible *would* + past verb forms are used.

I'd need some venture capital if I was / were to start my own business.
If I got a guarantee for the loan, I would lend them the money.
If I had invested my savings in the company I would have made a fortune.

3 If the verb is *had*, *were* or *should*, we can leave out *if* and put the verb at the beginning. The sentence is now more formal.

Had it not been for his help, we would not have survived.

Were it not for Patrick, we'd be in a terrible mess.

Should you require any further information, do not hesitate to contact me.

4 These words are also used in conditional sentences.

We'll meet tomorrow providing / provided (that) no one has an objection.
Even the best management teams won't be successful unless they are given the resources.
You can say what you like as long as you don't make any criticisms.
Supposing (that) we decide to use the Topsite service, how much would it cost?

5 Mixed conditionals follow a variety of patterns.

If you need help, just ask. (an offer)
If Peter wants to see me, tell him to wait. (an instruction)
If you hadn't invested in e-commerce our sales would be much lower. (this is true now, so wouldn't have been is inappropriate)
I would be grateful if you would give me an early reply. (a polite request)

8 Modal perfect

1 We use past modals to speculate about events in the past.

I thought I saw Yolanda in the car park but it may / might / could have been someone else.
The project might / could have been a terrible failure but turned out to be a great success. (we know it was a success, therefore may is not possible here).
I wasn't there myself but from what I hear it must have been a very stormy meeting.
She says she met me in Brazil but it can't have been me because I've never been to Brazil!

2 Past modals can also be used to express irritation.

She could / might have given me the information but she didn't bother.

3 Missed opportunities are also expressed using *could* or *might*.

She could / might have had a brilliant career but she gave it all up for love.

4 *Would have* and *wouldn't have* are used to make hypotheses about the past.

The team would have been stronger if she had been with us.
We wouldn't have achieved such good results if we hadn't worked together as a team.

5 *Should have*, *shouldn't have* and *ought to have* are used to criticise.

The report should have been submitted a lot earlier.
He shouldn't have resigned without having another job to go to.
You ought to have made a reservation – there are no seats left now.

6 Note the difference between *needn't have* and *didn't need to*.

I didn't need to come into the office because there was no work for me to do, so I stayed at home.
I needn't have gone into the office because there was no work for me to do when I got there.

9 Dependent prepositions

1 Here is a list of common verbs and the prepositions that follow them:

complain about	*insure against*	*react against*
hint at	*account for*	*hope for*
long for	*opt for*	*pay for*
strive for	*emerge from*	*stem from*
suffer from	*invest in*	*result in*
bet on	*insist on*	*rely on*
amount to	*lead to*	*object to*
refer to	*relate to*	*resort to*
associate with	*contend with*	*sypathise with*

2 Some verbs may be followed by more than one preposition, with a corresponding change in meaning.

How did you learn of his sudden departure?
I hope you will learn from your mistakes.
The team consists of two Americans and two Japanese. (= is made up of)
For her, job satisfaction consists in having almost no work to do. (= is based on)

3 Here is a list of common adjectives and the prepositions that follow them:

lacking in	*aware of*	*capable of*
representative of	*contingent on*	*intent on*
reliant on	*conducive to*	*essential to*
parallel to	*prone to*	*susceptible to*
vulnerable to	*compatible with*	*filled with*

4 This is a list of common nouns and the prepositions that follow them:

admiration for	*aptitude for*	*bid for*
demand for	*need for*	*remedy for*
respect for	*responsibility for*	*room for*
search for	*substitute for*	

ban on	*comment on*	*constraint on*
curb on	*effect on*	*tax on*

access to	*alternative to*	*contribution to*
damage to	*exception to*	*introduction to*
reference to	*resistance to*	*solution to*
threat to		

contrast with	*dealings with*	*dissatisfaction with*
involvement with	*relationship with*	*sympathy with*

10 Gerunds

1 The gerund is the *-ing* form of the verb used as a noun, either as the subject or object of the verb.

***Selling** is all about persuasion.*
***Getting through to** the right person isn't always easy.*
*My idea of relaxation is **going to** a fitness centre.*

2 Gerunds follow prepositions:

*We are committed <u>to</u> **giving** the highest quality.*
*We depend <u>on</u> **having** fast communications.*

3 They are often used to begin an item in a list.

Good leaders are skilled at:

- **fixing** goals
- **motivating** people
- **producing** creative ideas

4 Gerunds can be made negative, used in the passive, and with past verb forms.

*It's wonderful **not having** to get up early for work.*
***Being kidnapped** is not a pleasant experience.*
*He mentioned **having met** our main competitor.*

5 Many verbs are followed by a gerund (e.g. *admit, avoid, consider, deny, dislike, involve, mention, recommend, risk, suggest*)

*He denied **fiddling** his expenses.*
*I dislike **having** to eat at my desk.*
*She suggests **raising** the price.*

6 Some verbs are followed by either a gerund or an infinitive. The choice of one or the other usually leads to a change in meaning.

*Increased production may **mean taking** on extra staff at the weekend.* (= involve)
*I didn't **mean to** cause any offence.* (= intend to)
*He remembered **to buy** his wife a present.*
  (= he didn't forget)
*He remembers **buying** his wife a present.*
  (= he has a clear recollection of this)

11 Contrast and addition

1 We use link words, especially in formal writing, to signal the kind of connection there is between one statement and another.

2 We can use *while, although, whereas* to make a contrast.

While minor customer complaints can be dealt with by the Customer Service Department, serious product complaints must be dealt with by the senior management board to avoid damaging the company's reputation.

Although the company dealt with the crisis quickly, there was still a lack of shareholder confidence in future investment.

Whereas in some cultures promotion is based on merit, in others it is based on seniority.

3 *Whereas* can be used to express a clear contrast between two subjects in the same sentence.

Companies that communicate truthfully and promptly with their customers in a crisis receive a favourable response whereas those companies that try to avoid responsibility for service failures invite bad public relations and even lawsuits.

4 We use *although, in spite of* or *despite* before a statement that makes the main statement seem surprising or unlikely. *Despite* and *in spite of* are followed by a noun, gerund or a noun phrase.

The crisis, although serious, was managed more effectively than expected.

Despite /in spite of all their forward planning, the company did not prevent the crisis in time.

Despite receiving a lot of bad publicity last year, the company's profits this year have been extremely good.

5 We use *however* to link together two sentences which are in contrast to each other.

The hotel and tourism industry has been suffering in the last few years due to world events. However, statistics show that the number of business travelers has increased.

6 We can use *furthermore, moreover* and *in addition* to add extra information to a statement.

The economic downturn has had a negative effect on the hotel and tourist industry. Furthermore, changes in the weather have reduced the number of tourists to certain popular holiday destinations.

Effective crisis management is about handling a crisis quickly. Moreover, good crisis management is about reducing the number of dissatisfied customers.

Customers can make enquiries about any product at the customer service desk in-store. In addition customers can access our catalogue for full product details online.

12 Text reference

Read the following text and note how certain words refer forward and back to other words in the text.

Although more *women* are becoming sales managers, *they*'ll have to tailor *their* management styles to the gender of their employees if *they* want to have continued success. According to a *study* carried out by John Doyle and Jill Harris of the University of Hull, both female and male sales personnel welcome the newcomers. But *it* also points out that there can be a difference between *the management style* males prefer and *the one* that elicits their best performance.

In particular, the researchers wanted to discover differences in satisfaction and variations in sales performance under female supervision. Two management *styles* were identified. A transactional style is the more traditional of *the two*. Male managers are hands-off until something goes wrong. The philosophy is 'When *you*'re doing OK, *you* won't even know *I*'m around. But, when *you* mess up, *I*'ll be right next door.

Women take a more hands-on approach. A transformational mode encourages a more hands-on individual-orientated manner. *Women* more than *men* tend to motivate by encouragement and personal attention. *The former* relate to their staff emotionally and tend to foster new ways of thinking whereas *the latter* rely on rewards and punishments.

Grammatical reference

In paragraph 1:
they, their, they, refer back to, *women, it* refers back to *the study*
the one refers back to *the management style*
In paragraph 2:
the two refers back to *styles*
you, you, you, refers back to any employee working under a male manager
I, refers to the male manager
In paragraph 3:
the former refers back to *women*
the latter refers back to *men*

Lexical reference

Very often in texts, words belonging to the same family and synonyms and antonyms occur closely together.

gender ... men ≠ women, male ≠ female
John Doyle and Jill Harris ... the researchers
the newcomers ... women sales managers
employees ... personnel ... staff
differences ... variations
hands-off ... hands-on
something goes wrong ... you mess up ≠ do OK
style ... mode ... approach ... manner
individual ... personal
encourages ... motivate ... foster
encouragement ... rewards ≠ punishments

13 Headlines

The headlines in English-language newspapers can be difficult to understand as they are often written in a special style, with some specific rules of grammar, and words that may be used in unusual ways.

1 They are not always complete sentences:

Challenge for Euro

2 They may contain strings of three or more nouns:

Takeover bid drama

Office staff pay deal row

3 They omit articles and the verb *to be*:

Orange CEO likely to quit

4 They use simple forms and an infinitive refers to the future:

Nokia chief to stand down

5 If a continuous form is used *be* is omitted:

Prices going through the roof

6 Short words are used to save space. Here are some examples:

Axe = abolish, abolition, close down, closure
RST to axe 100 jobs
Chairman axed in boardroom clash

Blow = bad news
Peace talks blow

Flak = criticism
PM faces opposition flak

Hail = welcome
Bosses hail interest rate cut

Slam = criticise
Unions slam jobs plan

Top = exceed
Exports top $5bn

14 Prediction and probability

1 A number of modal verbs are used to make predictions. The modal indicates the speaker's degree of certainty.

*They **will** be there by now* (100% certain)
*They **won't** have any trouble finding our office, they've been here many times* (100% certain)
*They **must** have arrived by now* (80% certain)
*They **can't** have arrived yet* (80% certain)
*They **should** have arrived by now* (60% certain)
*They **may / could have** arrived by now* (40% certain)
*They **might** have arrived by now* (20% certain)

2 Conditional statements contain hypotheses about the way the future may turn out:

*If we use solar power, we**'ll probably** save money.*
***If** you try harder you **would be able to** do it.*

3 The future perfect and the future continuous predict what will be in progress or will have been accomplished in the future:

*By 2050 businessmen **will be taking** orders from the moon.*
*By 3000 scientists **will have discovered** how to transmit objects by electronic means.*

4 There are a number of lexical expressions of likelihood. These include:

about to   bound to   going to
*He's tapping his glass, I think he's **about to / going to** make a speech.*
*She's **bound to** be late, she always is.*

5 The following lexical phrases can be used to discuss the future: *certain, probable, possible, unlikely* or *impossible.*

*There's **certain** to be more changes in the world's weather systems over the next few decades.*
*It's quite **probable** that an economic upturn will start next year.*
***Maybe**, there'll be a change of management in the coming months.*
*It is **unlikely** that the retirement age will be increased to 75.*
*It is just **impossible** to imagine the World Wide Web having serious problems in future.*

6 There are a number of useful time phrases that can be used to talk about the future:

***In my lifetime** I will see China becoming a dominant world power.*
***Before long** the company will decide to merge with a bigger company.*
***In the near future** everybody will be using wind power.*
***In the next ... years** there will be a huge change in the way we travel.*
***Over the next decade** governments will start reducing air traffic.*
***By this time next year** I will be promoted.*
***By the end of this century** the way we conduct business in the world will be very different from now.*
***Sometime in the next decade /century** man will inhabit other planets.*

Are you in danger of burning out?

Do the quiz and discuss your answers with a partner. Then check your result on page 149.

You're turning up for meetings at the right time but in the wrong week. You're pouring milk into the waste paper basket rather than your coffee. You've lost your temper with half of the office, and the other half are cowering under their desks. You could be suffering from burnout, a debilitating condition caused by working too hard for too long and failing to prioritise. Try this quiz to see if you are in danger of self-combusting.

1 Your boss asks if you can work late for the third night in a row. Do you:

a Say yes without giving it a second thought?

b Laugh politely and close the door on your way out?

c Say yes, but feel like crying?

2 Some of your colleagues want to play a practical joke on your boss for April Fool's Day. Do you:

a Organise a brainstorming session to select the best idea?

b Tell them that there are more important things to be done?

c Go to your boss and tell them what they are planning to do?

3 You arrive home one Friday night with a pile of work only to discover that your partner has arranged a surprise weekend away. Do you:

a Leave the work behind and take Monday off to catch up?

b Tell them that you're sorry, but you can't afford the time?

c Agree to go but insist on taking the work with you?

4 There is a rumour going around that a proposed company merger may mean some job losses. Do you:

a Take a cursory glance at the job adverts in the paper and look for your CV?

b Bite your nails until your fingers hurt?

c Find yourself hyperventilating?

5 It's bedtime and you are exhausted after a stressful day at the office. Do you:

a Lie awake for two hours, then make a start on next week's assignment?

b Lie awake for five minutes, then sleep right through until morning?

c Lie awake for one hour, then read for a while until you fall asleep?

6 A colleague asks if you could help them with a problem but you're in the middle of a project with a tight deadline. Do you:

a Schedule some time in your diary to work with them when you're free?

b Agree to help, but become irritated when they don't grasp the solution straightaway?

c Tell them to speak to someone who cares?

7 There are a lot more things on your 'To Do' list than you realistically have time for. Do you:

a Divide the items into urgent and important and start with the urgent things?

b Pick out the easy tasks and start with them?

c Work overtime until they're all done?

8 An old friend you haven't seen for ages asks you to go out for a meal with them. Do you:

a Have a fantastic evening of reminiscence?

b Refuse the invitation as you are always too tired to go out on weekdays?

c Accept the invitation, and spend the evening telling them all about your job?

From the *Guardian* website: http://www.workunlimited.co.uk/quiz/questions

Writing file

Letters

TM Breweries GmbH

Baubergerstr 17
80991 Munich

Ms Teresa Winch
Vending Machines Inc
Box 97
New York

19 February

Dear Ms Winch

South East Asian opportunities

I was very pleased to have met you again at the open day we held in
our Munich brewery last week. I hope you enjoyed yourself and felt
that your visit was useful.

   I found our discussion about the activities of your organisation in
Korea very interesting. It seems to me that there are a lot of ways in
which our organisations could work together to our mutual
advantage in South East Asia. I have enclosed a brochure with
further information about our products. I propose that we get
together soon to discuss the matter in more detail.

   I hope this suggestion is of interest and look forward to hearing
from you.

Yours sincerely

Katherine Sell

Katherine Sell
Sales Manager

Encl. product brochures

Salutation

When you don't know the name
of the recipient:
Dear Sir/Madam (BrE)
Ladies and Gentlemen (AmE)

When you know the name of the
recipient:
Dear Mr/Mrs/Ms/Miss Winch
(BrE, AmE)

Note: In the US Mr. and Mrs.
include a full stop/period
e.g. Mr. Winch

Endings
When you don't know the name of
the recipient:
Yours faithfully (BrE)
Sincerely yours (AmE)

When you know the name of the
recipient:
Yours sincerely (BrE)
Sincerely (AmE)

Sign the letter, then print your
name and position under your
signature.

Common abbreviations
Re.   regarding
pp.   (on behalf of) when you
          sign the letter for another
          person
encs. documents are enclosed
          with the letter
cc   copies, the names of the
          people who receive a copy
          are included in the letter

e-mails

e-mails have two distinct styles: a semi-formal business style and a more informal personal style.

To...	james.scarfield@tmb.de
From...	alison.mcdermott@hasbro.com
Subject:	Meeting in Berlin

Dear James

You may remember we met at the Learntech fair in Kuala Lumpur last fall. You were interested in our company's automation equipment.

I am visiting Berlin at the end of next month and would like to visit you, if you are around. I will be there from 27–31 March.

Let me know if you have any time.

Best wishes

Alison

Alison McDermott
Product Manager
Has Bro Equipment Inc
Box 28
Chicago

email: alison.mcdermott@hasbro.com

The semi-formal style is similar to a business letter, but less formal and shorter. A likely ending is *Best wishes* rather than *Yours sincerely*. This style is best used for e-mails to people outside your company, or who you do not know well. The emphasis is on the efficient provision or exchange of information.

To...	james.scarfield@tmb.de
From...	jennifer.duncan@kingsland.co.uk
Subject:	Meeting in Berlin

Hi James

I'm over in Berlin from 6–8 November. Could we meet up some time? It would be great to see you!

Let me know when you're free.

Regards
Jenny

email: jennifer.duncan@kingsland.co.uk

The informal style is suitable for e-mails within your company and for people whom you know well. The greeting is often *Hi*, *Hello* or even *How are you?* The style is much closer to spoken than written English.

Faxes

J.D. Kingsland Ltd

Fax Transmission

To	Jenny Duncan
From	Zofia Nadstoga
Fax No	0044 1483 740675
Date	7 April
No of pages (including this)	1
Subject	Various

Jenny

Further to my message on your answering machine, I thought it might be helpful if I faxed you the points we need you to clarify on Monday:

1 Contacts inside Sataier-Bucht AG
We need to know what exactly we can say about your proposal to our contact inside the company. We have to ensure we do not breach any confidentiality agreements.

2 Technical documentation
Can you inform us about the technical documentation needed for the new equipment? Should it be in German as well as English?

3 Translator
Christine needs to give us more information about the technical writer required (French to English). The agency want an exact job description.

Regards

Zofia

Zofia Nadstoga
Office Manager

Faxes may contain the following headings: To / From / Fax numbers / Date / Number of pages / Subject

The style of the fax can be formal, as in a business letter, or more informal as here, depending on the subject and recipient.

Points can be numbered for clarity.

Memos

MEMO

To:	**All Staff**
From:	**Melanie Jury**
Date:	**15 July**
Subject:	**Purchase orders**

Please note that a purchase order (copy attached) must be completed for all purchases over €50.

Complete purchase orders should be passed to Christine Hantke to agree terms of payment with the supplier, and then sent to the Manchester office for final approval.

Purchase orders under €50 can be paid for from the petty cash account.

Many thanks for your co-operation.

MJ

Memos are usually for internal communications.

They should include the following headings: To / From / Date / Subject

They should be short and include only relevant information.

Points should be arranged in logical order. In longer memos, it is common to number points.

The tone of a memo may be formal or neutral.

It is usual to end with your initials rather than a signature.

Press releases

Press Presse Prensa

Automatix plc,
Semi Conductor Division

For the trade press
21 December

Opening of new production facilities in Johor Fahru, Balanesia.

At a ceremony attended by Automatix Chairman, Rocco Truffaldino, and the British Ambassador to Balanesia, Sir Edward Faulkner, Automatix plc's new semi-conductor chip facilities were opened in Johor Fahru on Wednesday.

'The new facilities represent our commitment to expanding our production of advanced memory chips. We aim to be the supplier of choice for the world's leading electronics companies, without damaging the environment' said Mr Truffaldino.

A special feature of the plant is the clean, no-waste production process, which aims to have zero impact on the environment.

For additional information visit our website
www.pr.automatix.co.uk
or contact Jerry Turner +44 (0) 1792 536012 (phone),
+44 (0) 1792 536723 (fax).

Date: 21 December
Title: Opening of new production facilities in Johor Fahru, Balanesia
Addressed to: The trade press
Author: Kylie Dawson

The header for a press release should make clear who it comes from, what the subject is and which part of the press it is aimed at.

The subject should be put in bold print so that the journalist can see immediately if it is relevant to him/her.

The main body should have a short introduction with names of people who might be interesting for the press, some description of what is new or interesting for the public and – if possible – a good quote which the newspaper could print.

The style should be formal and concise, with nothing irrelevant to the particular story.

Always include some information as to how the journalist can get more information about the subject if they want it.

Agendas

Management Committee Meeting

<u>Agenda</u>

Date: 7 April
Time: 14.00
Venue: Building B Room 10–213
Participants: JS, AH, RG, PK, TB

1. Apologies, minutes of last meeting and matters arising.

2. Sales projections for next quarter.

3. Recruitment and capital expenditure required for no. 2.

4. Company bonus scheme.

5. A.O.B.

6. Date of next meeting.

Always put the date, time and venue (place). It is also usual to include the initials of the participants.

The first point on the agenda is usually handled by the chairperson. He/she will explain why anybody is absent, check through the minutes from the last meeting, and allow participants to briefly comment on anything relating to the previous meeting (matters arising).

The points are then worked through. They should be arranged so that they lead logically into each other, if possible.

A.O.B. means *any other business*. This is for other relevant issues that were not included in the agenda.

Guidelines

Westpak Ltd
Company Guidelines

Welcome to Westpak, the company that cares!

As a new employee you probably have many questions that you wish to ask about your new position. To help you settle in quickly, here are answers to some of the most frequently asked questions.

1. How does the flexi-time system work?

All employees at Westpak are individuals with their own particular circumstances. We believe that it is your responsibility to work out with your supervisor a schedule that is fair to both you and the company. As long as your work is done as efficiently as possible, you can do it when you like. That is why our offices are staffed 24 hours a day.

2. How should I dress?

Most of you will be in regular contact with customers. It is important that they should feel confident about the service they will receive from Westpak. We suggest that you dress in a way which is smart and business-like as a mark of respect to our clients.

3. How are interpersonal problems dealt with?

Teamwork has always been the key to success at Westpak and anything which is likely to damage co-operation between team members has to be dealt with as quickly as possible. If you feel that efficient …

Guidelines vary enormously from company to company and industry to industry. It is important to distinguish between guidelines and regulations.

Regulations are required for ensuring the legally correct handling of a contract, or the safe operation of a piece of machinery, for example. The language used in regulations is therefore much more directive.

Guidelines are also important for ensuring the smooth operation of the company, but they often touch on areas of human behaviour where it is not easy to dictate to people. The language must therefore be more persuasive and less directive, or else personnel will object.

1

Action minutes

Minutes of the Management Committee Meeting

Date: 7 April

Venue: Building B Room 10–213

Participants: Jim Scarfield, Andrea Hevitsun, Robbie Gibson, Paul Keown. Apologies: Tony Barton

Always put the title, date, time and venue (place) of the meeting, plus the names of the participants.

Point	Discussion	Action
1. Management pay review	We agreed changes to the management pay review. AH will include these when the review is presented at the next meeting of the finance committee.	AH 26 April
2. Sales projections next quarter	We agreed that we need to produce better sales figures for the next quarter after the poor results so far this year. JS and PK will spend the next month personally visiting our top clients to check the reasons for the business downturn.	JS and PK
3. Recruitment and capital expenditure	We decided not to do any recruiting over the next quarter. However, we will buy the new accounting software to increase our efficiency in invoicing customers, if we can get a bigger discount from the software supplier.	RG
4. Company bonus scheme	Because of the present financial situation a bonus scheme can only work if it is linked to productivity. AH will review different possibilities for discussion with the finance committee, and report to us at the next meeting.	AH 3 May

The minutes can be an important record of what was really discussed at a meeting, so it is important to make sure that the summary of each point is as accurate as possible.

Initials are used to refer to participants.

The 'action' column is important for showing who is supposed to do what by when.

Next meeting: 3 May 14.00
Venue: Building B Room 10–213

If you are a participant at a meeting always make sure you check the minutes when they have been written up. If you think something has not been accurately reported then have it corrected.

Reports

Parry, Parry & Gibson

Site accident report

Executive summary

Damage has been caused to the emergency generator on the Witherby power plant site. It was caused by a fire started by the electrical contractors Mullet & Sons. Although the packing material that caught fire was left by another subcontractor, the personnel from Mullet started work before clearing the waste matter away, in contravention of contract regulation 2.3.8. Mullet & Sons should therefore pay for the replacement of the damaged equipment.

Introduction

This report will look at:

- the sequence of events
- the subcontractors involved
- the responsibilities of the subcontractors
- the financial compensation from the subcontractors
- recommendations to avoid future incidents of this nature

Findings

1. Fire broke out at 17.30 on Friday 13 October in the working area around the emergency generator. All personnel were cleared from the site and the fire service informed by 17.45. The fire service arrived at 18.00 and the blaze was extinguished by 18.30.

2. The electrical contractors Mullet & Sons started the fire accidentally when carrying out the connection work of the generator to the main power line. Packing material left on the ground by another subcontractor Harvest Macdougall plc caught fire and this quickly spread.

3. Although Harvest Macdougall are obliged to remove any packaging material they bring with them it seems that the electricians from Mullet told them to just leave it. We assume they wanted to get their own work done as quickly as possible so that they could finish for the weekend. Starting welding work without first making sure there is no inflammable material around is in direct contravention of contract regulation 2.3.8.

Conclusion

Mullet & Sons must pay for the replacement of the generator (€90,000) as they are solely responsible for the damage.

Recommendations

1. Mullet & Sons should not be offered any more work on site if they do not accept these terms.
2. Harvest Macdougall should receive a formal warning.
3. All subcontractors must be reminded of their obligation to follow all fire and safety regulations.

Normal Poole
Site Manager
19 October

1 A report should be well organised with information presented in a logical order. There is no set layout for a report. The layout will depend on:
   a) the type of report
   b) the company style.

2 The format used for this example is common for many formal reports:
   • Title
   • Executive summary
   • Introduction
   • Findings
   • Conclusion
   • Recommendations

3 Another possible structure would be:
   • Title
   • Terms of reference
   • Procedure
   • Findings
   • Conclusions
   • Recommendations

4 The *executive summary* is a summary of the main points and conclusions of the report. It gives the reader a very quick overview of the entire situation.

5 The *introduction* defines the sequence of points that will be looked at.

6 The *findings* are the facts you discovered.

7 The *conclusion* is what you think about the facts and how you interpret them.

8 *Recommendations* are practical suggestions to deal with the situation and ideas for making sure future activities run more smoothly.

Activity file

6 Risk, Skills, Exercise C, page 51

Manager A
You are not in favour of sending the executives to the area. You think the risk is too great. They could be kidnapped, or war could break out at any moment. Both executives are your personal friends and you fear greatly for their safety. If they did go, the company would have to hire an armoured car for them, at great cost. Try to persuade your colleagues to give up the idea of sending them.

3 Building relationships, Skills, Exercise D, page 27

Sales Manager
You are sales manager for a sports goods company. You are at a conference and see someone who you met briefly last year at a trade fair.
a) Reintroduce yourself.
b) Find out if the person is interested in becoming an agent for your company.

8 Team building, Case Study, page 74

Director one: Leader of meeting
You want to:
- get rid of Nigel Fraser by asking him to resign. You do not think he is a suitable person to manage the sales team.
- replace him with a new person from outside the company. The new manager would have a fresh approach to the team's problems.
- have more meetings and weekly sales reports.
- reorganise the sales team into mini-groups, for example all plasma sales staff working together. Commissions would be based on sales targets set for each mini-group.
- think of other suggestions for improving the performance of the team.

11 Crisis management, Case study, page 99

Directors, Titan Stores
Your objectives are:
a) to defend Titan Stores' reputation.
b) to explain what you are doing to deal with the crisis.
c) to handle the journalists' questions.

Your team will be lead by the Chief Executive of the company and could include: Director of Public Relations; Director of Human Resources; Head of Legal Department; Marketing Director; Consultant (crisis management firm).

1 Hold a meeting to discuss what actions you will take to deal with the situation.
2 Try to predict what questions the journalists will ask and prepare answers to them. You may be surprised by some of their questions as they have been carrying out some investigations to find out the truth.

You have made your own enquiries into the matter.
- You contacted your chief buyer. He says no one knows who placed the original order. According to him, it could have been a buyer who has left the company.
- You contacted the manufacturer of the game *Race against Time*. They were not helpful. They said they were still considering what action to take regarding the illegal copies.
- Staff turnover in Titan Stores has been high during the last two years. Because the company has suffered fierce competition, you have had to make over 2,000 employees redundant. You have to increase profits because the share price has been declining and shareholders are becoming restless.

8 Team building, Skills, Exercise D, page 73

Team leader
You meet a member of your team who is unco-operative and unhappy.
- Find out what the problems are.
- Try to offer solutions so that the employee performs better as a member of your team.

4 Success, Case study: Camden FC, page 37

Camden FC negotiating team

You have other companies interested in sponsoring the club if the negotiation with United Media fails. However, United Media is an international company with good management and a high profile in the business world. You want:

1 A four-year contract

The contract should have a total value of €80m, with no conditions attached. €20m should be paid within the first year as you need money to enlarge the stadium's seating capacity.

2 Limited advertising

Advertising of United Media at the club ground should be limited. You want the ground to keep its identity and intimate atmosphere. Too much United Media advertising will upset the fans.

3 Limited promotion by players

Players' appearances and promotional activities should be limited. Too much time doing promotion work affects performance on the field. If the team is knocked out of the European Cup though, you could increase players' availability.

4 Paolo Rosetti to stay at the club

You want to keep Paolo Rosetti at the club. Cristos and the head coach think he is a fine player who could play another three years at this level.

5 An additional payment

United Media should pay an additional €16m towards the cost of buying two star players. Cristos says this is essential to Camden's success in the European Cup.

6 Diversification into other areas

You have contacted baseball clubs in the United States. They are interested in renting the ground during the summer to play exhibition matches and promote baseball.

7 A deal with a football boot manufacturer

You want to make a deal with Sprint plc, a football boot manufacturer. Sprint have offered you €400,000 to be the official sponsor of the players' boots.

8 Perks

Try to get as many perks as possible from United Media, for example, €20,000 for each goal that a player scores over his individual target of 20 goals. Also, free cars for players, memberships to clubs, etc.

You can offer United Media

- the advantage of being linked to the most exciting young team in English football.
- the opportunity to work with one of the best managers in the Premier League.
- the benefit of working with a brilliant Commercial Director, Sophie Legrange.
- the possibility of becoming well known in China and the Far East.
- the use of a hospitality box with space to seat ten people.

14 The future of business, Skills, Exercise B2, page 121

Customer

It is 5 January. You ordered 20 microwaves from the German manufacturer on 4 December. You are very angry because the delivery is so late. These are the details:

- Order number BJP 201
- Model MX14
- Colours: black and cream
- Discount off list price: 4%
- Delivery: Two weeks from date of order

You wanted the microwaves for your pre-Christmas sale. Try to persuade the seller to give you a discount of at least 10% because of the late delivery.

4 Success, Skills, Exercise D, page 35

Chief Buyer (Retailer)

You want the shoe manufacturer to agree to the following:

Delivery time	One week after receiving order
Place of delivery	to individual retail outlets (20 around the country)
Price	Knee-length boots €280
	Ankle boots €160
Colours	Black, brown, green and red
Payment	60 days after delivery
Discount	6% for orders over 200
Returns	All unsold boots returnable up to one year after order

13 Takeovers and mergers, Case Study, page 115

Group A: Coffee ground plc
These are the notes you have made during your research. Use them, and any other information, to prepare your presentation on Coffee Ground plc.

Head office	London
Type of business	Coffee shops serving drinks (mainly coffee) and food.
Ownership	65% of voting shares: small shareholders + big institutions, banks, insurance company's pension funds, etc.
Founded	12 years ago. First outlet in Brighton, seaside town.
Location of outlets	All stores company-owned. Located high streets – major cities in UK.
Products	High-quality coffee – mainly Colombian, Kenyan + health food, low fat pastries, etc. Black low-fat chocolate very popular with customers.
Clientele	Mainly 18–35, a few older ones.
Atmosphere	Lively, quite noisy in the evenings. Music pop and jazz, but loud Latin music in the evenings.
Prices	Medium-high prices. Coffee drinks a little more expensive than rivals.
Décor	Large picture windows; bright colours, modern furniture, comfortable leather sofas.
Service	Friendly – sometimes over-friendly. Staff turnover high. Service varies a lot at stores.
Plans	Want to open new outlets next year in Italy or Spain.
Prospects	Difficult to say. Tough competition. Starbucks a formidable rival. Uncertain future. Company has lost its way a little.

11 Crisis management, Skills, Exercise D, page 97

Managers
You should defend your company's sales methods and persuade the journalists that your business has high ethical standards. The information below will help you to answer the journalist's questions.

- Your marketing strategy is to target older people (over 60s) because they need phones more than young people. Most phones are sold by phoning potential customers.
- Your sales staff phone potential customers in the evening because customers are usually at home then. Your staff ask for the customer's credit card details to check the customer's financial status.
- Your sales staff say that the monthly payment is £14 for the black, economy phone. Other models of phone are more expensive. Customers must pay extra for a small device that increases the volume of the voice they hear on the phone.

- Sales staff are trained to maximise sales revenue by offering the customer extra accessories, for example leather cases, straps, etc.
- They can also increase sales revenue by offering to 'adapt' the phone to a customer's requirements, e.g. by keying in numbers frequently called.
- Sales staff are encouraged to send phones quickly when the customer shows interest in buying a phone.
- Your sales staff are motivated, dynamic and enthusiastic. Some of them may occasionally try a little too hard to increase sales!

Are you in danger of burning out? page 137

Key

1	a) 2	2	a) 3	3	a) 3	4	a) 3	5	a) 1	6	a) 3	7	a) 3	8	a) 3
	b) 3		b) 2		b) 1		b) 2		b) 3		b) 2		b) 2		b) 2
	c) 1		c) 1		c) 2		c) 1		c) 2		c) 1		c) 1		c) 1

19–24

The Olympic Flame is more likely to burn out than you. You glow gently when necessary, but rarely get above Gas Mark three. This is because your stress levels are comfortably low and you know what to do at the first sign that things are getting on top of you.

11–18

You are smouldering slightly, and any spark could set you off. You may not think that you are a candidate for burnout, but you are heading in that direction. Try to develop your life outside work, and if it's the job itself that's causing the problem, think about looking for a new one.

10 or less

It is simply a matter of time before there is a little pile of white ash on the chair where you used to sit. Take some positive action to prevent total burnout before it's too late. Prioritise, delegate, improve your time management and above all, ask for help immediately.

4 Success, Skills, Exercise D, page 35

Sales Manager (Shoe manufacturer)

You want the retailer to agree to the following:

Delivery time	Four weeks after receiving order
Place of delivery	To the retailers' main warehouses in Frankfurt and Munich
Price	Knee-length boots €320
	Ankle boots €200
Colours	Black and brown
Payment	30 days after delivery
Discount	3% for orders over 100 pairs
Returns	Black boots only (easy to resell)

8 Team building, Case Study, page 74

Director two

You want to:

- keep Nigel Fraser as manager – you are a close friend of Nigel. You think he's an excellent manager of a 'difficult' team.
- send Nigel on a short training course which helps managers to develop team building skills.
- get rid of Martin. He is rude and upsets members of staff.
- have fewer reports and meetings.
- pay commissions based on the performance of the whole team. The team should be set challenging sales targets.
- think of other suggestions for improving the performance of the team.

11 Crisis management, Case study, page 99

Journalists

Your objectives are:

a) to ask probing questions so that you get the true facts and find out how the company is dealing with the crisis.

b) to gather information so that you can write a powerful and accurate article for your newspaper.

1 Work in small groups. Prepare some questions which you would like to ask the company's representatives.

2 Work as one group. Choose the best questions and decide who will ask each one.

3 When you ask your questions at the press conference, make sure you ask 'follow up' questions if you are not satisfied with the answers you receive.

You have made some enquiries and found out the following:

- The owner of the firm in the Netherlands which supplied *Race against Time* to Titan Stores was investigated five years ago.
- Two other games, manufactured by the firm which made *Race against Time*, have also been sold by Titan Stores in small quantities (approximately 200 each). The games *Space Gladiators 4* and *Endgame* are also illegal copies. They were supplied by another company based in Hong Kong.
- For the last two years, Titan Stores have been reorganising their business. They have reduced their workforce by making 2,000 staff redundant. Employees who left the company accused the management of being 'ruthless and dictatorial'.

8 Team building, Case Study, page 74

Director three

You want to:

- move Nigel Fraser to another department in the company.
- replace him with another member of the sales team – John? Denise? (you decide)
- hold a meeting of the whole department every two weeks, and allow members to express their opinions frankly.
- keep Martin in the team – you are Martin's closest friend. He is a difficult person, but a brilliant salesman, in your opinion.
- reduce the sales team from 7 members to 6 (you decide who should go).
- reorganise the teams (you decide how).
- think of other suggestions for improving the performance of the team.

1 Communication, Skills, Exercise F, page 11

Overseas agent

The Marketing Manager of an exclusive leatherware company phones you to discuss plans for advertising the company's new range of women's handbags and men's wallets before Christmas. You both have various ideas for promoting the sales of these two items. Try to reach agreement on a suitable advertising strategy. Note: you are on your mobile phone and the battery is low, so check all the details carefully.

You want to:

- spend a lot of money on cinema, local radio and television advertising.
- invite some well-known local sportsmen and women to promote the new products in large department stores.
- exhibit the products at the local airport, rail and bus stations, and on local transport vehicles.
- send mail order publicity to selected house and apartment owners.
- advertise online, but you have no experience in this area.

You expect the Marketing Manager to contribute at least 80% of the cost of the advertising. You expect this to be about €100,000. You could contribute 20% but this would greatly reduce your profits on the products.

9 Raising finance, Case study: Vision Film Company, page 83

Directors of European Finance Associates

1 **Financial terms**

You want to be repaid 120% of your investment ($6.6 million) within five years of the launch of the film, plus 70% of the net profits of the film. Your reasons are: it is a high risk investment; the producer and director have no track record in making feature films; they want to use unknown actors.

2 **Payment of instalments**

You want to pay the loan to Vision Film Company in the following way:

a) Pre-production (September) — 10%

b) Before the principal photography (March) — 40%

c) At the end of the principal photography (June) — 35%

d) When laboratory work is completed (July) — 15%

3 **Choice of director**

You do not believe that the present director has suitable experience for this film. You want to appoint someone with a good track record in feature films and offer that person a salary, plus a share of the profits.

4 **The leading actors**

You feel strongly that two European stars should have the principal roles. They would greatly increase the profit potential of the film and also attract major distributors.

5 **Distribution**

The director and producer of VFC do not understand that it is difficult to sign up distributors, especially when they do not have a track record in feature films. To do deals, you need contacts and skills. You can help VFC to make the necessary deals, but this will involve time and money!

6 **Artistic independence**

The film makers can have a great deal of independence – you will not interfere. However, they should bear in mind the following:

a) the film must have a happy ending. Film-goers do not like to leave a cinema feeling sad.

b) the film should contain some 'flashback' war scenes involving Alicia and Justin in order to attract younger film-goers.

c) There should be few, if any, erotic scenes as the film needs to appeal to a wide range of adults in various age groups.

7 **Launch date**

March (final year) at the latest, to follow up its expected success at the Sundance Film Festival.

1 Communication, Skills, Exercise F, page 11

Marketing Manager

You are the Marketing Manager of an exclusive leatherware company. You phone an overseas agent to discuss plans for advertising the company's new range of women's handbags and men's wallets before Christmas. You both have various ideas for promoting the sales of these two items. Try to reach agreement on a suitable advertising strategy. Note: you are on your mobile phone and the battery is low, so check all the details carefully.

You want the agent to:

- take out special advertisements for the new products in local magazines and newspapers, and do some limited cinema advertising.
- put additional posters in local stores
- advertise the products on buses, trams and key outside locations.
- contact a local marketing consultant for advice on online advertising:
  David Habershom   Tel: 01782 550378
  E-mail: d.habershom@JHPAssociates.com

You will contribute €60,000 towards the cost of the advertising. You expect the agent to contribute €40,000 towards the cost of advertising.

8 Team building, Case Study, page 74

Director four

You want to:

- hear the opinions of the other directors before making up your mind. You are not sure whether to keep Nigel Fraser as manager or not.
- have Eliana as manager if the other directors think Nigel Fraser should go. She is young, talented, and has good people management skills.
- get rid of Markus – he is lazy, selfish and unreliable.
- ask Vanessa Byrant to come back and advise Nigel Fraser for the next six months.
- send staff on regular team building courses.
- think of other suggestions for improving the performance of the team.

9 Raising finance, Skills, page 81

Owner of business

You want to:

- get an equity investment of 250,000 euros to make more products and market them.
- keep a shareholding of at least 50% so that you continue to own and control your business.
- get management advice from the angel, when necessary.
- keep control over recruiting senior managers.

In return, you expect to:

- offer the angel a 25% stake in the business
- give the angel a seat on the board of directors, but without voting rights.
- offer the angel a 10% share in the profits from any future products sold under the Eternity brand.

Negotiate a good deal for your business.

6 Risk, Skills, Exercise C, page 51

Manager B

You are very keen to send the executives because a sales office there would be highly profitable – there is a huge demand for mobile phones in the area. You don't think the risk is very great. The government controls the area firmly. There have been a few terrorist incidents, but that's to be expected. The executives can get advice before they go on what precautions to take (for example: deciding where to live, changing routes when they return home, locking their car doors, being alert at all times).

14 The future of business, Skills, Exercise B2, page 121

Sales Manager

You receive a call from an angry customer who has not received the consignment of microwave ovens ordered the previous month. Try to deal with the situation diplomatically and calm the customer down.

- Get full details of the order.
- Explain that there was an unexpected increase in demand for the product so not all customers could be supplied on time.
- Promise to give the customer a firm delivery date after you have talked to your production manager.
- Say that you will call back as soon as possible.

9 Raising finance, Skills, page 81

Business angel

You want to:

- invest 200,000 euros of equity capital in the jewellery business.
- help to manage the business.
- provide excellent contacts with sales outlets for this type of jewellery.
- put the owner in touch with other potential investors in the business.

In return, you expect to:

- have a 35% stake in the business.
- be offered a seat on the Board of Directors, with voting rights.
- have a 35% share in the profits of all future products sold under the Eternity brand.
- advise on recruitment of senior managers as the business expands.

Negotiate a good deal for yourself.

8 Team building, Starting up, Exercise B, page 68

Score 1 point for *each* of the following answers:

Doers vs Thinkers:	**a), d), f)**
Mind vs Heart:	**a), b), d)**
Details vs Ideas:	**b), d), e)**
Planners vs Improvisers:	**a), c), e)**

Score 2 points for *each* of the following answers:

Doers vs Thinkers:	**b), c), e)**
Mind vs Heart:	**c), e), f)**
Details vs Ideas:	**a), c), f)**
Planners vs Improvisers:	**b), d), f)**

18–24 points

You are definitely a creative type. You value original ideas over detailed planning. You are likely to show consideration for others. You can get bored easily and sometimes need to be under pressure to get results.

12–17 points

Clear thinking and careful planning are of great importance to you. You are not afraid of challenging others in order to get results. You are likely to be ambitious and well organised.

13 Takeovers and mergers, Case Study, page 115

Group C: Mario Ferrino

These are the notes you have made during your research. Use them, and any other information, to prepare your presentation on Mario Ferrino.

Head office	Genoa, Italy
Type of business	Delicatessen selling wide range of luxury food and drinks.
Ownership	Mario Ferrino, his brother Marcello, and family members (10). Two brothers own 40% of the voting shares.
Founded	35 years ago.
Location of outlets	North and Central Italy, spacious stores/cities and large towns.
Products	All Italian food, olive oil, canned fish, pasta, etc. Huge range + prepared foods made in three factories (lasagne, ravioli, spaghetti etc. + pasta sauces).
Clientele	Loyal customers, some have bought food from the stores for years.
Atmosphere	Friendly, noisy
Prices	Competitive
Décor	Bare walls, old-fashioned look, equipment out-of-date in many outlets, old wooden tables, brick walls.
Service	Staff knowledgeable and helpful, but slow. Long queues.
Plans	Mario and Marcello old (over 70). Want to retire. Relatives always arguing. No one keen to take over.
Prospects	Business not well managed. Owners tired, have lost interest. Used to have good image – quality, speciality dishes, authentic recipes. Famous all over Italy - Mario's avocado and bacon sandwich.

9 Raising finance, Case study: Vision Film Company, page 83

Director and Executive Producer of Vision Film Company

1 **Financial terms**

After repaying 100% of EFA's investment ($5.5 million) you will then share the net profits of the film on a 50/50 basis.

2 **Payment of instalments**

You want the loan to be paid in the following way:

a)	On signing the financing contract (April/May)	25%
b)	Before the principal photography begins (March)	50%
c)	At the end of the principal photography (June)	15%
d)	When the laboratory work is completed (July)	10%

3 **Choice of director**

Director: you have a brilliant track record in the advertising sector of the film business. You have also written the remarkable script for the film. Try to persuade EFA that you are the right person to direct this film.

4 **The leading actors**

You want to use two unknown actors in the main roles. They have agreed to perform in the film and you believe they have great 'star potential'. If you have to use established stars, this could add $1–2 million to your costs – perhaps even more.

5 **Distribution**

You are confident of signing up major distributors once the film is made and its quality is apparent to everyone (good story, wonderful script, plus your technical skills).

6 **Artistic independence**

You want complete independence when making the film, especially in two matters:

a) the film must contain several erotic scenes featuring the two lovers so that it will appeal to contemporary audiences' tastes.

b) it will have a sad ending which will highlight the high moral standards of the two main characters.

7 **Launch date**

Preferably July (final year).

A three-month publicity campaign immediately after the Sundance Film Festival is essential for the film's success in the United States.

11 Crisis management, Skills, Exercise D, page 97

Journalists

Many readers have complained to you about the dishonest methods used by the phone company. The complaints are related to selling by telephone. Use the information below to question the managers closely about their sales methods. Try to persuade them to offer financial compensation to all dissatisfied customers.

Readers say that the company's sales staff:

- target old people, using high-pressure tactics to persuade them to buy a phone.
- always phone late in the evening when people are tired and vulnerable.
- trick customers into immediately giving their credit card information.
- say monthly payments are only £14, then send bills for much higher amounts.
- persuade people to buy accessories, such as leather cases, which they don't really need or want.
- send mobile phones to people before they have decided to buy them, and include an invoice in the package.
- usually send the expensive deluxe models.
- promise that the customer can send back the phone if not satisfied. But when customers phone the company, they can't get through.

3 Building relationships, Starting up, Exercise D, pages 22–23

Key

1 a) 2	2 a) 2	3 a) 2	4 a) 2	5 a) 1	6 a) 1
b) 1	b) 1	b) 1	b) 1	b) 2	b) 2
c) 0	c) 0	c) 0	c) 0	c) 0	c) 0

0–7 Building relationships is not easy for you. Communication is the key. Make the effort to talk to people about problems. Ignoring them won't solve them and practice makes perfect.

8–9 You are making the effort to build good relationships but are you trying too hard? It might be better to spend more time developing the relationships you have rather than going out to meet more people.

10–12 Congratulations. You obviously enjoy good relations with many of your business associates. Can you use your skills to help those who work with you improve their business relations too?

4 Success, Case study: Camden FC, page 37

United Media negotiating team
Your negotiating objectives are listed below. Keep them in mind when you plan your strategy and tactics. You want:

1 A four-year contract worth €6om
In addition to €6om in sponsorship, you could offer Camden an additional €2om if the club wins the European Cup. Decide how much you wish to pay each year and when payments will be made. If Camden play badly and have to play in Division 1, the sponsorship deal should be renegotiated.

2 Maximum advertising at the football ground
- Four huge billboards advertising the company at the sides and ends of the ground.
- The company's logo on flags at all entrances.
- The main stand to be renamed 'The United Media Stand'.

3 Maximum promotion by players of United Media
- Players wear the company's logo on their shirts.
- The team's shirts and shorts should have a blue stripe – United Media's corporate colour.
- The two top goal scorers should do a minimum of 25 days promotional work a year for United Media (other players 15 days).

4 Discussion of Paolo Rosetti's behaviour
The player's behaviour is seriously damaging the club's reputation. If he continues to behave in this way, he will damage United Media's reputation too.

5 Approval of Camden's new ventures
If Camden FC wants to diversify into other businesses, United Media should be consulted. The new ventures must be in keeping with the company's image.

6 Cancellation of Camden's deal with Sprint plc
You have learned that Camden FC plan to make a sponsorship deal with Sprint plc, a football boot manufacturer. Sprint would become the official sponsor of the team's boots. You are against this deal because Sprint is owned by United Media's chief rival, Euromedia Group.

7 Use of a hospitality box
A hospitality box at the ground should be provided for the exclusive use of United Media staff and guests. There should be space for at least 30 people.

You can offer Camden
- a sponsorship package worth a maximum of €8om.
- perks, for example:
  - a car with the company logo on it.
  - free travel to holiday destinations.
  - cheap loans for apartment / house purchase.
- media training courses for players to improve their presenting and interviewing skills.
- financial help for older players to attend coaching courses or obtain academic qualifications.
- a financial contribution towards the cost of a new player to replace Paolo Rosetti – €4m maximum?

13 Takeovers and mergers, Case Study, page 115

Group B: Starlight plc
These are the notes you have made during your research. Use them, and any other information, to prepare your presentation on Starlight plc.

Head office	London
Type of business	Ground floor restaurant + cabaret nightclub below ground or on first floor.
Ownership	Joachim and Theresa Lopez (Brazilian) – 100% voting shares.
Founded	6 years ago.
Location of outlets	Mainly in beautiful old buildings in cities (London and southern England)
Products	Entertainment and food. Music: jazz, folk, world - local and international performers + cabaret + comedy. Cuisine – dishes from all over the world.
Clientele	Mixed crowd/ages – people who like varied, creative food dishes/entertainment. Cabaret appeals to romantic couples (all ages).
Atmosphere	Intimate restaurants. Lively cabaret clubs with late night shows. Themed parties can become noisy.
Prices	Variable. Cheap snacks, more expensive dinners, tapas at cabaret time.
Décor	Unusual décor in all clubs. Each club is very different.
Service	Smart, good-looking men and women. All nationalities. Lots of energy.
Plans	To create a national network with an annual turnover in excess of 100 million euros.
Prospects	Cannot grow at their present rate without setting up a more professional management structure. Need a Finance Director. Costs are beginning to rise. Locations more difficult to find. Copycat cabaret clubs have started up in the north of England.

4 Success, Discussion, Exercise A, page 31

SOLE BROTHERS
ADIDAS SALOMAN

The founder of Adidas was Adi Dassler. He made his first shoe in his workshop in Nuremburg, Germany in 1920. A passionate athlete, he was always present in person at important sports events.

5   In the mid 1930s, Adi Dassler was making 30 different shoes for eleven sports and had a workforce of 100 employees.

In 1948, he introduced Adidas as the company name and in 1949 he registered the company's
10 trademark, the three stripes.

The company's core product is athletic shoes, including tennis, running and basketball, but its three stripes logo appears on clothing, and even on sunglasses.
15 Adidas had problems surviving in a competitive and fast-moving market in the early days, but it made a comeback by shifting production to Asia and strengthening its marketing budget.

Adidas had always been a manufacturing and
20 sales company but when Robert Louis Dreyfus became CEO in the early 1990s, it changed into a marketing company, licensing products under the Adidas name and using its brand image to make the products successful.
25 In 1995, Adidas went public on the Frankfurt and Paris stock exchanges.

In 1996, the company equipped more than 60,000 athletes at the Olympic Games in Atlanta. This led to an increase in its clothing sales of 50%.
30 1997 was a significant date in its history. In that year, it acquired the Saloman Group, makers of ski and golf equipment. The company's new name became Adidas Saloman.

Many famous personalities from different sports
35 have endorsed Adidas products, such as Mohammed Ali, Franz Beckenbauer, David Beckham and Maurice Greene, the American sprint champion.

Adidas Saloman is continuing to expand worldwide by opening more of its own stores. It plans to
40 have an additional 25 to 35 stores by the end of the year, on top of the 200 stores it already operates.

8 Team building, Skills, Exercise D, page 73

Team member

You meet your team leader to discuss your performance at work. You are unhappy for the following reasons:

- You feel you are working harder than everyone else. You are always the last to leave work.
- Your hard work is not recognised and appreciated by the team.
- You recently married and are missing your partner and young child.
- You do most of the boring paperwork for letting the apartments while your colleagues are given more face-to-face contact with clients. You are not happy with how the workload is being distributed.
- You think the team leader is too young and inexperienced, and is not managing the team well. This is the main reason why you are unhappy.

6 Risk, Skills, Exercise C, page 51

Manager C

You can't decide whether the executives should go or not. On the one hand, the area has great sales potential and the company would be the first mobile phone operator to set up an office there. Also, at the moment, there is no terrorist activity. On the other hand, there is a real risk because in other areas of the country, executives have died as a result of terrorist activity or war. If they did go, you think they should have a special bodyguard at all times. This would, of course, be very costly.

3 Building relationships, Skills, Exercise D, page 27

Sports Goods Wholesaler

You have a wholesale business specialising in sports goods. You are at a conference and you see someone you think you recognise, but are not sure. When they introduce themselves:

a) show some interest
b) try to find out if there is any possibility of working together in the future.

Audio scripts

1 Communication

🎧 1.1

Good communicators really listen to people and take in what is said. They maintain eye contact and have a relaxed body language, but they seldom interrupt and stop people talking. If they don't understand and want to clarify something they wait for a suitable opportunity. When speaking, effective communicators are good at giving information. They do not confuse their listener. They make their points clearly. They will avoid technical terms, abbreviations or jargon. If they do need to use unfamiliar terminology they explain by giving an easy to understand example. Furthermore, although they may digress and leave the main point to give additional information and details where appropriate, they will not ramble and lose sight of their main message. Really effective communicators who have the ability to engage with colleagues, employees, customers and suppliers are a valuable asset for any business.

🎧 1.2 (I = Interviewer, AK = Anuj Khanna)

I   Is communication between companies and their customers better now than in the past, and if so, are there ways of improving it further?

AK Er communication between companies is much better, er now than in the past especially this great improvement in the last ten years and the reason for that is the introduction of new communication channels, i.e. the Internet, er mobile phones, er instant messaging er etc. So, it has definitely improved communication and become a two-way channel between customers but there are definitely scope of improving communication in terms of timeliness of the communication and giving more control to the customers so they control the communication with companies rather than companies communicating with customers without their permission.

I   Can you give some examples of really good communication between companies and their customers?

AK Sure, the best example of communication between companies and customers is where companies empower their customers to be in control of the information most needed by them and communicate only targeted issues which are of interest to customers. A good example of company communicating with customers is for example a bank keeping them updated by e-mail or SMS, commonly referred to as text messaging. When er, a customer's salary has been credited or he's crossed the overdraft limit. This information is useful to customers and adds value while making financial decisions. So, I would refer this as a good example of er customer communication.

🎧 1.3 (I = Interviewer, AK = Anuj Khanna)

I   Can you think of examples where a breakdown in communication seriously affected a business?

AK Breakdown in communication can bring the world to a halt today. We're living in an information society whose foundation is based on efficient communication. For example, recent breakdown in communication er of our country's A-traffic control system led to a twenty-hour closure of all airports in the country and a resulting delay in flights globally. Nowadays, companies and their suppliers are tied up with agreements where they pay huge fines, by the hour, for delay in fixing communication systems. This is more prevalent in the banking industry, where, for example, if a cash machine breaks down, every hour there is a delay in fixing the cash machine, there is a fine which is paid by the engineering company. And the reason for that is every hour when there is er, a delay, the bank loses money. This requires good communication between the bank and the engineering company, or it results in loss of money for both parties.

I   How do you see business communication developing in the future?

AK Business communication is under pressure to be more accurate, targeted and timely. There are stricter privacy regulations worldwide, which require explicit permission from customers if businesses want to communicate with them. We have all faced the problem of e-mail spam – messages which we never requested from companies who we have had er, no relationship with. Businesses in the future will give more control over two-way communication to the customers.

Nowadays, increasingly, apart from people communicating with each other, we have machine-to-machine communications. What I mean is where machines are imbedded with communication devices transferring information er to er information systems and computers worldwide. And this is primarily to improve business efficiency. For example, we have increasing number of cars, vending machines and equipment which is fixed with mobile devices which communicate with head offices of companies and service centres.

🎧 1.4 (KS = Koichi Sato, B = Bernard)

KS Yamashita Electronics, Koichi Sato speaking.

B   Hello, Koichi, this is Bernard Klebermann. How are you?

KS Very well, thank you. How can I help?

B   We need some more sales literature. We're planning a big advertising campaign for your new laser printer, the HG902 model. And there's a lot of demand for your other products too, by the way.

KS Good.

B   Can you send some more brochures, 5,000 would be good, plus some updated price lists, the same amount? Also we need point of sales literature, especially posters, and ... at least 200 and, oh yes, some of those pens and pencils with the company logo on, also 50 or so of the bags that we give out at exhibitions.

KS OK, I don't know if I can remember all that ... can you ...

B   Good. Another thing, you might like to know, we've managed to get a big new customer, Seelmayer.

KS Seel ... I don't think I know the company ...

B   We're very excited about it. They're a big restaurant chain. They've placed an order for 18 of the new lasers, please tell your boss, Mr Fujiwara, he'll be very pleased, I'm sure.

KS An order for 80 laser printers. Great! I'll let my boss know. He'll probably want to write to this company ... er ... Seelmund.

B   Yes, please tell him to write to them. That'd be good PR. They're expanding very fast in Europe and they'll probably order some computers and fax machines from us as well. They're planning a big roll-out here in the next two years. Tell him that.

KS Er yes, a big er roll-out, you say, er interesting. I'll tell him immediately. I'll need some details about the company, an address and the right person to contact and ...

B   Sorry Koichi, I can't hear you, it's an awful line. Anyway, nice talking to you. Speak to you soon.

🎧 1.5 (K = Koichi Sato, B = Bernard)

KS Yamashita Electronics, Koichi Sato speaking.

B   Hello Koichi, this is Bernard Klebermann. How are you?

KS Very well, thank you. How can I help you?

B   We need some sales literature. We're planning a big advertising campaign for your new laser printer, the HG903 model. And there's a lot of demand for your other products too, by the way.

KS That's good. Hold on a second while I get a pen ... OK? What do you need?

B   Could you send some more brochures, 5,000 would be good, plus some updated price lists, the same amount? Also we need point of sales literature.

KS Sorry Bernard, I didn't catch that. Could you slow down a little, please? I need to take notes.

B   Oh sorry. Right. I said, we need more brochures.

KS Right, I've got that so far. Could you give me some more details?

B   Certainly. Er 3,000 brochures for Switzerland, 1,000 for France and 500 each for Spain and Italy. Also, we need point of sales literature especially posters – at least 200 and oh yes some of those pens and pencils with the company logo on, a couple of hundred, also 50 or so of the bags we give out for exhibitions.

KS Let me check that, 200 posters, pens and pencils and 50 bags. Got it.

B   Good. Another thing, you might like to know, we've managed to get a big new customer, Seelmayer.

KS Seel ... sorry, could you spell that for me please, Bernard? I don't think I know the company.

B   Certainly, S-E-E-L-M-A-Y-E-R.

KS Thank you.

B   We're very excited about it. They're a big restaurant chain. They've placed an order for 18 of the new lasers; please tell your boss, Mr Fujiwara ...

KS Sorry, did you say 80 lasers?

B   No, 18, one eight.

KS Right, I'll let my boss know. He'll probably want to write to this company to thank them.

B   Yes, please tell him to write to them, it'd be good PR. They're expanding very fast in Europe and they'll probably order some computers and fax machines as well. They're planning a big roll-out here in the next few years. Tell him that.

KS Sorry I don't follow you. What does 'roll out' mean?

B   A roll-out is when a company plans to expand throughout a country; it's um a nationwide expansion if you like.

KS Ah I see. I'll tell my boss, Mr Fujiwara, immediately. But I need details about the company ... Sorry, it's a bad line. Could you speak up, please? I can't hear you very well.

B   Yes, the line's awful. What did you say?

KS Could you e-mail me the details, the address, the right person to contact, etc.?

B   Sorry, I still can't hear you. I'll call you back; maybe the line will be better.

1.6 (JM =Johannes Muller; KG = Karin Graf, CE = Caroline Eastman, PE = Peter Ellis, OD = Oona Daniels)

JM They want us to form new teams with staff we don't know and have never met before. They say we'll be more productive, but they don't tell us why. It's a stupid idea, this re-organisation. What's the point? Another thing, the management want our admin. staff to look after customers better, they tell staff, 'Be more proactive, ring customers up more regularly, find out if they have any problems, establish a real relationship with them. That's fine, but the staff expect more money for more work, and the management have kept quiet about that. No one trusts the management any more.

KG Last month, a director asked me to go abroad to try to hook a potential customer. 'It was urgent,' he said, 'drop everything.' I called our admin. staff - she was called Helen - and asked her to tell a couple of big customers that I wouldn't be back until the following week. She didn't do it; one of the customers got really angry and cancelled his subscription. I reckon we lost half a million euros on that one. I had a go at Helen. All she said was, 'I forgot, I was just too busy.' What could I say? Another point, why do I now have to write a report every two weeks, saying what I've been doing and what we've achieved? It's sent to all the top management but I never get any feedback from them. If you ask me, no one reads the reports; it's just a bit of red tape.

CE Customers constantly complain I don't explain their medical schemes correctly, and they get upset when they find out that the treatment's not covered by our contract. I think I'm a good communicator, I'm very persuasive. I explain the main points in the contract, and then let them go away and think it over. But, trouble is, we have so many different kinds of schemes tailored to every private customer's needs. And the policies are always being revised. I do my best but the customer only hears what they want to hear, know what I mean. We need three basic medical schemes, keep it simple, that's what I say.

PE It was a big mistake to move to these new premises outside the city. The administrative staff are in one building and all the other departments are in another, over a kilometre away. That's too far. A lot of internal post never arrives or it goes to the wrong department or is late. And that costs us money because we don't deal with customer complaints quickly enough.

OD I'm not happy at all. It looks as if we're going to lose flexitime. The unions are against it, but the management insist it's stopping us providing a good service for our customers. I don't understand it. I have to take the kids to school, like lots of other people in our department. What am I going to do now if I have to work normal hours?

1.7 (P = President, MD = Managing director)

P   I've just been talking to one of the new directors, Jean Rankin, she's our new HR Director. She thinks we should recruit a Communication Director, create a new post. She reckons we could get a top person for about 150,000 euros per annum plus the usual benefits, stock options and the like. We could offer a total package of, say, 200,000 euros. I like the idea. I think Jean'll really sort things out for us, Chris. What do you think?

MD I don't know, I thought we were trying to save money these days. Anyway, communication directors can be a pain in the neck; they're more trouble than they're worth. They interfere in everyone's business. And they want to change everything, to justify their fat salary. They start with the logo and the notepaper, and before you know it, they're costing the company a fortune. I know a bit about Jean Rankin, and I reckon she's an empire builder; she just wants someone to boss around. No, this isn't the time to be adding new management.

2 International marketing

2.1 (I = Interviewer, PS = Paul Smith)

I   How can a company prepare itself to market its goods or services internationally?

PS Once, having made the decision to market a company's goods internationally, there are a series of stages or steps which most marketing companies would approach it. Firstly, they'd look very carefully at the marketplace itself and whether it really is an attractive marketplace or not. And by that that means erm, does the market play to your strengths, erm, does it have a need for something that you have or that you can have access to creating and delivering? Er and this question about the need is very important. Is there a real need and that could be a conscious need or an unconscious need?

The next question they ask after that is, what is the profile of the buyer, that means, who would buy it? And there may be several different profiles, and surprising to say that most of the blue chip successful companies in the world today, most of them don't actually know who their customers are. They've got their names and addresses, they've got their buying details, but they actually haven't made sense of the profiles that they hold on the database to build segments of customers to help to profile and then to tailor other propositions for those particular customers. So, the second big question is who would buy it?

The next question would be can they pay for it? Do they have the income level, or do the companies have access to foreign exchange, erm, can they actually pay for it is a real question in overseas markets. Another question to ask as you move into an overseas market is can you beat competition? That means competition that exists right now or, competition that will be attracted into the marketplace as soon as competitors observe that you've got a market growing. The next question would be, do you need a local partner, and in many overseas markets local partners are absolutely crucial.

And, a few other questions to add are, you know, how easy is it to trade there, you know, are there taxes, are there barriers, are there borders, are there customs complications? Some countries do have it and this may just make it too complicated for both, the logistics, the delivery and the execution of the products and services. And lastly, the specifics of the marketplace are there any idiosyncrasies within the marketplace? Are there any unusual cultural characteristics we need to be particularly aware of? Is there a particular type of colour or language, or gesture that is not acceptable in that marketplace?

2.2 (I = Interviewer, PS = Paul Smith)

I   What typical problems can companies face in international marketing?

PS International marketing has a lot of challenges which domestic marketing obviously doesn't have. Er the typical areas or challenges that emerge are in the areas of language, literacy, colour, gestures, culture, media availability, legal restrictions and so on. Just to take a few of these, consider language, even the use of numbers within the same language have completely different meanings. For example, if you take the word trillion, in France and the USA trillion means one followed by twelve zeros. Whereas in Britain and Germany, trillion means one followed by eighteen zeros. Now that's a huge difference if you are negotiating a financial contract around anything to do with trillions. A classic example of the difference in language.

2.3 (P = Paul, S = Stephanie, C = Courtney)

P   OK, thanks for coming along this morning. As I said in my e-mail, the purpose of the meeting this morning is for us to brainstorm ideas, promotional activities that we are going to carry out to make sure that the launch of the Business Solutions website is a success from the start. I'm going to open up to you to come up with the ideas that you've formulated over the past couple of weeks. Anything goes, we've got no budget at the moment but you know, fire away.

S   Oh great, no budget constraints.
C   That's great. Television and radio.
S   Well, it's starting big.
P   Excellent.
C   Well, we haven't got a budget, err, well, I think we could reach a wide audience, something like that, and err, we could focus on some of the big sort of business financial network television if we want to reach a global market, if that's what we're working to do and extending to all areas I think.
S   Yeah, that's been quite successful for some of the banks and stuff.
P   That's right, but definitely focused advertising.
C   Focused on specific networks that would reach, that you know ... businessmen are watching network television.
S   Well, I've been working more on cheaper solutions than that just in case there are budget problems. I thought we could do some effective online promotion, which is actually very cheap, and I think we should aim to do anyway. Direct mailing but also register the site effectively with search engines so anybody who goes onto the Internet and is looking for business solutions would come up with our website.
C   Yeah, we should definitely do some of that.
P   Absolutely, yes.
C   What about press advertising, traditional newspapers, business magazines, journals?
P   Yes.
S   Yes, great, I mean we've done that very effectively in the past.
P   Yes, we've had some very good response rates to for the ads we've placed before.
S   Yes, and that could be something we could do, not just once but a kind of campaign over a period of time.
C   Yes, build it up.
P   Yep, use a campaign, OK.

2.4 (P = Paul, S = Stephanie, C = Courtney)

S   And then, going back to cheaper solutions, we could use the contact base we've got, the market research we've been doing for this new website. We've got some very good contacts where I think we could send out glossy brochures, maybe a CD demonstration, CD ROM demonstration of the site to human resource managers, training managers.
C   Yes, that's a good idea.
P   Great.
S   As we've already got contacts with lots of those and I'm sure we should.
C   ...exploit them.
S   Yeah, we could build that up.
P   Yeah.
S   And direct mail them.
P   With information packs or..?
S   Yeah, we could do a big either CD ROM walk-through as part of a glossy brochure pack. That might be one way and err, or information brochure if we didn't have so much money.
C   Yeah, would it be worth it sponsoring some kind of event, I don't know?
S   Oh yeah.
C   You know, inviting the real movers and shakers of art, you know, are target customers, the ones we can count.
S   It would be great to do a presentation maybe on a boat going up the river or something. That would get the press in.
P   Yes.
C   Yes.
P   That's a good idea Courtney, excellent. OK, What are the other areas of press advertising could we do, do you think, I mean, you know, we've done bill board advertising before but...
S   Bill boards, what about that?
C   I don't know.
S   I hadn't thought of that for this but...
C   I don't know what the costs are related to that, I think we would have to look at that. Underground, airports, maybe some of that.
P   Yep, OK, well, I'm going to wrap the meeting up now. We've come up with some really good ideas, we've got TV, radio advertising, obviously that's going to be dependent on the budget we've actually set at the end of the day. Online promotion which is cheaper but obviously we've got certainly have some degree of online promotion. Press advertising, business journals, billboards, maybe depending on the budget again. The contacts with the human resources departments, definitely, I mean that's an area that we've really got to explore and certainly a sponsorship of a major event to tie into the launch would be a great idea.

C   OK, so when will we meet next?
P   I think we're scheduled for three week's time.
S   Yes, that's right.
P   By which time we'll have more of an idea of the sort of budget that we're working with.
S   Shall we cost some of these things and see... So that we can...?
C   I've got some research I can look at.
S   OK, then we'll bring that to the next meeting.
P   Great.
S   Great.
C   OK.
S   OK, thanks.

2.5 (I= Interviewer, G = Gonzales)

I   Good morning Mr Gonzales.
G   Good morning.
I   It's been a very good year for your company, hasn't it?
G   Yes, an excellent performance. Our turnover was over 150 million euros, up 15%, and our gross profit roundabout 18.5 million. Very satisfying. And of course, our main product, Zumo, has done exceptionally well.
I   Yes, it's certainly been a winner in Europe. How about the rest of the world? Any plans?
G   Yes, of course, we would like to build on our success in Europe and market the brand internationally. Obviously Spanish speaking countries would be good markets to break into, like Argentina and Mexico, they would provide the base for us to develop a global brand.
I   At present, you market Zumo as a Spanish drink. It's got a strong Spanish image. Would you need to adapt the product for the global market?
G   Well, we haven't decided yet, but obviously it's got to have a wide international appeal. Also, of course, as Zumo is almost unknown outside Europe, a marketing campaign would have to raise awareness of the Zumo brand. So it would have to be a very imaginative campaign with a standardised advertising theme.
I   Interesting.
I   Tell us a little about the competition. Who are your competitors?
G   Oh, Coca-Cola, Pepsi, Heinz, they're all trying to take the market share from us, but we have a big advantage.
I   Yes.
G   Zumo's got a secret ingredient, called 'herbora' It's made from the roots of rare African plants, and it gives the drink its unique taste.
I   Really.
G   Herbora's the key to Zumo's popularity and its thirst-quenching ability. But Zumo has other qualities. People's bodies can absorb Zumo faster than water and other soft drinks - scientific studies have proved that. And it contains things like caffeine - a small amount - lots of vitamins and glucose.
I   Thanks very much, Señor Gonzales for giving up your time to talk to us today.

3 Building relationships

3.1 (I = Interviewer, WL = Ward Lincoln)

I   Ward, what are the key factors in building good business relationships?
WL I believe that relationships, business or otherwise, are about trust. And in order to gain trust, you must be honest; you must be transparent, clear. Don't promise what you can't deliver. There is nothing worse in a relationship than being let down. It is also about being clear, being explicit - people present their products in brochures, pamphlets, flyers, e-mail, videos. All of those media - they're all very effective, but it must be clear. The customer must understand very quickly, what you are selling, what price you're selling at. The speed of that information, the speed of the response - it must consistently be fast. The restless customer of the 21st century does not have time on his or her hands and there are a million other providers, all ready and eager to sell to that customer. In order to continue that relationship, maintaining the relationship, consistently answer their queries, respond quickly in a simple format.

3.2 (I = Interviewer; AC = Agnes Chen)

I What do you have to consider when building relationships with customers overseas?

AC Well, I think if you are selling in a global market, you're doing business in markets at different stages of development. So if you want to expand internationally, you have to build good business relationships and understand the cultures and business behaviour of the people you deal with.

Well, let's take some examples. If you want to do business in South America for instance, you have to be aware that Latin people are warm and friendly. Personal contacts are very, very important to them. They like to get to know you well before they do business with you. So they may have long business lunches or dinners - not 15-minute 'power' lunches like in the US - and they like to take their time before doing business with you.

In China, a country I know very well, the Chinese like to work with friends and relatives. So you often have to find an intermediary to help you, someone who knows the local people and organisations, who can help you to establish good relationships. Chinese people will trust you if you are loyal to them, and show respect. To do business there, you have to win people's trust and respect.

Also in China, expensive gifts such as high quality branded goods, and extravagant entertainment are part of business practice. You must be aware of that. It shows the status of the person receiving the hospitality.

Understanding business culture is important too. But I think the best way to build a relationship is to make yourself valuable to a customer, and to be available to give them expert advice. Also, you should show appreciation of what they have done for you. Small talk will help to strengthen a relationship in an informal way so that you upgrade yourself to 'friend' level instead of remaining at a business partner level.

3.3 (I = Interviewer; AC = Agnes Chen)

I What are the key factors to bear in mind when building a relationship?

AC At the beginning of a relationship, it's important to have clear objectives, so both of you know what you're trying to achieve and deliver. And then it's a good idea to review your relationship from time to time, to see if it's still what you want. Personally I like to have as much face-to-face contact as possible, so that you build a real relationship. And you've got to have an open and sharing relationship, that's vital for building up trust. I mean, most businesspeople will tell you, trust is the foundation of any effective business relationship. So, you must do what you say you will do. And you have to deliver. And don't promise more than you can do.

3.4 (A = Manager A, B = Manager B)

A How's it going in France, Gina? We didn't do too well there last year.

B Yes. Our results were terrible. We tried to build up market share but it just didn't happen. We just managed to hold on to what we had.

A What exactly was the problem?

B Unfortunately, our agent let us down. We thought we could count on him to boost sales but he had no commitment, no motivation.

A Well, I suppose you terminated his contract then.

B Yes, there was no way we could renew it. We sounded out a few possible replacements and found someone else. We get on really well.

A Good. Let's hope he'll be better that the last one.

B He should be. He's got a very good track record. We'd set up a meeting on Friday, but he had to call it off - something came up.

A Well, I hope you get a result. I must be going. I've got to draw up an agency agreement myself; I've put it off far too long already.

B All the best. Speak to you soon.

3.5

Conversation 1

A Haven't we met somewhere before?

B Really?

A Yes. Wasn't it last year at the conference in St Petersburg?

B You mean the one on database management?

A That's it! We both went to that presentation on the first day and we were talking afterwards.

B Oh, yes ...

A I'm Jill Davis from Trustwood Marketing.

B Yes, of course. Harry Kaufman. Good to see you again.

Conversation 2

A So, you work for Delta Systems. Do you know Henry Willis? I've been trying to get hold of him.

B No, I don't think I do.

A He's a designer with you.

B Where's he based?

A Well, he was in Seattle the last time we were in touch ...

B Oh, that division's been restructured. Maybe he moved on. You could try to track him down through our New York office.

A OK, thanks. I'll do that.

Conversation 3

A Excuse me. Are you Gabriella Dietz?

B Yes, I am.

A I'm Tim Ross. I was given your name by Jon Stuart.

B Oh, right.

A He said you'd be a good person to talk to about Italy. We're trying to find an agent there.

B Well, yes, I should be able to help. Look, I have to go right now. Here's my card though. Why don't you give me a call at the office next week. And say hello to Jon for me!

Conversation 4

A I see you're with UGC ...

B That's right.

A Are you on the sales or product development side of things?

B Sales. I'm responsible for our new range of kitchen systems.

A Oh, really? How's the response been to your new publicity campaign?

B Pretty good. It generated a lot of interest and orders are starting to come in.

A Do you do much business outside Europe?

B It's early days but we're beginning to get enquiries from Latin America and Asia.

A We've been working with some very good people in Singapore. Maybe we could help you out there.

B Ah, now that's a market we're definitely interested in.

3.6 (A = Valentin Perez, B = Call recipient)

A Hello, my name is Valentin Perez, I'm a friend of Silvana Belmonte.

B Oh yes.

A I hope you don't mind me phoning. Silvana said it would probably be OK. Is it a convenient time to ring or could I call you back at a better time?

B No, it's OK. I'm not busy at the moment. How can I help?

A Silvana mentioned that you might be able to advise me on franchising contracts. We're thinking of setting up a franchising network here.

B Mmm, I don't know, I could maybe give you a little help, but I know someone who's an expert in that area. Her name's Stephanie Grant.

A She sounds interesting. You haven't got her phone number by any chance?

B Certainly, hold on a moment. I'll look it up in my book. I'm sure she won't mind if you call her. Just a minute, now...

A Can I mention your name when I call her?

B By all means. She's a close friend as well as a colleague.

3.7 (A = Director A, B = Director B)

A There's a lot we can do to keep our customers and learn more about them. But we need to be creative and come up with some good ideas. I've been thinking a lot about this ...

B Good. I'm listening.

A Well, for one thing, why don't we offer a really good discount to our existing customers if they buy one of our new models? Really encourage them to stay loyal by offering a financial incentive. I don't know, maybe 20 percent off a new purchase.

B Hmm, reward them for their loyalty. Interesting.

A Another idea I have. Why not send our company magazine to customers, free of course? They'd get all the latest news about us and know about our plans. We could even do a feature each month on some of the owners of our cars. People would like that, I'm sure. It would make them feel special.

B Hmm, maybe.

A Well, how about this then? We should be generous when customers buy one of our new models and trade in their old cars. We should encourage our dealers to offer customers a really good deal on trade-ins.

B Do you think the dealers will like that? It's a pretty competitive market, you know. They're complaining already about their profit margins.

A   Well, we would have to put a bit of pressure on them. It's in their interests as well as ours to treat customers well.

B   Yes, you're right I suppose. Actually I had one or two ideas for the loyalty programme. You know our customers are not very impressed with our after-sales service. Well, how about offering them free after-sales service for the first, say, three years after they buy one of our models?

A   Interesting. It'd be popular, that's for sure, but could be costly for the company.

B   Well, to get customer loyalty, you have to spend money. You can't do it on the cheap.

A   True.

B   One other idea, it's about getting more information about people who buy our cars. I think we should offer an expensive pen with our logo on it if they complete and send in a new questionnaire on their lifestyles and buying habits. What do you think?

A   Don't know about that. But we do need a better response to our questionnaires. That could be one way of getting it.

4 Success

🎧 4.1 (I = Interviewer, CN = Catherine Ng)

I   What factors have made your business successful?

CN   First of all, the advent of LCD watch technology in the 1970s created a vast opportunity for us. You see although the Swiss were the first to develop a quartz watch, the support of the Swiss manufacturers was not strong as they overlooked the phenomenal growth potential of the market. They believed their mechanical excellence would keep them leaders of the industry and that the quartz watch was only a gimmick and that it would soon fade out. In fact this poor judgement eventually led to the downfall of some companies.

As demand was greater than the supply, therefore it wasn't difficult for me to get entry to this market when I first set up my company. At the end of the first year the number of employees increased to 20 and we moved from office premises to a factory. Our floor space increased from the original 600 sq ft to 2,000 sq ft by the end of the first year, and the company grew more than tenfold in the next five years.

And then a few years later, prices started to become very competitive as the retail market became saturated. So I had to think about certain strategies to tackle this problem, I had to think up a short-term strategy and develop some long-term planning.

Like all our competitors, we developed new products such as giftware and luxury items. For example, we designed products with a time device in them and customers could print their logo on the product for promotional purposes. However competition became severe. It reached a point that any product which had a time module in it became less valuable.

In the short term, we had to cut our costs. However for certain customers who are less price conscious, I was able to upgrade the quality of our products, for example, by offering better batteries, a longer warranty, etc. We did not want our customers to think we were ripping them off of course if we charged a higher price. For customers who were less focused on quality, we had of course to reduce our prices. In the end, our customers all thought that our company offered quality products, which were value for money while most of our competitors struggled for survival and cut prices in a very competitive market. Some were even forced out of the market.

On the other hand, we also switched our capacity to producing clocks, cutting our watch production line and training our workers to assemble clock products. Watch production was based on an assembly line. Well we bought components from suppliers and assembled the watches. Clock products involved more components, we had to make them in house and the company started to install machinery, hire designers and the work flow became more sophisticated and today, we have become one of the best known manufacturers in the world, with ISO 9001 certification.

🎧 4.2 (I = Interviewer, CN = Catherine Ng)

I   What are the critical factors behind your success?

CN   The critical factors of our success, I would say, were our vision and our strategic planning. From time to time, we utilise management tools such as SWOT analysis to review our situation and make necessary adjustments. Furthermore, we have made use of the Internet to promote our products, for example, we used an e-catalogue to start with, and lately we have developed a customer relationship management system.

If I was asked what advice I would give to people looking for success in business...erm.. Well I would say to people: Be well prepared. Seize an opportunity once it emerges. And finally, stay open-minded, as business can be developed by individuals, alliances, partnerships and joint ventures.

🎧 4.3

1   Could you go over that again, please? Why can't you deliver by the end of May?

2   Let me make a suggestion. Why don't you hire an outside haulage firm to deliver the cars to us?

3   We want all the vehicles to be painted in our company colours - green and black.

4   I'm not sure I follow you. Do you mean that the discount is reduced if we want them all green and black?

5   I've got a question for you now. Are you willing to consider payment by instalments?

6   OK, we agree then. The colours will be green and black but the discount will only be 10% however you'll let us pay in two instalments.

7   Could you clarify one point for me? It's about the length of the warranty.

8   We'll give you a five year warranty if you want, but you'll have to pay a little extra for that, I'm afraid.

🎧 4.4 (P = Presenter, B = Bill)

P   Let me ask you about Camden now, Bill, do you think they'll beat Real Madrid and get into the semi finals of the Champions League.

B   Frankly, I can't see it happening. I don't think they're good enough to progress further.

P   Yeah, most people seem to think that, but they've got Paolo Rossetti, he's a brilliant player. You never know ...

B   Yes, he's a fine player, agreed, but he's very unreliable.

P   True, and also very short-tempered. That could affect negotiations over sponsorship. I understand United Media are interested in making a deal with Camden.

B   Yeah, I heard about that too. I don't think it's just a rumour. But if you ask me, there'll be a lot of talk about Paolo. United Media have a very good image; will they want to be linked with a team whose star player is Paolo?

P   Know what you mean, he's thirty now, and he's certainly been getting a lot of publicity lately. And the bad kind, unfortunately. It's not just that he's missed a lot of training, there have been several newspaper articles about the way he treats his wife. They obviously have serious marital problems. And on the football pitch, he's very rough. Always getting into trouble with the referee.

B   Yeah, he would be problem in any deal. But let's face it, Camden have a great future if they can buy more players. The club's making a lot of money, as you know.

P   Can you expand on that a bit?

B   Certainly, Sophie Legrange, their Commercial Director, has been tremendously successful exploiting the brand. The club owns a travel agency which their fans use a lot. Their hospitality facilities are very popular with businesspeople. Companies pay a lot of money to entertain clients in the boxes. Camden have a joint venture with an insurance company, and they run training courses on leadership in their conference rooms. They've got a finger in a lot of pies.

P   Very impressive, Sophie Legrange seems really on the ball.

B   She is. She's done a lot to increase their turnover and profits. The club's very secure financially, and they'll make even more money soon, because TV rights will be re-negotiated, and Camden will get a share of the income. Also of course, there's the sponsorship deal, if they can pull it off.

P   Mmm, things look pretty good for them.

B   I'd say so. They'll be in a strong position when they negotiate with United Media. They should be able to strike a good deal. Who knows, in a few year's time, they could be the new Manchester United.

4.5

Now some hot news for football fans. Paolo Rossetti is leaving Camden at the end of the month. Rossetti's agent, Sam Whimster, has confirmed that Rossetti will be joining a Spanish club for a transfer fee of five million euros. Whimster refused to name the club, but most experts believe it could be Real Madrid, and that Rossetti will be offered a contract for two years.

This is a blow for Camden. The club was confident that Rossetti would renew his contract with them. Although he has had problems and received a great deal of negative publicity, he is a superb player. Without him, Camden has no chance of reaching the semi final stage of the European Cup.

5 Job satisfaction

5.1 (I = Interviewer, HT = Helen Tucker)

I A recent survey rated Procter and Gamble as one of the best workplaces in the UK. How does the company create job satisfaction among its staff?

HT First of all we listen to our employees. We run a survey annually across our whole corporation, that's globally and we take it very seriously, we ask a number of questions looking at people's pride in the company, their work/life balance, how they're learning and developing themselves. How their manager is managing them and developing them, and if they understand how their work fits in? We also ask if they have a trusted counsellor and mentor in the company to give them guidance and if they understand about all their benefits and compensation and if they feel they're getting adequately rewarded for the work that they do? So, you can see it's a very comprehensive survey and you get a lot of data back from that and we take it seriously and look at what are the action steps that we then take from that survey in order to make this a wonderful place to work.

5.2 (I = Interviewer, HT = Helen Tucker)

I In your experience have job priorities among employees changed much over the last ten years?

HT Yes, they certainly have changed in the last ten years. We've seen a huge move in terms of how people want to get their work done, some want to work on a reduced work schedule, that's something very new. Others want to work from home as opposed to having the commuting time coming to the office. Other people want to work exceptionally hard but they still want energy left at the end of the day and time left at the end of the day and end of the week in order to give something back to the communities that they live and work in, in order to have a social life outside work whilst still making a significant contribution to their business. One of the areas here that's important is flexible work arrangements. As an employer you can really help generate a very positive working environment and one where individuals are very satisfied by offering a range of different options. So, for example, looking at part-time work, not just for mums coming back from maternity leave, but for, not just for jun, junior managers, but also for senior managers potentially working four days a week; one of our board in finance, he works four days a week spending the fifth day with his children. And we look at parents' ability to manage child care, what happens if your child is sick so that you can have an emergency cover for your children, so you can then get back to focussing on your work knowing that your child is being very well taken care of even if they're too sick to go to their nursery or day care place. We look at what happens if someone has to travel on an emergency basis and perhaps they're looking after an older relative at home, or have young children, or even pets that they need to take care of and how do we help them with that provision. And the other area that people are very interested in in terms of job priorities is understanding the environmental impact of where they're working. So some people will be choosing their workplace based on the ethical standards and the principles and values of their employer and I think that's more than you ever saw even ten years ago. There's a lot of emphasis on sustainability, meaning from a manufacturing point of view are they using raw materials from renewable sources, for example, or in an office environment is there significant recycling of waste materials happening. We've recently introduced a car share scheme here at the office so that we're not having as much emissions and as much traffic for the local area because it's very busy here and it impacts everybody coming to the office because the traffic is so bad in the mornings.

5.3

Conversation 1

A Good morning, John Slater.

B Hi John. I'm just calling to confirm the arrangements for your trip. We've organised a really full programme. Everyone's looking forward to meeting you.

A Luis, I was about to call you. I'm really sorry. We're going to have to reschedule things. Anne's just resigned and I've got to cover for her until ...

Conversation 2

A ... and then I said we can't possibly have it ready by then. I mean the deadline's only three weeks away after all ...

B Look - sorry but could we talk about this later? It's just that I'm already late for a meeting.

Conversation 3

A He just doesn't listen to a word I say. It goes in one ear and straight out of the other.

B Yeah, I know what you mean. You're not the only one who feels like that.

Conversation 4

A I'm up to my eyes at the moment. Would you be able to give me a hand with these progress reports for tomorrow's meeting?

B I'm sorry, I really can't. I'm busy with next year's budget. Maybe Janice can help.

5.4 (KJ = Karl Jansen, CN = Claudia Northcott)

KJ Well Claudia, thank you very much for coming to see me. Erm, what exactly is the problem in the general office?

CN Well, it's a bit difficult to say, to explain, but one of the problems, the main problem seems to be that Derek is, we think, I'm speaking on behalf of the part-timers ...

KJ Uh huh.

CN Well, we think Derek is giving too many hours to Petra.

KJ I see.

CN And well, this makes the rest of us, the rest of the part-timers feel, well between irritated and angry, really.

KJ Right.

CN And it's now become very obvious, I have to say.

KJ And is it affecting the work of the department, would you say?

CN Oh, I don't know about that, but it does mean that, er, if she has so many hours, one wonders how well she can do the work on a part-time basis, but also it means that there are one or two of us who would quite like the extra hours, and don't get a chance, or haven't been given a chance.

KJ Er, well that's obviously unfair.

CN Although it's work we could do equally well, we are sure, it's nothing personal, nothing against either Derek or Petra, but we would like a bit more openness, a bit more transparency about what's going on.

KJ Right. So this is obviously a situation that we'll have to deal with.

6 Risk

6.1 (I = Interviewer, AS = Allan Smith)

I What types of risks do companies face?

AS Firstly the risk of simply doing nothing. Another type of risk is what's called credit or guarantee risk. There's also political risk and a final example I'd like to give is the risk of catastrophe or other disruption happening to a business.

6.2 (I = Interviewer, SF = Steve Fowler)

I What are the main types of risk that companies face?

SF Well, all organisations face a wide range of risks. Indeed, risk and reward are intrinsically linked. The company or the individual that risks nothing achieves nothing and generally speaking higher returns involve greater risk. Understanding risk is therefore fundamental to effective business. Good risk management maximises the probability of business success and the likelihood of failure. Risk can be categorised into four types. Firstly, operational risks, for example, regulatory non-compliance, supply chain failure, or failure of governance within an organisation. Secondly, financial risks. For instance, cash flow, credit or exchange risks. Thirdly, hazards. For instance safeguarding the health and safety of employees and the public, natural events and consequent business interruption impact, or environmental impact. And finally, strategic risks, for instance, market changes, increased competition, or failure to adapt or change by an organisation.

Risks can be internally driven i.e. within a firm, or externally driven i.e. by the market or the environment in which the company operates. Companies should think laterally when considering risk. Don't just consider the obvious risks, but do think about 'what if'? Learn to understand who to listen to and how to assess risk as well as what to review. Having good risk radar is therefore vital for the successful enterprise. By considering emerging trends, organisations not only can prepare better for potential future adverse events but can also capitalise upon opportunities before their competitors.

6.3 (I = Interviewer, SF = Steve Fowler)

I   And how can companies begin to manage risk?

SF   Risk management's everyone's business. By following an agreed systematic process you can ensure that everyone in your company or organisation is engaged. There are five key steps to effective risk management. Firstly, be clear about your own organisation's objectives. Secondly, identify and describe the risks to those objectives. Thirdly, evaluate and rank the risks mapping the likelihood of occurrence against potential consequences. Fourthly, take action to deal with the highest ranking risks. This might involve exploiting the risk or opportunity, ignoring it, introducing controls, changing a process or product, protect, protecting against consequences for instance, fire protection, preparing to deal with the consequences, for instance, through business continuity planning or financing or outsourcing the risk, for instance, through insurance. And finally, reporting on both inherent and residual risks to the organisation's key stakeholders. The Board of an organisation must actively own the organisation's risk management strategy, but individual business units must own and manage their own risks within the framework of an overall risk management policy. This policy may be determined by either a part-time risk champion, working with the Board or, in the case of a larger organisation a full-scale risk management department. Internal audits turn, in turn, is to provide assurance that the strategy has been effectively implemented. Finally, assigning and rewarding responsibility for risk is much more likely to achieve effectiveness than adopting a loose structure, after all what's paid for, gets done.

6.4 (I = Interviewer, SF = Steve Fowler)

I   And can you give us some examples of effective risk management?

SF   By their very nature, it's difficult to give examples of effective, rather than failed risk management. The failures tend to be high profile, whereas the successes tend to go unnoticed. The success of companies in responding to the year 2000 computer bug, however, is a good example of effective risk management. So is the survival of those companies affected by the 9-11 attacks where appropriate business continuity arrangements had been put in place and tested beforehand. Sadly, where plans had not been implemented the firms affected tend to no longer be in business. This is not just about planning however, as Marshall Petain said on the eve of battle at Verdun in 1917, 'a plan is always perfect till battle commences.' Don't let your control systems swamp managerial commonsense. More recently, the prompt action taken by the Coca-Cola Company to withdraw Dasani bottled water from the UK market in the wake of a possible contamination scare, was a prime example of good risk management, minimising long term reputational damage to either the Coca-Cola or Dasani brands. This contrasts with the public vilification of Shell in the 1990s for its environmentally sensible principle to sink the Brent Spa oil platform in the North Sea in the absence of a climate of supporting public opinion.
To take another example, a major retailer sought to introduce corporate risk standards, which all of their suppliers would adhere to. The strength of their brand enabled them to work with their suppliers to share risk knowledge across the supply chain. This in turn led to an improved culture of no surprises and strengthened business partnerships.

6.5 (P = Paul, S = Stephanie, C = Courtney)

P   Right, if you remember from the last meeting we came up with a list of ideas where we wanted to spend this budget that we've just been set for the launch of the website. We came up with TV, radio advertising, online promotion, press advertising and a launch event of some kind. We've got the costs in. You can all see them. We've got this budget; we've got to decide where we're going to spend it. Does anybody have any strong feelings about any particular areas that we came up with?

S   Well, unfortunately I think we'll probably have to abandon plans for an event and probably TV advertising because this is so expensive.

C   Well hold on, I'm not sure if I agree with that. I mean do we have to, I think that those are both really valuable ideas and that there's a lot of potential in them if we target on the network television that reaches our customers.

S   Well, if we had to choose one that was targeted I think that the event's arguably more targeted than the TV advertising.

P   I think I agree with you there Stephanie.

S   But they're both so expensive if we look at the cost.

P   Yes I don't think ....

C   Is this the final budget?

P   It is the final budget, I don't think we're going to get any more money allocated to this budget but I certainly think there's not enough money there to do both the TV advertising and the sponsorship, the launch event.

S   Well I would say I don't even think there's enough money to do effective TV advertising. I mean we don't really have any positive experience, or much experience with television advertising ourselves, although other companies have done it effectively so I would say it's really risky to put so much money into that one...

P   But then all our competitors do that and they have a fairly high profile.

C   Yes, we're going to miss out on a whole lot.

S   All our competitors, we're one of the first to come out with an online training set of solutions, I don't agree because we actually are one of the first to have an online business solutions website.

P   But they're advertising their traditional training provision.

S   OK.

C   All right, well if our budget doesn't stretch for TV, what about if we focus it on business magazines.

S   Yes, I would agree with that.

C   Traditional press, newspapers, journals.

S   Yes, we've been really successful with that so we know the readership.

P   Yes, we've had some good responses to those adverts.

C   And we can reach a really wide audience whilst still making sure that it's our target audience.

P   Yes, I think that's important, we've got to make sure it's focussed.

S   Yes, I would say it's that as well as some much more targeted initiatives. I said last time, and I keep on going on about this, but it's very important that we use the contacts that we've already got and build on the market research we've done with big companies' human resource training managers and use that as pre-sales. They're ready to buy this product.

P   Yes, and it wouldn't be that expensive really.

S   Not really, I mean, a CD ROM that would be the biggest we would see from the cost, the biggest, the biggest erm, contributory cost but ..., and the brochure, but it's not bad really. Could we combine the two, maybe?

C   Well, yeah as long as we allocate enough to the press advertising I just think we have a customer base and find we can exploit them, but we also need to build our base and by reaching a wider audience that's how we're going to do it.

S   But if we cut the event and we don't do the TV we are going to have enough money to balance the two and do some online stuff because that's under £500 what we're proposing. That's nothing.

C   OK.

P   I mean the risk is that if it's unfocused and we lose a lot of impact we're not touching the right people but as long it is focused.

S   And then the word of mouth, if we hit the right ones and they talk about us that's going to be as effective as anything else.

P   OK. Well, can I just clarify that I think we've all agreed that the sponsorship event and the TV advertising is too expensive and we're going to blow the budget if we go along, go down that route. So online promotion as we said but also focused advertising in business journals and we've got the list in front of us.

S   Great.

P   And the approved journals.

C   And newspapers and magazines.

P   And newspapers and magazines absolutely OK. But also this, building on the established contacts we've already got with HR departments as well.

C   OK.

P   Which is a fairly cheap option.

🎧 **6.6 (JD = Jack Dexter, A = Anita Taylor)**

JD I think we made some progress at the meeting, Anita.

AT Yes, you've obviously ruled out two of the options.

JD Right. I made it clear I'm not interested in doing a deal with a German manufacturer. We're a British firm, we're proud of our heritage, and I want to keep it that way. Everyone seemed to agree, so no problem there.

AT Yes, and you're also against getting the engines made in Asia - I think you're right, by the way.

JD Yeah, I'm dead against it. For a start, we won't be able to get the same quality of engineering at the prices they have in mind. They're bound to cut corners when producing the engines to keep prices down. Another thing, there's an active terrorist group in the country, causing a lot of trouble. Think of the risk to our engineers if they went out there.

AT Yes, the option's far too risky. No doubt about that. What about the other options, putting our brand name on a small car, aimed at green consumers?

JD It's interesting. Worth looking into, perhaps. It'd be a big challenge for our designers, I'm not sure we could do it, and the market's very competitive. Could we compete against Smart cars and the new Mini, I wonder.

AT What about cutting profit margins and reducing prices? How do you feel about that?

JD It's quite a nice idea. We'd gain market share probably, and we need to do that. But I think we'd have to look at cutting costs throughout our business, and we might run into resistance from the Unions.

AT You seemed to like the idea of automating production.

JD I do. That would cut costs, increase our production capacity, and improve the bottom line. Raising prices at the same time by say 20% seems a good idea to me as well. That would provide us with the cash to modernise the factory, we can't put that off for ever.

AT What about the US market? You talked a lot about that at the meeting.

JD Yes, I am attracted by this option. If we could raise the finance to make a serious attempt to break into the US market, I'm for it. Selling in the US could transform our fortunes in the long term. I'm going to suggest we carry out a study of the market, and take it from there.

AT Good idea, I'm sure that's a very positive step.

7 e-commerce

🎧 **7.1 (I = Interviewer, JK = Jeff Kimbell)**

I Would you describe how Dell's online business model works?

JK Dell's online business model really is centred around the customer. So, erm, as most people are aware of by now Dell's business model is one in which we have direct relationships with our customers so we don't sell through the channel or through distributors in any way, we have a one-to-one direct relationship with our customers set and our online strategy and therefore our online tool set really reflects that strategy, so we offer information to our customers that they tell us they need in order to make a purchasing decision or in order to further research the technology that they are considering and then we obviously err, also transact a lot of business online. So erm, customers can go to the Dell dot coms around the world and configure a system and purchase a system online without ever having to interact directly with a Dell sales representative if that's how they choose to interact with us.

🎧 **7.2 (I = Interviewer, JK = Jeff Kimbell)**

I And what are the reasons behind Dell's success in doing business online?

JK We really feel that er the core reason why we have been so successful doing business online is the fact that we do have direct relationships with our customers and therefore we hear first hand from them what type of information they want from the company as well as how they would like to interact with us online. So, er whether it be a consumer part of the business where people often need information to compare different technologies and different configurations of systems, or they are looking for a specific promotional offer, we, we do lots of activity around those areas. Erm, in addition to that we have large Corporate customers who, er we develop customised web pages for that offers very customised pricing and customised configurations of machines and customised information for them based on topics that are relevant for them. In order to build a successful business online it's really critical to

erm have a very clear understanding of what your customers want from you in terms of their interaction with you online. So, erm for Dell it's a combination of providing information as well as a commerce area whereby people can procure items online.

🎧 **7.3 (I = Interviewer, JK = Jeff Kimbell)**

I What developments in e-commerce do you see in the future?

JK Well, really if, if you consider the future of e-commerce, really you know the main trend is gonna be a continued acceptance of both erm, sharing information and doing business online as people whether they be home users, or large corporations or Public Institutions get more comfortable with transacting business online both from a security point of view, as well as er from the point of view of being able to shop around and see the product online through 3D tools etc. erm really the adoption of online technology is just going to continue to explode in the future.

🎧 **7.4 (RM = Roger Marris)**

Part 1

RM OK, let's get started. Good morning everyone and thanks for coming. For those of you who don't know me, my name's Roger Marris and I'm the Head of Business Development at Smarterwork. Perhaps I should start off by asking how many people here have heard about Smarterwork. Can you just raise your hands? OK, and of you people who have heard of it, how many of you have used the site? ...Thank you.
This morning, I'm going to talk to you about Smarterwork. I'm going to begin by giving you an overview of Smarterwork, then I'll go on to tell you about our two types of users and finally I'll explain how it all works. Feel free to ask any questions you like as we go along.
OK, what is Smarterwork? Well, I think *Internet magazine* were able to sum up what we do very well. They said, 'Smarterwork does an excellent job of matching freelance professionals to organisations looking for particular skills.' For example, finding someone who can translate your instruction manuals into a foreign language. We've been around for 14 months. We have 60,000 users of the site, which means that we have people who have come to the site, have registered and are using the site, er, on what we call a regular basis. There are 90 people in our company and I think that's interesting because I think people have an impression of online companies that it's just a site and there's no one behind it. Smarterwork is very much the leader within the UK and now Europe in providing business services online. We've built a platform that will allow small companies to come on to the Internet, post their requirements and then meet an approved supplier to do that work in a sort of quality controlled environment.
OK I'll now move on to tell you about our two types of users. We have clients on one side and suppliers on the other. Our clients are typically small businesses like yourselves. Our suppliers have all been pre-screened. What that means is that if they want to work through the Smarterwork platform, they have to prove their ability. All our suppliers have quality ratings, which have been given to them by other clients - again like yourselves. Now these suppliers could be in any part of the world, so it means that businesses like yourselves in the South of London can work with suppliers in India based on a quality rating. The great thing about the Internet is that it's a community bringing together clients and suppliers from all over the world.

🎧 **7.5 (RM = Roger Marris)**

Part 2

RM Right. The next thing I'd like to do is explain how it all works. Let's look at the chart. As you can see, it outlines the steps involved. Firstly, the client posts a project, and we can help you with this. You post this project in an area in Smarterwork called 'My office'. Then the suppliers visit the site and make bids and include their CV or company resumé detailing the type of work they've done before. After that the client evaluates the bids. I'd just like to highlight one of Smarterwork's USPs here. We provide account managers free of charge, a free service to help the client choose the supplier. At the next stage, the client assigns the project to a supplier and then the client transfers the agreed fee to a secure holding account. The client and supplier then develop the project. The work gets completed. The client is happy. Finally the client signs off the work and the money is paid to the supplier - and that's where Smarterwork makes their money, we take a commission.

7.6 (MJ = Michael Johnson, HD = Hanna Driessen)

MJ Frankly, Hanna, I'm really worried about the way things are going. It's pretty obvious we have serious problems. And I think we need, you know, a really radical solution. We've got to get out of high street retailing altogether. Now's the time to do it. If we wait around, hoping for things to get better..

HD Hold on. What do you mean, in what way should we change, Mike?

MJ Go completely online. Sell all the stores, every one of them, it wouldn't be too difficult to do that, and use the money to set up an e-commerce operation. A 100% online operation. Think of the saving in costs, lower overheads, wage bills. Surely the market's telling us this is the way to go?

HD Come on, it's not as simple as that. We've got no experience in that area whatsoever. And look at what's happening to dot com businesses. They're going bust every day. I think they're just a fad. And people will soon come to their senses. They're not the answer, believe me.

MJ OK, so what is the answer? We've got to do something, that's for sure.

HD I'm not against online selling, Mike. But it won't solve our problems. We've got good products and a loyal customer base. Where are we going wrong? Well, I think we're not promoting our goods properly. We've been doing all our marketing in-house - it's a mistake. We should be out-sourcing our advertising and promotion. We need to get a really creative ad agency who'll work on our image and rebrand us.

MJ That's it? That's your solution?

HD Not just that. I think we ought to pay more attention to the findings of the study done by the Marketing Department. Another thing - why not get a consultant to look at our product range? Have we got it right? Do we need new products and services? Do we need to target different segments of the market? But we must stay in the high street. That's the business we know.

MJ I can't agree. Our profits are falling, costs are increasing. Most of our customers are over 40; we're not bringing in the younger ones at all. We can't stay as we are. It's just not an option. Look at our share price, it's half what it was a few years ago.

8 Team building

8.1 (I = Interviewer, JG = Janet Greenfield)

I Why is team building important in an organisation?

JG If you want to be successful in business, everyone in the organisation must work together to increase revenue, maximise profits and keep costs down. You can only do that if everyone is focusing on the main objectives of your organisation.

I How can you build effective teams in a business?

JG There are many things that contribute to effective team building. Let me mention three key points.
Firstly, it's important to have in your organisation a corporate culture that encourages teamwork. That means, the management recognise the value of teamwork and reward it as much as they do individual contributions to the company. The management will emphasise the value of teamwork at all times, so that it becomes a core value of the business. The pay, bonuses, reward system will all be linked as much to team performance as to individual achievements.
Secondly, a team can only be effective if the members understand what is expected of them. Each person must have a clear idea of what their objectives are, and how these relate to the overall objectives of the company.
Finally, members of a team must feel that their contribution to the organisation is recognised and valued by the management. Therefore team members must receive feedback regularly on their performance.

8.2 (I = Interviewer, JG = Janet Greenfield)

I In the United States who has influenced ideas about team building?

JG Well, er, most people would probably say, Vince Lombardi. He was coach of the Green Bay Packers, a highly successful American football team in the 1960s. He's an iconic figure in our sporting history. People giving seminars on team building these days often mention his ideas.

I Interesting. Can you give some examples?

JG Certainly. Lombardi believed that to create a championship football team and he did it several times by the way - you need to teach the basics, the fundamentals, he called them. Each player must know exactly how to play his position and how to play it well. So, that meant discipline. Every player was treated the same, there were no prima donnas in a Lombardi team, no people who thought they were more important than the others.
These were his basic ideas but to create a championship team, a team needs more than this. In his opinion, to play together and win as a team, each player had to care about the others. Each player had to think 'how will the other players feel if I don't play my very best.' Some people call it team spirit; anyway it creates a winning team.

I How does that apply to business?

JG OK, it means, each employee must know the basics of their job, and they need the right training to perform well. Also, it means there must be discipline in the company. For example, a company policy spelling out how staff at all levels should behave and conduct themselves. And above all, the company must develop that team spirit that Vince Lombardi talked about, that special feeling that produces a winning team.
How to do it? There are so many ways, aren't there? Company functions, like picnics and parties, departmental bonuses, company holidays, erm, motivational events, like seminars, paint ball games, inter-company competitions. In fact, anything, any event which enables staff to spend time together, get on better with each other, and care for one another. Team spirit is at the heart of every successful team.

8.3 (K = Karen, Head of Department, L = Larissa)

K OK, Larissa, I think I understand now. What you're saying is, you're unhappy with Sophie, you don't think she's pulling her weight in the department, and it's putting pressure on you and the rest of the team. Right?

L Yeah, we're meant to work as a team, aren't we? And she's the most experienced member. But she's not doing her job. She's never around to give us advice, or help us deal with difficult clients. Preparing the annual report is a big job, but we're getting no input from her at all. Another thing ...

K OK, I've got the picture. I understand your feelings, Larissa ...

L I hope you do. I'm really fed up with her, it's not just me, it's the whole team.

K OK, let's keep calm. What do you want me to do? Fire her?

L Oh no, not that ... of course ... but you could give her a good talking to. You know, tell her to make more effort, and then if she doesn't do anything, well, you'll have to take serious action, won't you?

K Mmm ... . I think there's one thing you could all do, maybe you should talk to her, tell her how you feel, that'd help, I think. But I'd like to put off doing anything else for a while.

L Oh, why's that? How would that help?

K Let me explain. Sophie's getting married early next month. She's got a lot on her mind at the moment, and it's not work, it's the wedding. That's her priority at the moment ...

L Yeah, OK, but even so ...

K Why don't we wait for a while? Let her get the wedding out of the way, I think you'll find that she'll be the Sophie we used to know then, she's always been a good member of the team, she hasn't changed overnight, has she?

L Mmm, I don't know, maybe ...

K Look, let's talk about this in a few weeks' time. We can review the situation then. Meanwhile, you and the others can talk to her, in a friendly way, I hope, and, OK, I'll have a quiet word in her ear.

L All right, we'll see if that works. Thanks for listening, Karen.

8.4 (NF = Nigel Fraser, M = Martin, J = John, E = Eliana, D = Denise, MK = Markus)

N I think we all agree that we need to work a lot better as a team. I've got some suggestions for improving our teamwork. I'd like to share them with you and see how you feel about them. OK, let's start with meetings. At the moment we meet once a month. That's not enough. In future, I'd like us all to meet once every two weeks. I would expect everyone to attend, and to be on time - that's not the case at the moment as you know. So Martin, what do you think?

M Totally against the idea, to be honest. Once a month is fine, surely. I'm making the most money for us at the moment and I can't go on doing that if I have to attend meetings all the time. Anyway, when we do meet, we spend most of the time arguing with each other. A lot of them are a waste of time. No, keep things as they are.

N Thank you, Martin. John, what do you think? Meeting once every two weeks. Compulsory attendance.

J   It's a good idea. Why not? We need to spend more time together to sort out problems, share ideas, that sort of thing. Actually, I think we should meet once a week.

M   Rubbish.

N   Now Martin, calm down. You've had your say. And nothing's been decided yet. But thanks John for backing me up on this one. Eliana, how do you feel about this?

E   I'll go along with whatever you say. It really won't affect me much. My main problem, as you well know, is I want to move from data projectors. I'd like to sell plasma screens, they're in great demand at the moment, that's why Martin tops our sales, it's not difficult to be the best when you have the best products to sell.

M   I thought we were talking about meetings, Nigel. Do we have to listen once again to Eliana's complaints?

N   No, we don't Martin. You're right, we're getting off the point. Denise, let's hear from you now.

D   Thanks, I'd like more meetings, once a week would be OK for me, but I don't know if attendance should be compulsory. But yeah, people should turn up on time, not drift in as they do at the moment. If we had more meetings, I'd get a chance to make a few suggestions for improving our sales. And maybe I wouldn't be interrupted so often by Martin and Markus. John seems to be the only person here who listens to me.

M/D/other members   Oh come on now. Nonsense. Right. True.

N   Could we come to order, please? Everyone calm down. Markus? Meetings once a week, once every two weeks, or keep to once a month? What do you think?

MK Keep it as it is, once a month. That's enough. When we do have a meeting, two or three people seem to take over, and no one else can get a word in edgeways. Frankly, Nigel, our meetings are not very productive, and that's the real problem. I'd prefer to spend the time meeting our customers and trying to drum up more sales. That's what we're paid for.

N   OK, Markus, thanks very much. Let me get a few more opinions ... . Robert ...

9 Raising finance

🎧 9.1 (I = Interviewer, PG = Patrick Grant)

I   How do you approach a bank or other lender if you want to get a loan?

PG Well, firstly, before you start, you need to have prepared all of your key documents, erm you'll have a good business plan, and should also have recent financial statements available, plus projections for the business - they'll be in your business plan, of course - and a repayment plan. Banks, and other lenders, want to know when they'll get their money back. And finally, you'll need collateral, security for the loan.

I   What types of collateral would be suitable?

PG There's a whole range a lender might consider. For example, real estate - your house or apartment, the buildings your business owns, or hard goods, like the equipment your business has. Or you might offer stocks and shares as collateral, other personal assets or even a personal guarantee.
Banks usually want to see you're making a personal investment in the business. They're much more likely to give you a loan if the owners of the business have a stake in it, if they invested a good percentage of the start-up capital, for instance.

I   What else will the bank want to know?

PG OK, look at it from their point of view. They are interested in how the loan will be used, and if you have a realistic plan for paying the money back. There are really three types of loan.
Firstly, short-term loans for a start-up business, that's to say to get the business going, if you like. This sort of loan is usually for a year, maybe less.
Next, there are the intermediate loans to help a business buy equipment and cover the expenses at this early stage of development. These loans could be from, say, one to three years. And finally, there are the long-term loans to help a business grow, for equipment, furniture, buying a long lease, that sort of thing. They are generally from three to seven years, and the business will pay back the money by instalments.

🎧 9.2 (I = Interviewer, PG = Patrick Grant)

I   What should someone do if a lender rejects a request for a loan?

PG Well, remember first that one lender may say 'no' but another may say 'yes' after looking at the same loan request, the business plan and other documents. So it's good to persevere and try to find another lender. But if several lenders reject a request for the same reasons, you may have to work on certain areas, for example, produce a more convincing business plan, improve your credit rating, or perhaps decide to purchase the land for your business at a later date.

I   And do you have any other advice?

I   Yes, once you get the loan, you need to negotiate the terms. You need to think about things like: What's the interest rate? Is it competitive with other available loans? Can you negotiate a lower rate if you're really persuasive? How will you pay the money back? In one lump sum or by instalments at set times? When is the final amount due? And could you extend the final date for repayment, if necessary? When you consider the payment schedule, you should also be thinking of your projected cash flow. You don't want to have to make payments at the wrong time.
One other thing, it's probably a good idea to get a lawyer to review any loan agreement. Some terms are common in any loan contract but others are often negotiable.

🎧 9.3

1   Can you offer any collateral?
2   There seems to be something wrong with your figures.
3   Let's go over what we've agreed.
4   What sort of loan are you looking for?
5   Let me clarify my last point. What I meant was, we would want to retain control of the business.

🎧 9.4 (A = Bank manager, B = Client)

A   I've looked at your business plan and I like some of your ideas for expanding your business. Could I ask you, what other people are providing finance for you?

B   Well, two family members have offered 100,000 euros for a small stake in the business, I haven't decided anything yet, and my partner is also investing some more money. We're still discussing the exact amount.

A   Have you approached any other bank, if I may ask?

B   Yes, two banks, but they turned me down.

A   Sorry to hear that, these are difficult times to raise money. I'd like to make a suggestion. Why don't you revise your business plan? And especially, put in a bit more about your competitors, for example. That'd help.

B   Certainly, I can do that.

A   Good. Could I ask what sort of repayment terms you have in mind?

B   I'm pretty sure we could repay a loan, the whole amount, that is, within three years.

A   Right. That might be a bit optimistic, I'd say. Anyway, suppose we were to offer you a loan of, say, 250 thousand euros, once you've revised your business plan? How would you feel about that?

B   Let me clarify what you've just said. The 250 thousand would be for working capital, and to hire more staff, a finance director, marketing people, money for the extension of the factory ...

A   Well, we can talk about that a little later. Your first task is to strengthen the management as we discussed earlier.

B   OK. Well in that case, 250 thousand would certainly help me to achieve some of my objectives in expanding the business.

A   Good. We seem to be getting somewhere now. Let me sum up what we've agreed so far then we can talk about your marketing strategy.

10 Customer service

🎧 10.1 (I = Interviewer, SA = Sarah Andrews)

I   At Harrods how do you define good customer service?

SA Good customer service here at Harrods is about exceeding our customers' expectations. Erm the customer's expectations here at Harrods are generally higher than most other retailers and most other Department Stores, in that they may visit one of our competitors like erm a food retailer or another Department Store and they would expect to get a general level of customer service. In Harrods they expect to be bowled over with the service that they receive. They expect our staff to go the extra mile at every given opportunity and to receive something quite exceptional. We actually set erm a minimum level of service, a framework that all of our staff work towards, that when they join the business we train them on these seven steps to exceptional service, then going forward we mystery shop, which is basically we have erm real Harrods customers that we recruit and go and test the Departments and experience the service and report back to us what they've experienced. And if our staff get 100% they get a Certificate from the Chairman, they get £50 worth of vouchers to spend in the store and they get, you know, high recognition within their Departments and obviously if we have consistent poor performers that aren't meeting that minimum level of service then we, we would manage their performance.

🎧 10.2 (I = Interviewer, SA = Sarah Andrews)

I   Do you think companies generally pay enough attention to customer service?

SA I think companies, er retail companies are recognising erm more recently the importance of good customer service. Erm, it's very important to retailers to have customer loyalty. It is difficult in these days to have a point of difference to the product that you offer because most of the things that are available also here in Harrods are available elsewhere er, in London or in the UK it is no longer unique to Harrods, so we have to make the difference with great customer service, which means that when the market may be tough, our customers continue to come and shop with us because they know they are going to get a great experience. I think there are, there are some companies that have not yet recognised that and I think they pay for that with a transient customer that doesn't, doesn't stick with them and may move from one retailer to another dependent on what's on offer. I think it's hugely important.

I   And is new technology helping in the improvement of customer service?

SA I, I think that er there is new technology available to erm measure customer service, Marks and Spencer for example, have a, a unit at their till points that when customers pay they can, they can press different buttons and say whether they were happy with the service they received today, erm, personally, and for here at Harrods I'm not sure how effective that is. I believe the most effective thing is to get real customers' feedback on what they experience and really look at the retention of our genuine customers, so, how many of our customers here in Harrods, that, that possibly own a Harrods credit card come back and shop with us on a regular basis and for me that's the absolute best test and measure of what level of service we are delivering to our customers.

🎧 10.3 (I = Interviewer, SA = Sarah Andrews)

I   Can you tell us how you prepare your staff to give the best customer service?

SA We have a set of standards here in Harrods that we call 'sell the experience'. So to sell the experience of Harrods erm, we have seven steps that erm, we work through which starts from the customer arriving in the Department until they purchase their goods and leave. The first step is to welcome our customers within one minute of entering the Department, so our customers are treated as guests in our home of Harrods and when they walk into the store or into the Department they are greeted in some way. So that may be a smile, that may be a more formal good morning or good afternoon, or it may simply be eye contact.

The second stage is to approach customers at an appropriate time and initiate a conversation. So we train our staff to erm, monitor customers' behaviour and look for an appropriate time to go and start a conversation with the customer. Some customers may look like they are happy browsing and don't want to be interrupted, some customers may give signals that they have spent a long time at a particular rail possibly looking for sizes, which is an indicator that they may then need to be approached.

The next stage is for us to ask questions to establish our customers' needs, which is a very important part of the service process. Erm our staff are trained on how to ask the right questions to really ascertain what the customer is looking for.

The next stage is for them to use their product knowledge and to select items to meet those customer needs. So it's very important that they listen to the answers when they've asked the relevant questions and then to use their knowledge to match the customers' needs with the products we offer.

The next thing we ask them to do is to highlight the features and benefits to customers, so this is about talking about the product, 'this is a beautiful painting madam; what a wonderful shade of red the dress is made in' and it's to really talk about the product and really focus on the real beautiful features and benefits of what the customer is looking at.

The next think we do is to offer related products to maximise the sale or service. So this where a customer, a gentlemen is buying a shirt, maybe we will introduce a matching tie, or a matching suit, so that the customer can get the whole experience of Harrods. Then we ask our staff to introduce the Harrods card. We believe the Harrods card is a big benefit, both to the store and to our customers, so it's important that our staff introduce those benefits to each and every customer that shops in the store.

And, finally to make sure that we finish the whole process very well, the staff are encouraged to thank customers and invite them to return.

🎧 10.4

Conversation 1

A   It was just before Christmas ...

B   OK.

A   I went into this wine store and bought two bottles of red wine. I bought them because they were promoted as 'wine of the month', so I thought they must be good. When I tried one of them, I found the wine was much too sweet, like fruit juice almost.

B   Fruit juice?

A   Yes, Really! I offered a glass to my neighbour, who was our guest. She took one sip and asked me if I had anything else!

B   So, what did you do?

A   Well, I took the bottles back to the store and complained about the wine. The salesman didn't argue. He took the bottles back and told me to choose another two bottles. 'I'll look for some at the same price,' I said. 'Don't do that,' he said, 'choose any two bottles you like.' I chose two which were quite a bit more expensive and thanked him. I always go to that store for my wine now because I like the way they treat their customers.

Conversation 2

A   I flew to Spain recently with my family and I was really impressed with the level of customer service we received. We were flying with a relatively cheap, no frills airline and they didn't promise much - no meals for example, but what they did promise, they delivered.

B   Really?

A   Yes. The service was excellent and friendly - it was service with a smile. They were particularly friendly and helpful to people with small children. We took off on time and arrived on time. We'll definitely be using them again.

Conversation 3

A   Something so irritating happened recently with a delivery that I'd ordered. I certainly won't be using the supplier again.

B   What happened?

A   Well, I work from home as a translator for a leading bank. My printer had broken and I needed a new one urgently. The person who took my order was extremely friendly and promised it would be there the next day.

B   OK.

A   It didn't arrive and I had waited in all day to receive it! When I phoned the supplier I got the same friendly helpful treatment again - they were very sorry - it would definitely be there the following day. But they let me down again. This went on for the rest of the week.

B   How awful!

A   I was very put out indeed. It was all talk and no action.

10.5 (C = Customer, E = Employee)

C I'm calling because I went into one of your shops this morning to look at some phones. I really have to complain about one of your sales staff.

E Oh dear, what happened?

C They were on me as soon as I got into the shop. I don't know if they're on commission or not but they really pounced on me.

E Oh?

C And didn't listen to me at all. They seemed to be pushing a particular package which was far too expensive and not suitable at all. I'm a pensioner; I have to be really careful with my money.

E I quite understand. Sorry you felt you were being hassled. Which branch was it?

C Your main branch.

E So, do you remember who served you?

C Yes, but I don't want to say.

E Well, if you want me to take this seriously, we need to know who was at fault.

C It wasn't just one person. They were all bothering me. In my opinion, you ought to look into your training methods. It's just not good enough.

Recorded Message

Hello, my name is Irma Schultz. I'm leaving a message because I haven't been able to get through on your helpline. I've called several times, but without success. I recently bought a new phone from one of your stores. I was persuaded by the sales assistant to spend a lot more than I intended on the latest top-of-the-range model, but it's much too complicated for me to use. The instruction manual is the size of a dictionary! I felt under pressure in the shop to make a decision and the sales person was rather 'pushy' which is why I now have this high-tech phone which I cannot use. Could someone please call me back? My reference number is ZX3450. Oh and my phone number is . . . .

11 Crisis management

11.1 (I = Interviewer, Mike Seymour)

I What are the commonest crises that businesses face today?

MS Today companies face crises in three areas. The first is when a brand or a product has a failure or a perceived failure or problem. The second area where there is perception that management or corporate behaviours have been not up to the requested standards and the last area are problems that have been highlighted by interest groups and activist groups. Of course, in crises perceptions are more important than the facts.

11.2 (I = Interviewer, Mike Seymour)

I How can companies prepare themselves to manage crises?

MS Firstly, they have to accept that crises might happen and secondly, they have to make sure that they realise and understand all their audiences and groups that may take an interest when a crisis hits. And thirdly they need to prepare their plans and then test and validate them through exercises and training.

11.3 (I = Interviewer, Mike Seymour)

I Can you give us some examples of crises which were handled well?

MS Yes, I'll give you two examples. The first one, and probably the most well-known in the crisis management field is Johnson and Johnson's handling of the Tylenol case. This is when some headache pills were spiked with cyanide which led to some deaths. Johnson and Johnson were very open and were very clear in what they were doing and they successfully brought the brand back to market. In the second case, Heineken erm, out of Amsterdam were faced with the problem of having 17 million bottles of beer with glass in them and these were in a 152 markets and again, through open communications and pro-active erm, response, they successfully managed the recall and maintained brand confidence.

I And can you tell us about some poorly managed crises?

MS Two examples. The first one would be Union Carbide's handling of the Bhopal tragedy in India, this is when a leak from a chemical plant killed many of the local community and in this case Union Carbide was secretive and slow to response and they were seen to be handling it very badly. And today there are still liability cases going on from this particular incident. The second case would be the Mercedes handling of the Baby-B, a new small car, which when it was tested by journalists in Scandinavia were found to be unstable

and in spite of video evidence of the vehicle rolling, erm, Mercedes, for three days continued to deny that this could possibly happen. Of course the public and the media became very cynical about the new product and it took some time to be able to win back this trust.

11.4

1 Could you answer my question?

2 Would you mind answering my question? What is your policy about gifts to customers?

3 Could you please tell me how many sales staff you employ?

4 Could you tell me how many sales staff you employ?

5 Do you deny that bribery is a common sales strategy of your company?

6 Could I ask why you're replacing your Sales Director?

7 Do you mind if I ask how many letters of complaint you have had from doctors?

8 I'm interested in knowing whether you consider yourself an ethical company.

9 Isn't it true that you don't care how your staff behave as long as they meet their sales targets?

10 May I ask why you didn't investigate the allegations more quickly?

11 Surely you're not saying that no payments were made?

12 Could you clarify what gifts can be offered to customers?

11.5 [CD = Carla Davis, HS = Hugo Stern]

CD Let me tell you a bit about what's happened. You've read the article in Euronews, so you know the basic facts. Our CEO was interviewed and denied everything. We're now investigating the matter, of course, and we're not happy with what we've found out.

HS Oh, is there any truth in the accusation?

CD Well, yes, there is unfortunately. Someone in the buying department ordered the games from a supplier in the Netherlands. We contacted him, the supplier I mean, and after a lot of persuasion, he admitted the games were from an unusual source and could be illegal copies. He said he'd bought them from a firm who had gone bankrupt. He bought them in good faith, he said, and wouldn't accept any responsibility for them.

HS Mmm, why didn't you buy the games from the manufacturer?

CD Well, we did when they first came out, but it seems this supplier made us an offer we couldn't refuse - 30% off the usual price, so we snapped them up. There's a lot of competition in computer games, you've got to take your opportunities when they arise.

HS What are your relations like normally with the game's manufacturer?

CD Well, they're pretty good actually. We supported them in the early days when they started up. We bought several of their products when no one else seemed very interested in them. We got them going really. But you know, like all manufacturers, they don't like to hear that their games are being pirated.

HS What about your stocks of *Race against Time*? Have you sold most of them?

CD We've sold most of the original consignment. But we bought another 50,000 last month, and they're lying around in our distribution centre. Heaven knows what we'll do with them!

HS There are a lot of questions I'd like to ask you. I don't need to tell you, this is a serious situation and we need to work out how you'll handle it. One of the first things you must do is form a crisis management team and bring in an expert from outside the company to advise you.

CD Right.

HS I can help and suggest someone suitable for the job.

12 Management styles

12.1 (I = Interviewer, NF = Niall Foster)

I What are the key qualities for a successful manager today, compared to the past?

NF Today a key manager must listen. A key manager must ask questions. So, for example in terms of cultural style before I go into any contact I ask my local erm, personnel or a local friend or contact in a country to give me ideas as to what I should and indeed should not do in any meeting situation, or over dinner or travelling in a car. What are the things I should do, should I shake somebody's hand, should I wait for them to give me their hand first? So to answer you, ask, listen. The days of telling are over.

🎧 12.2 (I = Interviewer, NF = Niall Foster)

I Which management style do you think gets the best out of its team or its people?

NF The first style, the first point in that style is to really show recognition, compliment staff or any others, publicly or in face-to-face situations as often as they can. Basically the more you compliment the less you need to have to criticise.
Second point is then to communicate very clearly your decisions. Management have decided, I have decided. And this is always important because managers are there to actually deliver, they have that responsibility.
Then the third point is then to give very specific reasons why a decision has been taken and in any organisation it is very important that the senior management team agree together what reasons they are going to give right across the organisation. This we find stops rumours.
Fourth point should be then to explain the benefit of this decision to the individual, to the organisation, to its customers. Er, we find that that really gives clarity and, you know, very clear understanding erm, as to why decisions are made and this is very important.
The fifth point is then often to ask for people's commitment to working with management to realise the goal and we find that when you ask for somebody's commitment, 'Can I count on you working with me on this?' ninety nine people say yes. The role of the employee is now enhanced and their motivation is improved and enhanced by the manager now asking 'what are you going to do to help me realise this?'

🎧 12.3 (H = Host, V = Visitor)

H Ah good morning Mr Crane. How was your connecting flight from London?

V Terrible. There was a lot of turbulence and several people were sick. It was a nightmare. Anyway, I'm glad to finally get here. It's really very nice to meet you.

H Have you been to Rome before?

V Yes several times. I've been on a couple of short business trips and, I came on a school trip a long time ago. I don't feel I know the city at all though.

H Where are you staying?

V Right in the centre, the Grand Hotel.

H Oh yes, what's it like? Not too noisy I hope.

V No it's great thanks. It's very comfortable and the service is first class.

H And how's business at the moment?

V We are doing really well thanks. Business is booming! It's been our best year so far, but I seem to be working all the time.

H No holidays coming up?

V No, I'm afraid not. Not for a while at least! It's all systems go at the moment, until we get this new office up and running.

H Yes. I know what you mean. So... What do you do to relax, to keep the stress away?

V Oh I enjoy tennis, when I get the time, which isn't very often these days!

H Well you must try and see some more of the sights this time. What do you think about the city?

V I'm really impressed. The architecture is fascinating. I hope I have time to take it all in.

H I'll make some recommendations if you like.

V Thanks, that would be great.

H Now, would you like to go for a coffee?

V Yes. Thank you. I'd love to.

🎧 12.4 (TM1 = Team member 1, TM2 = Team member 2, TM3 = Team member 3)

TM1 Ryan just wasn't right for the job. He was hard-working and decisive - that was good. But I think he made decisions a little too quickly. He didn't like people to talk back to him; in fact he hated anyone to disagree with him.
I don't think he was good at giving instructions. He told us what to do, and if we didn't get it right, he'd say, 'Do it again'. I once had to re-write an email five times. He never had time to tell me what I was doing wrong, so I couldn't improve my performance. I never got any feedback from him.
And another thing, he just didn't want to spend time with team members. It's not that he didn't like us; he just couldn't be bothered to get to know anyone.

TM2 Ryan had some good points. He was a strong manager, always decisive and direct with us. He didn't like it if people made excuses for not doing a job properly.

He gave clear instructions, but they were a bit brief - some people say he needed to explain things more.
In my opinion, he didn't set clear goals. If he wanted you to write a report, he didn't tell you how long it should be and when he needed it by. And then he would call you, and say, he wanted it on his desk by the following week. Another time, he wanted information about incentives to staff, but didn't tell me how I should get the information

TM3 I don't have much work experience, I'm a new employee. so I liked certain things about Ryan's management style. He told me exactly what to do and if I didn't get it right, he gave me an opportunity to do it again, and yet again if necessary.
But he wasn't a good manager. He never gave me any work to do that was really interesting or challenging. I think he tried to do too much himself. He didn't seem to trust me.
I like warm, friendly people. Ryan wasn't like that. He wasn't really friendly with anyone, he had no real friends in the team. Also he didn't adapt to the different people and nationalities in the group. He used the same approach with everyone. I think he had no team building skills - that's why he had problems.

13 Takeovers and mergers

🎧 13.1 (I = Interviewer, S = Susan Barratt)

I What are the essential preparatory steps in a successful acquisition?

SB Well, I think the first thing to establish is what strategic goals you are trying to achieve through that acquisition and they might be various in terms of market share, er, maybe some economic benefits with vertical integration or international presence, etc., etc. Having established those strategic goals, I think it's essential then to establish your target. Who you're gonna try and buy, who is that acquisition company you're gonna go for? So, there is a lot of preparatory work in identifying the target. Having identified the target, it is obviously essential to put a valuation on that target, er and erm, and that valuation is obviously absolutely essential in terms of determining how much you are going to pay for it, which in turn will determine the success or failure of that acquisition.
Having put together the strategy and identified the target and the valuation of that target, er, you need to make sure the funders, er, of the acquisition are on board, be they institutions or private funders or banks, etc. Er and they need to fully understand what you are trying to achieve, er and have confidence in the financial er data that you've put together.

🎧 13.2 (I = Interviewer, S = Susan Barratt)

I And once the acquisition has happened, what needs to be done to ensure the successful integration of the new business?

SB I think er, erm, an acquisition and the success of the integration of that acquisition is all about planning in reality. It, it can be a very complicated, intricate process and it has to be planned very carefully er and very precisely in my view, erm and then I think there are two sides of success, one, what I would describe as hard success criteria and the other as soft success criteria. Er and both are equally as important erm, but I think really it's very hard to establish the hard success criteria without getting soft success criteria correct. Now the hard, by hard, I mean the financial side of things. So, we are looking at making sure we achieve those strategic and financial goals we set out to achieve. And make sure they happen within a timetable that's acceptable, so, erm, if you're trying to, if you're rationalising er units or rationalising locations, er rationalising departments in any way, you need to get on with that very quickly, er, and make sure that the implementation of that action is planned and thought through and done properly. On the soft side of things, it about communication. I think it's, once you go through an acquisition then people generally, huh, generally think the worst if there's a vacuum of communication, huh, if there's a vacuum of knowledge of what's going on, people will think the worst but then that's human nature. So, communication of what's happening, er telling people exactly what's gonna happen and by when is vital to make sure there's a, a good integration of a, a business.

I And how do you know whether an acquisition has been successful or not?

SB I think that's quite easy really, er and that's er basically driven financially. Er you know you acquire a business to add value to your own business, er and if you've added value then the acquisition has been successful and er, it's pretty straightforward I'd say. So, um it's about making sure you get a return on the capital you've invested er to add value to the business that you're running.

🎧 **13.3 (I = Interviewer, S = Susan Barratt)**

I From your own experience, can you give us an example of a successful takeover?

SB Erm, yes I can, I've been involved in erm several periods of change erm, when I started my career actually, my very first job was at Coopers and Lybrand er the accountancy company, erm, who were, who merged with the Deloittes Haskins and Sells when I was there. Now I was a humble accountant er pretty early on in my career, er but from the position I sat, you know, that the, that seemed to me to be a very successful integration er and the reason for that and I was like I say from an employee's point of view it seemed successful, was because we were well communicated to, we knew exactly what was happening, er the name changed very quickly on everything, literature changed, processes were solid. There wasn't, a, not at one point did we oh I don't know how to do X erm and so I think that was successful, certainly from my point of view as an employee.

🎧 **13.4 (J = Jeremy)**

J ... So as you were saying a few minutes ago, Dave, there are so many pitfalls in takeovers and mergers that you really have to plan carefully, be rigorous in your analysis and be flexible about the way you approach things at the same time. And your experts will help you with that - your mergers and acquisition experts.

But what are the sort of things that the experts forget generally. There are three things in my mind and the first thing is, you've got to recognise the constraints that your organisation is under with regards to communication - legal and confidential documents that you tie yourself up in through a merger and acquisition.

At the time when you most need it i.e., when your people are most uncertain, that's when suddenly you're hamstrung in your communications and the only answer to this is to be absolutely honest with everybody about what you're doing and about the process you're going through and be clear with them where you cannot communicate with them and why. You've got to create that trust as the basis of managing the change moving forward.

The second thing for me is about being ... beware of the sycophants in your organisation - remember with a merger or a takeover, you're bringing two organisations together, two management teams - all of their roles probably duplicated - and in that process, you're going to get a whole lot of people vying for the same jobs. Of course they're going to be saying Yes! Yes! Yes!

But actually, often they won't believe in that and when they go out and engage the business and taking it forward, what they will do is, they will fail to collaborate. They will be nervous of collaboration with the employees, because they don't really believe in what they're doing and so the only answer to that is, to create that space with them beforehand, where they can genuinely express their concerns - draw them out as valid concerns, such that you can get a really good understanding of what they believe in, so they can take it forward.

And lastly, everybody works for an organisation with a core meanings to their work and a good example of this is the National Health Service, where people are very much focussed on, for example, caring as their primary task. They don't care about cost savings and they don't care about efficiencies. And the whole resistance to change in the National Health Service is based on that. When you bring your two organisations together, people are going to have this core purpose, whatever it might be for each of the organisations, the reason why they joined that organisation in the first place. Spend some time understanding that and helping them to re-establish one with the new organisation. Before I finish - I'd just like to run round the room, just would be ever so grateful, if you would tell me - What's missing? What haven't I explained properly?

🎧 **13.5**

And now for some news about Mario Ferrino – the Italian delicatessen business. Some experts believe that the British restaurant group, Bon Appetit, is looking hungrily at this struggling Italian chain of delicatessens.

Mario Ferrino used to be a fine business. But now it's clearly in trouble. Turnover has fallen by eight percent in recent months, and there've been a lot of complaints about the food and service in the restaurants.

Let's face it many people say that Mario Ferrino no longer has a reputation for quality, creativity and good service. The chain needs new managers, new technology, new ideas and investment especially in marketing and PR. It's a business ripe for a takeover.

14 The future of business

🎧 **14.1 (I = Interviewer, TK = Tamar Kasriel)**

I What new business opportunities do you see developing in the future?

TK Well, I think that in developed markets, consumers over the last 10, or 20, or even 30 years have got more and more money for spending and so we are going to see a development in services and in luxuries and in the kind of sectors where companies can be more targeted onto a particular group of consumers. For example targeting older people who are going to be a growing and important segment, and also things like beauty services for men, for example, things that we don't really need but we feel that we want.

I And which business sectors do you see expanding and contracting in the future?

TK Well, I think in many market places we are going to see a split into two extremes. At one extreme we are going to see areas where the supplier, the company can be very price competitive for example, if you think about the growth of discount supermarkets across Europe and also in the United States. At the other extreme we are going to see the growth of companies where they can charge a premium, they can charge consumers for something a bit special and we'll see there the growth in services and luxuries.

🎧 **14.2 (I = Interviewer, TK = Tamar Kasriel)**

I We usually assume that more business technology will lead to greater efficiency; do you think this is true?

TK Well, I think when it comes to lots of manufacturing processes we have seen a very significant growth in efficiency erm, a lot of manufacturing processes are now able to produce far faster and with far less waste but I think there are a lot of examples where in fact technology has made us less efficient. For example if you think about e-mail, we now spend a lot of time reading and writing e-mails and it also means that people are able to do personal activities in the office, for example arranging their social life. Also if you think about technology in general and computers, what many people do is receive a document electronically and then they print it off in order to be able to read it, so we all end up with piles of paper on our desks, which surely can't be that efficient.

I How do you think companies will organise themselves in the future to be more efficient, more competitive and more successful?

TK Well, I think in the 1980s a lot of companies focused on efficiency and they tried to remove costs wherever they could. Very often they removed the middle management level. Erm, now these companies have become more efficient and if they really want to improve that they are going to have to look outside the company. So, they may try and squeeze suppliers, or they may focus more carefully on their customer, on their consumer in order to be more competitive. I also think within companies there's been a shift in understanding that it's important to invest in people, in the people who work for the company because if the people are happier they are going to be more productive and more efficient.

🎧 **14.3**

Dialogue 1 (CM = Carla Martinez, KT = Ken Tang, S = Switchboard, DC = Dan Chen)

CM Hello, Carla Martinez speaking. Could I speak to Mr Li Wang, please?

KT Sorry, you seem to have got the wrong extension. This is Ken Tang here. Accounts Department.

CM Oh I see. Well could you put me back to the switchboard, please?

KT Certainly. Hold on a minute.

S Hello. How can I help?

CM Erm, I wanted to speak to Mr Li Wang, but you put me through to the wrong extension. I got the Accounts Department.

S Oh I'm so sorry. I thought you said Mr Tang. I'll put you through to Mr Wang right away.

DC Hello, Dan Chen speaking.

CM Hello, Carla Martinez here. I'd like to speak Mr Li Wang, please.

DC I'm afraid he's out of the office this week. Can I help you at all?

CM Oh, really, I didn't know that. Actually, I need some information about one of your products. Your hairdryers - the Fairfax range.

DC Of course, but first of all, could I ask you, have you got our brochure and price list?

CM Yes, I have thanks, but I need to know a bit more about the product. For example, about colours, designs, speed settings, and so on.

DC OK, shall we have a look at the colours first?

Dialogue 2 (C = Customer, S = Supplier)

C Hello, Michael Bishop here. I'm calling about the cash machines we ordered. I'm really very unhappy. I want some action on this. They're now more than two weeks overdue. Our customer wants them urgently. What on earth's going on?

S Hold on, Mr Bishop. Could you give me a few details, please?

C Details? What do you want to know? Surely you've got everything on file.

S Yes, but let me just check. When exactly did you place the order?

C What, you want to know the precise date?

S Er, yes, if you don't mind.

C Erm, wait a minute, let me get it up on the screen, er right, it was the … it was November the fourth.

S Thank you. And what was the model you ordered?

C Oh it was the TX40, your latest model, the one you've just brought out.

S Right. Could you tell me one more thing? What's the order number please, the order form number?

C Oh, it's erm, let me see, it's C, er, 270. And we ordered 50 registers.

S OK. I'll check it out right away and find out what's gone wrong. I'm sorry to hear about this problem. I'll call you back as soon as I can.

C Well, thank you. Goodbye.

Dialogue 3 (C = Customer, S = Supplier)

S Can we go through it again, please? You want 80 items, reference number JG 905.

C I'm sorry, I didn't catch that. What did you say the reference number was?

S JG 905

C OK. I've got that, I think. JE 95.

S No, that's not right. I said JG - J for Juliet, G for Golf - nine, O, five. OK?

C Fine. Shall I just read that back to you? JG nine, O, five.

S That's it. And you want delivery by June the 30th. Right?

C No, not June the 30th - June the 13th - at the latest.

S OK. Sorry. I've noted that. June the thirteenth. It shouldn't be a problem.

Dialogue 4 (C = Customer, S = Supplier)

C I'm calling about the sales invoice I've just received from you - for 50 car CD players.

S OK. What's the problem?

C Well, there seems to have been a misunderstanding. I haven't actually placed an order for them.

S Sorry, I don't follow you.

C Well, when I called your office last week, I was just making enquiries about the players - prices, availability …

S Are you saying you don't want them? My assistant told me you needed them urgently. We've packed them and we're just about to send them off to you.

C I'm sorry. To be honest, I was getting quotes from several suppliers. If I'd wanted to place a firm order, I'd have given you written confirmation. Your assistant was a bit too hasty, I'm afraid.

S OK, well, I suppose we'd better cancel the order then. I take it you don't want the CD players.

C I'm afraid not. We've ordered them from another source this time. I'm sorry if this has caused you any inconvenience.

S Don't worry. I'll have a word with my assistant; I don't want him to make the same mistake again.

C Yes, I think you should do that. Well, goodbye for now.

🎧 **14.4 (L = Lam, Y = Yamashiro)**

L You asked me to include in our report an analysis of the major trends in the industry. We've done quite a lot of research, would you like to know what our findings are so far?

Y Yes, if we know the major trends, it'll help us to shape our strategy. So what have you found?

L There are some trends which you need to be aware of when you make decisions. Firstly, as I'm sure you know, Japan has an ageing population, people are living much longer, so the over 50 segment of the market is getting much bigger. It'll offer you opportunities for growing your sales, there'll be a lot of potential there.

Y Yes, we'll bear that in mind - it's clearly a very important trend,

L Also, our surveys and research show that most Japanese consumers want, they look for, value for money. They like to feel they've got a bargain.

Y Ha! Just like the Americans, then.

L Exactly, they have that in common. They're very price-conscious. Another thing, many people say, 'Oh, the Japanese are very brand-conscious, they'll pay anything for a top brand, especially if it's a foreign one'.

Y You surprise me, that's not true any longer. Well, of course, Japanese people still love brands, look how many women wear Burberry scarves, for example, but you should be aware that sales of 'no-brand' goods are increasing fast - people are very price-conscious, and they want value for money.

L Yes, I get your point.

Y OK, what else?

L We believe that Japanese society is changing. It's moving from a luxury culture to a convenience culture.

Y What do you mean exactly?

L Well, increasingly, people want services that make life easier for them, or which save them time. That's why the convenience stores, with their 24-hour service, are doing so well. Customers can go there when they want, and they won't pay high prices. They offer flexibility to the customer.

Y I see.

L The last trend I want to mention is, women are marrying later in life. Let's put it this way, the single woman under thirty market is getting bigger and bigger.

Y Well, thank you, Susan, I know you'll be talking about these trends when you have your next meeting. I'm looking forward to getting your report, I'm sure it'll be very helpful to us.

Vocabulary file

Numbers following the words indicate which unit the word first appeared in.

Describing people

Adjectives
arrogant 8
articulate 1
bossy 12
charismatic 8
coherent 1
communicative vs
  uncommunicative 8
considerate 12
decisive vs indecisive 8
diplomatic 12
efficient vs inefficient 8
eloquent 1
enthusiastic vs unenthusiastic 8
extrovert 1
flexible vs inflexible 8
fluent 1
focussed 1
hesitant 1
honest vs dishonest 8
imaginative vs unimaginative 8
indifferent 10
inhibited 1
inspiring 12
logical 12
loyal vs disloyal 8
moody 8
organised vs disorganised 8
outspoken 8
persuasive 1
passionate 4
practical vs impractical 8
rambling 1
rational 12
reliable 8
responsible vs irresponsible
reserved 1
responsive 1
sensitive 1
sociable vs unsociable 8
stable vs unstable
succinct 1
supportive 12
tolerant vs intolerant 8
unhelpful 10

*She is a **very effective
communicator** who has a
remarkable ability **to engage with**
employees and customers. 1
He was very **critical** of his
colleagues' opinions. 8
He is a good **team player**. 8*

Nouns
charisma 4
dedication 4
discipline 4
drive 4
foresight 8
imagination 4
intuition 4
ruthlessness 4
stamina 4
toughness 8

Products, marketing and advertising

Nouns
advertising agency 2
advertising campaign 2
advertising slogan 2
billboard advertising 2
brand awareness 2
brand loyalty 2
direct mailing 2
marketing campaign 2
marketing director 2
market sector / segment / niche 2
marketing strategy 2
online promotion 2
press advertising 2
product features 2
product range 2
purchasing behaviour 2
questionnaire 2
survey 2
teaser campaign 2
TV and radio commercials 2

Verbs
carry out promotional activities
commission a market survey 2
develop a (global) brand 2
draw up a customer profile 2
endorse 4
increase customer loyalty 2
introduce 2
launch 2
launch a campaign 2
license 2
outsource 4
phase out 2
position a product 2
relaunch 4
reposition a product 2
roll out 2
phase out 2
set up a focus group 2
snap up 4
withdraw 2

*Our new soft drink has to **compete
against** similar products. 2
Their products are
targeted at **niche markets**. 2
It is one of the fastest-growing
global brands. 2
The company has **rolled out**
fifteen stores since **launching** its
first. 2
Its price is in the medium range. 2
They bought **a top-of-the range**
car. 8*

Markets, the economy, and trade

Doing business
consumer protection laws 2
developing market 2
domestic market 2
economic downturn 11
emerging market 2
expanding market 2
export licence 2
extremely volatile exchange rate 2
growing market vs a declining
  market 2
international market 2
labour market regulation 14
large-scale unemployment 14
niche market 14
offshoring 14
outsourcing 14
overseas market 2
worldwide market 2

Verbs

enter / penetrate / break into a
    market 2
get a foothold in a market 2
retain competitive advantage 14
retreat from / pull out of a market 2

*Our company wants to **go
international.** 2*
*Their company **saturated** its home
market. 2*
*Government bureaucracy can
hinder a company's **entry into** a
market. 2*

Finance and money

invoice discounting 9
leasing 9
merchant bank 9
overdraft 9
profits before tax 13
profit margin 6
stake in a business 9
turnover 2
venture capital 9

Verbs

charge (for a service or product) 3
chase debts 14
cut prices 4
default on debt interest or
    repayments 9
generate revenue 2
increase / raise prices 6
make a bid 13
overdraw one's current account 9
produce added value 13
refund 10
share costs 3
take a stake 13

*AIG has a **capitalisation** of $166
billion. 3*
*We are close to **bankruptcy.** 4*
*The increased **revenue** was
achieved only by heavy
expenditure on promotion. 7*
*The **interest rate** on the **loan** was
ten percent. 9*
*A large number of companies use
equity to finance **acquisitions.** 9*
*We could not finance our
expansion plans from **cash flow**
alone. 9*
*Borrowed money is often **secured**
on business **assets.** 9*

*I expect a **return** on my
investment. 9*
*I felt I had been **ripped off.** 10*

Nouns

business executive 3
distributor 2
equity investor 9
just-in-time delivery 6
retailer *vs* a wholesaler 2
sales rep 8
shareholder 9

Verbs

consider new ways of doing
    business 2
issue shares 4

*Their **sales figures** were really
impressive. 2*
*Our **balance sheet** is improving
rapidly. 2*
*We've been **flooded** with orders. 6*
*We **pride ourselves** on providing
quality products at affordable
prices. 11*
*Our goods **appeal** particularly to
young adults. 11*

E-commerce

Nouns

dot-com 9
Internet shopping 7
Internet start-up 7
online retailer 7

Verbs

browse / search a website 7
do business online 7
do a search (for something) 7
shop on the Internet 7

*Our website receives many more
hits than our competitors'. 7*

Companies and organisations

Nouns

alliance 13
conglomerate 13
corporation 4
employee retention 5
flagship store 4
limited partnership 4
MBO (management buyout) 13
merger 13

sales point 2
subsidiary 4
takeover / acquisition 13

Verbs

acquire a company) 4
build employee loyalty 5
build up market share 3
denationalise a state company 4
establish a branch office 3
establish / set up a company 4
franchise an outlet 2
go bust 7
go out of business 6
licence a store 2
mismanage (a company) 4
open a store 2
take over (a company) 4
go public (on the stock exchange) 4
retain employees 5

*The company **expanded** from its
home market to Japan in the '90s. 2*
*Copy-cat chains have **emerged,**
only to be **swallowed** by our
company or forced to **merge** with
competitors. 2*
*They wish to **set up a joint venture**
with our firm. 2*
*Our company has a **workforce** of
600 employees. 4*
*Bamelco has **gone into
administration** with debts of
about €100 million. 9*
*Our company is known for its
integrity and high **ethical
standards.** 11*
*Grennix started by selling
stationery and later **branched out**
into magazines and music
products. 11*

Work

Nouns

autonomy / independence 5
fringe benefits / perks 5
golden handshake 5
high staff turnover 5
incentive 5
management consultant 13
motivated workforce 4
pay / remuneration 5
pay rise 5
performance appraisal /
assessment 5
project manager 12
redundancy 5

self-employment 9
severance package 5
shop floor 13

Verbs

achieve / reach goals 12
assess performance 12
change jobs 5
deal with red tape 5
establish goals 12
implement decisions 12
meet standards 12
renew a contract 2
reach decisions 12
set standards 12
take time off 5
terminate a contract 3
work flexible *vs* fixed hours 5

She is **Head of Marketing** at IPD. 1
He is **Vice President** of global IT at
Gearbulk. 1
My job was **on the line**. 3
Several sales staff
underperformed last year and
didn't meet their sales targets. 4
She's working in Poland **on a
fixed-term contract**. 4
Overwork can lead to **burnout**. 5
Some of our employees are not
happy with their **work / life
balance**. 5
His new position is less
challenging with little **opportunity
for promotion**. 5
We have to **work to tight
deadlines** and **under constant
pressure**. 12

Problems and difficulties

Nouns

communication breakdown 1
delay (in doing something) 1

Verbs

assess / calculate / estimate /
evaluate 6
break off (relations) 3
endanger (relations / the success
  of something) 3
face / encounter 6

get to the bottom of the problem 10
jeopardise (relations / the success
  of something) 3
lose sales / market shares 6

make a loss 6
minimize 6
mitigate 6
overcome / solve / resolve a
  problem 1
predict / foresee 6
prioritise 6
reduce 6
sort out a problem 10
sour (relations) 3
spread 6

Adjectives

faint 6
negligible 6
serious 6
significant 6
slight 6
substantial 6

Global companies sometimes **face**
language difficulties. 1
A number of serious
communication problems have
arisen. 1
The product had a design **fault**. 2
The incident **damaged** the
reputation of the company. 3
The strike **disrupted** production. 3
Their image has been **undermined**
by poor after-sales service. 3
He has been badly treated by the
management and wants to take
his case to **an industrial tribunal**. 5
Our company went **through a
difficult period** a few years ago. 8
When you **handle complaints**, it is
important to be diplomatic. 10
My job is to **come up with
solutions** to our customers'
problems. 10
The goods we ordered are more
than a month **overdue**. 14